NELL
GWYN
Royal
Mistress

Courtesy of the Metropolitan Museum of Art

NELL GWYN BY SIR PETER LELY

NELL GWYN
Royal Mistress

by

JOHN HAROLD WILSON

Pellegrini & Cudahy
New York

Louise Wilson
Her Book

ACKNOWLEDGMENTS

FOR FINANCIAL and other aids in the long process of preparing this biography I am grateful to the Trustees of the Guggenheim Memorial Foundation, to Louis Booker Wright and the Trustees of the Folger Shakespeare Library, and to Paul N. Hudson, Dean of the Graduate School, and James F. Fullington, Chairman of the English Department, the Ohio State University. I am indebted also to many friends and colleagues for suggestions, information, encouragement, and criticism, particularly George K. Boyce, of the Pierpont Morgan Library, William Van Lennep, of the Harvard College Library, James M. Osborne, Richard D. Altick, Charles E. Ward, William Charvat, Claude M. Simpson, Jr., Myra T. McCrory, John W. Nichol, Bernard R. Jerman, and, above all, William Riley Parker.

CONTENTS

I

The Gwyns
of Covent
Garden

1650

I

LIKE CLEOPATRA or Helen of Troy, Nell Gwyn belongs as much to folklore as to history. The facts about her life and character have been overlaid by fable and anecdote. Many people remember her as the mistress of a king, but like Huck Finn they are not sure *which* king. "My, you ought to seen old Henry the Eighth when he was in bloom," said Huck. "He *was* a blossom. He used to marry a new wife every day and chop off her head next morning, and he would do it just as indifferent as if he was ordering up eggs. 'Fetch up Nell Gwyn,' he says. They fetch her up. Next morning, 'chop off her head!' "

Better informed than Huck, we know, of course, that Nell was the mistress of King Charles II, a monarch not given to maiden beheading. But our further knowledge of her has been drawn from more than two centuries of anecdotes, romances, sentimental plays, and popular biographies. We are conditioned to think of her as "sweet Nell of Old Drury," a happy-go-lucky child of the slums who flourished in good King Charles's golden days, rose from poverty to a palace, and died repentant, leaving behind her a trail of good works. The moral Victorians, whenever they wrote about her, suppressed or bowdlerized her bawdy sayings, choosing to ignore those facts of her life which collided with the legend of her goodness; they even overpainted portraits which displayed an embarrassing expanse of her uncovered bosom. They canonized her as Saint Nell the Good, disinfected and triumphant, a kind, generous, charitable, unseeking, loyal, friendly—and completely mythical—character.

Nell was not a divinity but a woman, composed of good and evil, capable of kindness and of meanness as well. Compelled to earn her way in the world, she lived precariously as actress and mistress, keeping herself from disaster and achieving an astonishing social and economic success largely by force of her physical attractions and her broad humor. She was coarse, friendly, extravagant, generous, giddy, loyal, greedy, humorous, and ambitious—in short, an extroverted human being who lived a full, interesting, and not so very merry, life.

Our information about Nell comes from a variety of sources, not all of which are reliable. There are some legal facts: deeds, wills, warrants, state papers, theatrical records, and the like, which are not to be challenged. Information derived from contemporary newspapers, letters, diaries, memoirs, and histories varies in value with the honesty of the writer. Anecdotes, especially if told by Nell's contemporaries, are always useful, but anonymous stories have a bad habit of floating about loosely and attaching themselves to any prominent person. Finally we have a number of prose and verse lampoons or libels, usually anonymous and always infused with the spirit of slander. Circulated in manuscript or printed and sold as broadsides, these satires served the function of modern editorials and were often as well informed. From all these sources it is possible to draw the story of Nell's life and the world she lived in.

In the middle of the seventeenth century, London, with a population estimated at half a million, sprawled loosely along the curving north bank of the Thames, which was at once its highroad and its sewer. The older part of the metropolis, the "City," still bound within its medieval walls and gates, was a roaring confusion of narrow, cobble-paved streets, shops, and warehouses. Hackneys and drays fought for the right of way, apprentices before every shop cried their "What d'ye lack?" at pedestrians, and everywhere hawkers bawled their wares: fruits and vegetables in season, milk, custards, herrings and oysters, old clothes, and Newcastle coal. The ancient plaster and timber houses, leaning wearily against each other and threatening to topple into the streets, were fire-traps teeming with rats, lice, and people. No one had the least notion of sanitation. Refuse, human and animal offal, was heaped up on noisome laystalls about the city or was dumped into the streets and flushed down the kennel (the gutter in the middle of the street) when it rained.

A mile westward from the limits of the City was Westminster, with the old royal palace of Whitehall, the Parliament buildings and Westminster Abbey, piles of brick and stone set without plan along the river bank. Behind them, away from the river, were St. James's Park, St. James's Palace, and the new, exclusive neighborhoods of Pall Mall and St. James's Square. Midway between these western suburbs and the limits of the City was the Covent Garden district, bounded by Drury Lane, Longacre Street, St. Martin's Lane, and the Strand. This was the scene of Nell's childhood.

According to her horoscope, still preserved in the Bodleian Library at Oxford, Ellen Gwyn was born at six o'clock on the morning of Saturday, February 2, 1650, with the Sun, Venus, Mercury, and Mars all happily in conjunction. Properly Mars should have been in the ascendant; Nell came into a world torn by revolution and troubled by rumors of war. Only a year earlier the English nation had deposed its lawful monarch and chopped off his head. For the moment England was a republic governed by a council of state (with John Milton as foreign secretary), backed by the power of Oliver Cromwell, general of the Roundhead army and soon to become Lord Protector of the realm. King Charles II, twenty years old, was in Scotland, suffering under the fire-and-damnation sermons of covenanting preachers as he sought support for an invasion of his lost kingdom. Meanwhile many an English cavalier prayed daily for his return and was destined to continue praying for ten long years while enduring a regime which proscribed actors, cut down May-poles, forbade music, dancing, games, sports, and holidays, made adultery a capital crime, and took all the fun out of life.

Nell was born somewhere in or near the Covent Garden district, a curiously confused region, with the open piazza of Covent Garden and the spire of St. Paul's Church as its center, surrounded by fashionable residences cheek by jowl with lodging houses, ale houses, shops, brothels, and the hovels of the poor. To the north, in the mid-seventeenth century, lay open fields, and to the south were the great palaces and gardens of the nobility, and the broad reaches of the Thames. Two streets in the Covent Garden district have long competed for the honor of Nell's nativity: the Cole-Yard, a squalid alley off Drury Lane, northeast of Covent Garden, and the Hop Garden, a shabby little by-way off St. Martin's Lane, southwest of Covent Garden. Since both streets have long since disappeared in the rush and roar of modern London, their competition must continue on an academic plane.

Nell's father was a yeoman too insignificant to leave his mark—much less his first name—upon the records of the times. His surname suggests that he was of Welsh extraction, but Gwyns in Wales are as plentiful as blackberries. So far as we know Nell herself never mentioned him, and it is a reasonable presumption that he died while she was still an infant. The anonymous author of a lampoon on Nell, "A Panegyric" (1681), asserted that her father died in a debtors prison in Oxford, and that in the days of her wealth Nell "gloried"

> In giving others life and liberty,
> So pious a remembrance still she bore
> Ev'n to the fetters that her father wore.

Nell's mother was much better known. Off St. Martin's Lane, a stone's throw south of the Hop Garden, was St. Martin's Church. Here, in the south aisle, there long stood a monument with the legend, "Here lies interred the body of Helena Gwyn, born in this parish, who departed this life the 20th of July MDCLXXIX, in the lvi year of her age." In the burial register of the parish for July 30, 1679, she is listed as "Mrs. Eleanor Gwyn, Widow," but the discrepancy in Christian names is not important. Her contemporaries called her "old Madam Gwyn," or merely "Madam Gwyn," and we may follow their example.

Old Madam Gwyn was a thoroughly disreputable char-

acter. She was an enormously fat woman who smoked and
drank to excess and had been in her youth "skilled in arts
of gallantry." There are good reasons for believing that
at the time of Nell's birth and for some years afterward
she kept a bawdyhouse in the Covent Garden district. Nell
herself made no bones about the matter. In 1667 two
slightly different versions of her retort to the taunts of a
fellow actress, Beck Marshall, were circulated. In one Nell
was quoted as saying that she was "born in a bawdyhouse"
and "brought up in a playhouse," in the other that she
was "brought up in a bawdyhouse to fill strong waters
[brandy] to the guests."

Until Nell came to her mother's rescue some time after
1670, took her into her own home and eventually set her
up in a house in Chelsea, old Madam Gwyn lived a precarious life. According to a usually reliable contemporary,
Sir Francis Fane, one day (about 1670) Nell was driving
through the city in her coach and saw her mother selling
apples in the street. Stopping her coach, Nell called to her
mother, bidding her serve God and He would provide for
her as He had provided for Nell! Having had her joke,
Nell relented, turned visible providence and not only
maintained her mother but kept her well supplied with alcoholic beverages. In July, 1679, after a hearty debauch,
old Madam Gwyn fell into a stream near her home and
was drowned.

Her death was the occasion for a libelous chorus of
poets to rake over her lurid past, asserting that she had been
"Maid, punk, and bawd, full sixty years and more," and
that "Bawd was her life, and common-shore her death."
The author of a black-bordered "Elegy upon that never to

be forgotten matron, old Madam Gwyn," (1679), professed to mourn as much for the brandy merchants as for
the dear departed, their best customer,

> That in one day could twenty quarts consume,
> And bravely vaunt she durst it twice presume.

In the intervals of drinking,

> She would a pipe with expedition fill,
> And then could force the vapor to abound
> That clouds of smoke would oft invade her round.

She was so fat that the poet was at a loss for comparisons:

> I will not say with Tryphon's her vast bulk
> O'erspread nine acres, yet her mighty hulk
> Six foot in compass was supposed to be,
> Too ponderous for a common destiny.

Finally the mock-elegist called upon those of her own
kind to follow the hearse: the "Red-noses" who "live by
drinking," the "social topers," and the "Sons of Vulcan"
who "Belch perpetual fume," and those light ladies

> Who are most skilled in arts of gallantry,
> As such who scorn to turn their backs on men,
> But if they close will close with them again.

The author of a "True account of the late most doleful
and lamentable tragedy of old Madam Gwyn, mother to
Madam Eleanor Gwyn" made much of the deceased's profession. She was, said he, a "chief matron [bawd]" who
had recently been at great expense "to find out an ingenious method to restore lost maidenheads, that so she might
to her abundant profit make a double mortgage to such
buffoon beauty hunters who daily accosted her for the

procuration of some rose-buds though June be passed, as likewise to find out a private tincture for to sprucify her daughter's decayed physiognomy." Her death, he concluded, "caused a universal grief among the buxom bona-robas [prostitutes]."

Rose Gwyn, Nell's older sister, made up for a misspent youth by a respectable maturity. In December, 1663, when Rose was at least fifteen and probably older, she was charged with theft, a capital offense in that day. Convicted at the Old Bailey, she was reprieved by the intercession of a higher authority and allowed to appeal for a pardon. While she lay in jail waiting for the slow machinery of state to grind into motion, she was visited by two young courtiers, a Mr. Browne, Cupbearer to the Duke of York (the King's younger brother), and Henry Killigrew, Groom of the Bedchamber to the Duke.

Killigrew was the son of Thomas Killigrew, Groom of the Bedchamber to the King and Master of the King's Theatre. He was also, by virtue of his recent marriage, brother-in-law to Sir Charles Sedley ("Little Sid for simile renowned"), a Court poet and dramatist. At twenty-six Killigrew was notorious as a humorist, duellist, drinker, and liar—particularly the last. Within a few years he was to become even more famous as founder of "the ballers," a group of courtiers who paid regular visits to "Lady" Bennet's brothel and danced naked with her nymphs. Quarrelsome, dissolute, and incapable of ever holding his libelous tongue, Killigrew was involved in one lurid scrape after another, and usually managed to escape punishment, thanks to his drollery and masterly prevarication.

On December 26, 1663, Rose wrote to Browne, thanking him for "his and Mr. Killigrew's civil visit," and begging that she might be admitted to bail until her pardon was ready. She denied that she had ever been a thief and pleaded that her pardon had already been granted (by the King), although not yet passed by the proper authorities. She complained that her father had "lost all he had in service of the late king," Charles I—a common enough claim in the early years of the Restoration, and one not to be trusted. Her letter had an immediate result: four days later she was out on bail. Her pardon followed in due course.

There can be only one explanation of this sequence of events: Browne and Killigrew had a more than friendly interest in Rose's welfare. If Rose was not technically a member of the Oldest Profession, she was at best a demi-mondaine with whom the two young rakehells had become intimate during their rambles among the dives of Covent Garden. If Nell served strong waters to the guests in her mother's bawdyhouse, what did Rose serve? Certainly Rose was sufficiently notorious in tavern society. The author of "The Haymarket Hectors" (1671), who referred to Nell as "the sister of Rose," expected his readers to know the older sister as well as they did the younger, and by that time Nell was the King's mistress!

Some time in 1671 or 1672 Rose married one John Cassels, a captain in the Duke of Monmouth's guards. This gentleman, as his widow wrote twenty years after his death, had "for many years served the crown to the great expense of his fortune"—another common and doubtful claim. But it was certainly not his long and arduous services which, on November 8, 1672, secured from the grateful crown a pension of £100 a year "to Capt. John Cassels and Rose his wife" out of the Irish revenue—the usual source for funds granted to the King's mistresses and favorites. Two years later Cassels was killed at the battle of Enzheim. The kindly King took good care of sister Rose; on October 30, 1675, he increased her pension to £200. Some time before 1679 she was further consoled by a new husband, a Mr. Guy Forster.

Rose was never wealthy, but as long as Nell lived her pension was always paid, and she was never in want. The two sisters kept in close touch, and Rose occasionally did little services for Nell. In 1675, for example, she did some shopping for Nell and submitted the bills for her purchases with little notes in her own hand. Otherwise Rose remained an undistinguished and harmless person who spent her life trading on her sister's fame. She was still alive in 1694, petitioning for the renewal of her pension, unpaid since the accession of William and Mary. She described herself as "Rose Forster, widow, sister to Mrs. Ellen Gwyn, mother to the Duke of St. Albans."

Besides her sister and her son, the Duke of St. Albans, Nell had (or chose to remember) only one other relative still living when she made her will in 1687. This was one William Cholmley, a "kinsman" to whom she bequeathed £100. The author of "A Panegyric" (1681), after touching on Nell's father and mother, concluded,

> Nor must her cousin be forgot, preferred
> From many years command in the Black-Guard
> To be an ensign;
> Whose tattered colors well do represent
> His first estate in the ragged regiment.

The origins of this cousin, like Nell's, were low: the members of the "Black-Guard" were tattered waifs, link-boys, whose smoking torches lighted wayfarers through the pitch-black streets at night. But the power of a royal mistress could easily transform a vagabond into an officer and a gentleman. On October 17, 1678, a commission was issued for "William Cholmley to be ensign in Colonel John Russell's regiment of Foot Guards." By 1681 Cholmley had risen to the rank of captain in the Coldstream Guards. The accounts of Nell's executors list on January 25, 1689, "Paid Mr. Warner for Mr. Will. Cholmley—£100." The use of "Mr." instead of the military title was by no means unusual, and the fact that Mr. Warner, Nell's chaplain, collected the money, suggests that Cholmley was abroad at the time, probably with his regiment.

These, then, were the Gwyns of Covent Garden: a nameless father, a dipsomaniac mother, a notorious sister, a vagabond cousin, and Nell herself. And the setting for this family? A bawdyhouse, a debtors prison at Oxford, the Old Bridewell of London, the narrow dark streets and evil slums of Covent Garden. Out of this dungheap grew a lily—a tiger lily.

I I

From Barmaid to Actress

1 6 5 0 – 1 6 6 4

II

ONE OF THE greatest triumphs of Nell's life was her ability to survive infancy and childhood. In seventeenth-century England more than half of the babies born each year died before they reached the advanced age of two, and in the slums the proportion of deaths was much higher. But Nell was tough-fibred and fortunate. She survived bad air, filth and vermin, childhood diseases and the far more dangerous treatments of physicians, the small beer which even children drank in preference to water, and the food which at best was coarse and monotonous. She grew up—a small girl, but active and wiry, lively, cheerful, and fun-loving.

Nell was less than two years old when young King Charles led an army of Scotch Covenanters into England in a desperate gamble for his throne. At the Battle of Worcester (September 3, 1651) the outnumbered and out-generaled invaders broke and fled before the pikes of Cromwell's Ironsides. For a month thereafter "Charles Stuart, a long dark man, above two yards tall," with a price of £1,000 on his head, wandered through England, disguised as a country bumpkin, and accompanied only by such faithful friends as Lord Henry Wilmot and Father John Huddlestone. Passed on from one loyal subject to another, he hid in ditches, lofts, and peasant cottages, and once spent a long day in the sheltering boughs of a hollow

oak, thereafter immortalized as the Royal Oak of Boscobel.
Finally he reached a seaport and escaped into France, bearing with him a story which he never tired of retelling in
later years—to the weariness of his listeners.

Nell was three when the Long Parliament—the last fee-
ble remnant of lawful government—was finally dissolved,
and she was nearly four when Oliver Cromwell took his
seat in Whitehall Palace as Lord Protector. There were
wars going on with Holland, Portugal, and Spain while she
was still under six. England lived by martial law under the
government of major-generals, one for each of twelve sec-
tional divisions. Puritanism lay like a blight over the islands,
while on the continent exiled King Charles vainly sought
support from the crowned heads of Europe. The king
without a country and his family of refugees were church-
mouse poor, nibbling at the crumbs dropped from royal
tables. Charles's mother, the French princess Henrietta-
Maria, secretly married again to Henry Jermyn (later Earl
of St. Albans), supported herself, her husband, and her little daughter Henrietta on a pension granted by her nephew,
Louis XIV of France. Louis would gladly have helped his
royal cousin with money and arms, but he was still a youth
(nine years younger than Charles) and under the firm grip
of his wily prime minister, Cardinal Mazarin, who had
formed an alliance with Cromwell. Charles's other sister,
Mary, widow of William II of Orange, had little money
and less power, and his two younger brothers, James, Duke
of York, and Henry, Duke of Gloucester (who died in
1660), to stave off starvation took service with the armies
of Spain in its endless war with France.

Hopelessly King Charles wandered from Paris to Cologne, Bruges, Brussels, and Holland, pursued by Cromwell's relentless enmity, followed by a host of hungry courtiers, and supported always by the calm strength and financial wizardry of Sir Edward Hyde (later Earl of Clarendon and Lord Chancellor), who never lost hope. For diversion the King played with a succession of light damsels, rioted with such boon companions as the brilliant, unstable George Villiers, Duke of Buckingham, and vainly proposed marriage to a number of wealthy and well-connected heiresses, among them Hortense, the youngest of the three beautiful Mancini sisters, nieces of Cardinal Mazarin. Young King Louis fell desperately in love with the two older sisters—first Olympia, then Marie—but the Cardinal stubbornly refused to let him marry either. His nieces were not good matches for the King of France; they were too good for the refugee King of England.

In 1658, when Nell was eight years old, the King's fortunes were at their lowest ebb, and the flighty Duke of Buckingham deserted the ship of monarchy, returned to England, made his peace with Cromwell, and married Mary Fairfax, the heiress of a Roundhead general. In August that year, a terrible storm fell upon England, blew down great trees, unroofed houses, wrecked ships in harbors, and brought his last sickness to Oliver Cromwell, "the Beast in Revelations." He died on September 3. King Charles received the happy news at Hoogstraeten in Holland, and his small Court went mad with joy. Nell Gwyn was too young to be interested in anything but the storm. Besides, the news of great events filtered slowly through the seacoal smoke and fog of London, and the people of the slums, lost in their own small lives, had no ears for the affairs of the nation.

But the stirring news of the next two years penetrated even to the alleys of Covent Garden. In May, 1659, the members of the old Long Parliament returned, to be scornfully nicknamed the "Rump" Parliament. There was growing talk of the King's return; with him would come a flood of high-living, free-spending gentry. The liquor sellers of Covent Garden had profited during the Puritan regime—when all other amusements were forbidden, men turned more than ever to the pleasures of wine—but the clothiers, haberdashers, and jewelers had sold little to the dank Puritan politicians. Even the children were excited. Their elders could remember better days when there were football games in the open area of Covent Garden, puppet shows, and mountebanks and quack doctors with their zanies; when there was music in the Spring Garden in St. James's Park and dancing in the streets to tunes scraped out by vagrant fiddlers.

When General Monk entered London with his army on February 3, 1660 (the day after Nell's tenth birthday), and declared for a free Parliament, the whole city turned out to greet him, and in every street that night rumps of beef were roasted at open fires to celebrate the end of the Rump Parliament. And when King Charles came back to London on May 29 (his thirtieth birthday) and paraded down the Strand to Whitehall with a glorious company (including the disloyal Duke of Buckingham, renovated and forgiven), the city exploded with joy. The streets were strewn with flowers, the church bells clanged, the fountains ran with wine, the City Companies appeared in livery.

with banners and golden chains, the windows and balconies along the Strand were crowded with ladies and gentlemen in velvet and gold and silver, there were blaring trumpets and thundering drums. It was a brave new world indeed. (And that night King Charles slept in the arms of his newest mistress, Barbara Palmer, wife of Roger Palmer, Esquire, daughter of William Villiers, Lord Grandison, and cousin of the Duke of Buckingham.)

The Restoration era opened in glory, and poets prophesied an age of peace and prosperity. The exiles swarmed back to England; Parliament met and poured gold into the King's lap; the nation crowned him in a roar of loyal fervor that made the welkin ring twice; there was a year of honeymoon, saddened only by the deaths of Henry, Duke of Gloucester, and Mary, Princess of Orange. Queen Henrietta-Maria returned to England to break up a projected marriage between her son James, Duke of York, and Chancellor Clarendon's daughter Anne, but she was too late. The lady was already with child by James, and the Duke obstinately insisted upon making an honest woman of her. Little Henrietta ("Minette," the King's favorite sister) came to England with her mother but within a few weeks returned to France to marry Philip, Duke of Orleans, brother of Louis XIV. King Charles gave himself up to luxury with Mrs. Palmer, whose husband he created Baron of Limerick and Earl of Castlemaine in the peerage of Ireland, with remainder to "the males got of the body of this wife, the Lady Barbara," said Pepys, "the reason whereof everybody knows."

Barbara was tall, supple, fair, blue-eyed, and so beautiful that many observers considered her the "finest" woman in England in her time. Her education in sex had started before she was quite fifteen, with Philip Stanhope, Earl of Chesterfield, as her tutor, and the vicious Lady Anne Hamilton (later Lady Southesk) as his assistant. (For a short time the three had a *ménage à trois*.) After Barbara's reluctant marriage to Roger Palmer, and even after she had entered upon her liaison with King Charles, she continued to see Chesterfield. To entertain a husband and two lovers at the same time was no great feat for a nymphomaniac who by the end of her sensational career could hardly count the number of men in her life. Barbara was spoiled, petulant, and imperious. When she flew into a tantrum—as she often did—her eyes flashed and her tongue poured forth a torrent of profanity and abuse. She was intensely avaricious and extravagant and for years kept the King poor paying her debts and complying with her demands. "She was a woman of pleasure," said Bishop Burnet, "and stuck at nothing that would either serve her appetites or her passions; she was vastly expensive, and by consequence very covetous; she was weak, and so was easily managed"—by politicians, not by the King, whom she managed in turn. Nine months after the Restoration Lady Castlemaine presented her royal lover with a daughter, insisting that he was the child's father. The parentage was promptly acknowledged by the Earl of Castlemaine and, some years later and only after much bullying, by the King. The gossips insisted that the Earl of Chesterfield was the real father.

In some ways it was a far cry from Whitehall Palace to a Covent Garden bawdyhouse, but in the reign of Charles II the palace—home of the King, his family, and his swarms of functionaries—was the greater brothel of the two. In fact, a seventeenth-century bawdyhouse was not strictly a brothel; it was a drinking establishment with a woman proprietor who served also as a bawd. The true brothels were large establishments in Moorfields, Whetstone Park, and Dog-and-Bitch Yard, kept by such famous procurers as "Lady" Bennet, Madam Cresswell, "Mother" Temple, and Damaris Page. Annually during Lent (when flesh was forbidden) the London apprentices attacked such houses and partially demolished them, to the great amusement of the constables. Bawdyhouses were more like the "pitiful alehouse near Bartholomew Fair" where the diarist Samuel Pepys went once with a friend and "had a dirty slut or two come up that were whores," or like a little place near the House of Lords where he went one day to drink wormwood ale, and which "doubtless was a bawdy-house, the mistress of the house having the look and dress."

A bawdyhouse was often no more than a cellar, or a barren room above a shop in some unsavory street. Although there might be a seedy-looking husband in the background, the place was usually presided over by some old, weatherbeaten trull who, aided by a young girl, served her guests ale, wine, or the more expensive Nantes brandy. The equipment was cheap: a few plain tables with candles, some stools and chairs, and the necessary jugs, bottles, and glasses. The professional damsels, who appeared on signal, lived elsewhere but had rooms in the building at their disposal. They sold their favors at almost any price from a shilling to a crown, and when trade was bad they would rather accept sixpence than go without employment. The guests ranged from courtiers, law students, tradesmen, and soldiers, to thieves, pickpockets, and Mr. Pepys.

It was in some such place that Nell Gwyn served strong waters to the guests. In a world which looked upon a girl as marriageable at the age of twelve, a ten-year-old was no longer quite a child. It took nerve to move about through a roomful of ribald men, carrying bottles and glasses and evading the clutch of lecherous hands. It took impudence if not wit to bandy profane repartee with the customers; it took cunning to protect money from pickpockets, and agility to duck flying bottles when a brawl broke out. It was a rough school for a youngster.

According to the lampoon writers of later years Nell engaged in a variety of occupations. Of course such writers depended on hearsay, and their fancies took over when rumor flagged. Mr. Lacy, the author of "Satire" (1677), claims that Nell's

> . . . first employment was, with open throat
> To cry fresh herrings, even at ten a groat.

The writer of "A Panegyric" (1681) asserts that she first raked cinders, then sold apples about the streets, and at last became an orange-girl:

> Even while she cinders raked, her swelling breast
> With thoughts of glorious whoredom was possessed.
> But first the basket her fair arm did suit,
> Laden with pippins and Hesperian fruit.
> This first step raised, to the wondering pit she sold
> The lovely fruit, smiling with streaks of gold.

In "Mrs. Nelly's Complaint" (1682) she is made to cry to the reader,

> You that have seen me in my youthful age
> Preferred from stall of turnips to the stage . . .

The alleged poet who wrote "The Lady of Pleasure" (1687) agreed that Nell's first vocation was cinder raking and drew a charming picture of her in the street,

> With face of potlid black, unshod her feet,
> And in a cloud of dust her cinders shaking.

But his lubricous imagination brought forth an interesting explanation for her rise to the stage. He accused her of charming "a cully of the city" who, after enjoying her for a while, "grew Nelly-sick" and sent her to the playhouse,

> Where soon she grew, being in her proper sphere,
> The pride and envy of the theatre.

During the years from 1660 to 1663, while Nell was furiously busy serving strong waters, selling herrings, apples, turnips, and Heaven knows what other comestibles (and seducing cullies of the city in her spare moments!), the groundwork of her future was being prepared elsewhere. Shortly after the restoration of King Charles two major theatrical companies were formed: the Duke's Company, headed by Sir William Davenant, and the King's Company, with Thomas Killigrew as master. Both companies were quickly established in Lincoln's Inn Fields, northeast of Covent Garden, in tennis-court buildings converted into theatres. Almost from the first, women were employed for feminine rôles, a revolutionary novelty imported from France. Boys and young men had played such parts from Elizabethan times up to the closing of the theatres in 1642. Even with women playing women's rôles, there was such a shortage of capable actresses that for some years men played some of the feminine parts in a number of productions, in accordance with the old tradition. One well-worn anecdote tells that King Charles, coming a trifle early to a performance of *Hamlet*, sent backstage to learn why the play did not begin at once. The messenger brought word that the queen (played by Edward Kynaston) was not yet shaved. "Ods fish," cried the King, "I beg her majesty's pardon! We'll wait till her barber has done with her."

It was not long before the prospering King's Company began to feel cramped in its small quarters. Early in 1662 it began the construction of a more commodious theatre in the Covent Garden section, between Bridges Street and Drury Lane. Of course twelve-year-old Nell was too young for the stage, but the new theatre would employ a number of people in other capacities; there might be some kind of post for her. She had influential friends: her sister Rose was intimate with Henry Killigrew, son of the theatre's chief shareholder and manager.

In February, 1663, the King's Company granted to Mrs. Mary Meggs, a widow, the right to sell "oranges, lemons, fruits, sweetmeats, and all manner of fruiterers and confectioners wares" in the new theatre, which was nearly finished. She was to be allowed three assistants and room under the stairs backstage for the storage of her goods. Mrs. Meggs had employment for three girls as assistants. Their function would be to parade about with their baskets of eatables or to stand in the pit with their backs to the stage, on the alert for customers and crying their wares between the acts. For such duties she needed pretty, quick-witted, impudent girls, attractive to the gentlemen who paid half a crown for the privilege of sitting on the backless benches of the pit, and capable of coaxing or shaming the said gentlemen into paying sixpence apiece for small "China" oranges, the staple commodity. For such a post Nell Gwyn, now thirteen, was thoroughly qualified by nature and previous experience. And "Madam" Rose, her sister, was in a position to get her the job.

Mr. Lacy (who *may* have been John Lacy, actor and playwright), in "Satire" (1677), summarized Nell's history by calling on King Charles to

> Witness the royal line sprung from the belly
> Of thy anointed princess, Madam Nelly,
> Whose first employment was, with open throat,
> To cry fresh herrings, even at ten a groat;
> Then was by Madam Rose exposed to the town,
> I mean to those that would give half a crown.
> Next, in the playhouse she took her degree,
> As men commence in the university—
> No doctors till they've masters been before—
> So no player till first she has been a whore.
> Look back and see the people mad with rage
> To see the bitch in so high equipage;
> And every day they do the monster see,
> They let ten thousand curses fly at thee.

The high equipage and the curses were both still far in the future; meanwhile Nell had her first real step up in life. The King's Theatre, brave with paint and scenery, opened its doors on May 7, 1663, and if Nell was not one of the original orange-girls she soon became a member of the sorority.

Economically this was a considerable promotion for her. An orange-girl worked six days a week (the theatres were closed on Sundays), and her small earnings were often eked out with a coin pressed in her hand by a gentleman as payment for running an errand, or as earnest of future reward for favors to be granted. She was better dressed: in smock, stays, petticoat, shoes, and a coarse "stuff" gown with a handkerchief about her neck. But best of all was the glamorous excitement of the ever-changing world of the theatre.

The King's House was a large, barn-like, wooden structure, about a hundred feet long by sixty wide, with a glazed cupola which let in some measure of daylight and, in bad weather, so much rain that the people in the pit were forced to flee. The building was draughty and heated only by the animal warmth of the audience and by the flames of candles along the walls and over the stage. The young bloods of the town sat in the pit (2s. 6d.), bantered with the orange-girls, flirted with drabs wearing vizard masks and pretending to be ladies of quality, laughed, fought, and showed off their wit at the expense of the playwright. The beauties of the Court and most royal and noble dignitaries sat in the side boxes (4s.), raised so little above the pit that amorous exchanges took place between the two levels. More sedate folk sat in the middle gallery (1s.6d.), and the poorest crowded into the upper tier (1s.) where footmen and coachmen were admitted free near the end of the play. Musicians under the stage discoursed sweet music before the play began and between the acts. Performances began at three o'clock in the afternoon. There were no reserved seats. Fashionable folk sent

their footmen to hold places for them and, as always, arrived late.

Here, under the tutelage of Orange Moll and her Rabe-
laisian customers, Nell completed her education in vulgar
repartee and profanity. She became particularly adept at
the latter. Years afterward a Court lady was so tactless as
to commend Nell's wit and beauty in the presence of her
bitter rival, the Duchess of Portsmouth. Nell's friend
spoke of her skill at diverting the King with her repartee
and boasted that she made a very fine appearance, that she
seemed to be as much a lady of quality as anybody. "Yes,
madam," said the duchess drily, "but anybody may know
she has been an orange wench by her swearing."

Nell studied other subjects, some with less success. She
was ambitious, and there before her eyes daily were the
actresses of the company—Mrs. Corey, Mrs. Eastland, Peg
Hughes, Mary Knepp, Anne Marshall, and Susanna Up-
hill—young women of little education or training and only
slightly better backgrounds than Nell's. They wore splendid clothes; they were paid what seemed to her fabulous
sums (twenty to fifty shillings a week—worth about as
many dollars today); and in the greenroom when the play
was done they were praised, pawed, and petted by elegant
gentlemen who took them out to dinner and sometimes
home to bed. Who would not want to be an actress?

If she had not earlier done so, Nell had to learn to read
and write now that she was almost an actress. The members of a stock company were required to read and memo-
rize dozens of rôles in the course of a season; skill at
reading was essential. Writing was another matter. Rose
wrote a good plain hand, but Nell never really learned to

write. She signed all documents with a childish "E.G.", so painfully formed as to show a learning process barely begun.

Nell did much better with lessons in singing, speaking, and dancing. She had willing teachers. The need for actresses was so great that the chief men of the King's Company—Charles Hart, Edward Kynaston, Michael Mohun, and John Lacy—were constantly on the lookout for likely young wenches. They themselves were experienced actors who had all been on the stage in some capacity or other before the closing of the theatres. Hart and Kynaston had played female rôles and could teach an aspiring orange-girl how to imitate a fine lady on the stage. Mohun was not only an excellent actor but a good singer. Lacy had been a dancing master at one time and now served the theatre in a triple capacity: as actor, dancer, and choreographer. Nell was an apt pupil; she learned to dance the vigorous jigs which so delighted the audiences, the bransles and corantos commonly performed "by the entire company" to conclude a comedy, and in time she became Lacy's partner in comic dances and spectacles.

She studied also the ways of the world. At fourteen a girl of the slums was wise beyond her years and cynical about such mere abstractions as truth, honor, and virtue. An orange-girl was in daily contact with a godless lot of men, on stage and in the audience. From their stations in the pit the orange-girls saw the by-play between the King and his mistress, Barbara Palmer, Countess of Castlemaine, and watched the Court nobles making love to so-called Maids of Honor while the play went on unheeded. They carried love-notes from one member of the audience to another, looked on as the vizard-masks made assignations with their victims, and responded daily to dozens of coarse suggestions from their customers. They saw that the way to rise in the world was not by merit and hard work but by friends, flattery, and compliance. One played the game according to the rules.

It would not be at all surprising, then, if Nell, following a time-honored procedure, eased her way to the stage by sleeping with some man of influence—in short, no player till first she was a whore, in this case to the leading actor, Charles Hart, a tall, handsome fellow in his late thirties. But whether she was "eased of her virginity" by Hart before she came upon the stage or after (or whether, indeed, she had not lost that dubious article to some earlier lover) is of no particular consequence. Certainly Hart was one of her "keepers," if not the first, and the identity of Christian names among her known lovers—Charles Hart, Charles, Lord Buckhurst, and Charles II—later gave her the cue for one of her broadest jokes: she called the King her "Charles the Third!"

In November, 1664, Thomas Killigrew was preparing one of his own rambling, long-winded plays, *Thomaso, or The Wanderer*, for production. (If it ever appeared, no one bothered to record the fact.) Accidentally prophetic, he wrote the name "Nelly" in the list of actors after the bit part of "Paulina, a courtesan of the first rank." This is the earliest reference to Nell as a member of the King's Company. Now, nearly fifteen years old, the little barmaid, itinerant vendor, and orange-girl was entitled to call herself by the proud title "His Majesty's Servant."

III

His
Majesty's
Servants

1 6 6 4 – 1 6 6 5

III

NOT LONG AFTER Nell became a neophyte actress she moved to lodgings in Drury Lane, in a house next door to the Cock and Pye Tavern, opposite Wych Street. There on a fine May-day a couple of years later Pepys saw her standing at her door—"a mighty pretty creature in her smock sleeves and bodice"—watching the troops of flower-decked milk-maids dancing through the streets with a fiddler before them. Her reason for moving to Drury Lane was obvious: it was just a step around the corner to the Russell Street entrance of the King's Theatre. All her colleagues lived as close to the theatre as they could. Since the company presented as many as two or even three plays in a single week, the players practically lived in the theatre, spending the mornings rehearsing new plays (or old plays not acted for some time) and the afternoons from three to five or later acting in the current production. Their evenings they devoted to more ignoble activities, following, it must be admitted, the custom of the time.

Partly in reaction against Puritan repression, partly in obedience to their natural bent, a good many Restoration Londoners went to excesses of drunkenness and lechery, and the actors were not the least of the sinners. The great mass of the English people were sober and God-fearing; the wastrels and rakes were little more numerous in proportion to the total population than at any other period, but because of lax law enforcement they were more open in their wickedness. When young gentlemen, heated by wine, ran riot in the streets at night, broke windows, beat up harmless pedestrians, and skirmished with the watch, there were many indignant outcries but few punishments. The King himself was given to hard drinking, and the popularity of the habit among his subjects is suggested by the words of a popular song:

> Good store of good claret supplies everything,
> And the man that is drunk is as great as a king.

The widespread addiction to lechery could be illustrated by hundreds of examples, from Pepys and his hole-in-a-corner affairs with servant girls and workmen's wives to the King's mistresses, flaunted in public to the rage of respectable people. A locksmith of Nantwich, convinced that the sin of "keeping" was becoming a national diversion, proposed that all unmarried females above twelve years of age should wear padlocks until they were married, and that he himself should be "the maker and fixer of the same." The Covent Garden slums which produced Nell Gwyn would have thought his notion of the age of consent a bit naïve, and the gentry, who guarded their own daughters—and sometimes their wives, too—would have been incensed. But the gentry considered other men's wives and daughters fair game—especially milk-maids, servant girls, shopkeepers' wives, and actresses.

In the pyramidal class system of Restoration England, with the broad base and most of the core of the pyramid composed of honest, industrious artisans, farmers, and "citizens" (tradesmen and merchants), the apex was a small, tightly-knit society ("the Town" as opposed to "the City") which played the sedulous ape to King and Court in speech, dress, manners, and morals. Love and gaming were the two principal pastimes in the rambling galleries and chambers of Whitehall; consequently both diversions, but particularly love, were indulged in by the gentlemen of "the Town." "Keeping" became so much a matter of fashion that Francis North, Lord Guildford, a sober lawyer and courtier, was seriously urged to "keep a whore," because his failure to do so made him "ill looked upon at Court." By the same token many an amorous lady ventured her person and reputation with a gallant, and the husband who resented his wife's lewd conduct was considered a fool and a spoil-sport. When the Earl of Chesterfield, fearing an intrigue between his wife and the Duke of York, dragged the reluctant lady off to his country estate, the young blades of the Court—such cuckold-makers as Lord Buckhurst, Sir Charles Sedley, the Earl of Rochester, and George Etherege—diverted everybody with witty ballads at his expense.

Many of the Court intrigues shifted so rapidly that even the best informed gossips could hardly keep track of them. King Charles, a patient man, was more dogged in pursuit and more constant than most in his keeping; although his affections might shift, he rarely discarded a mistress, preferring to add to his hand. In 1664, while Barbara, Countess of Castlemaine, was his semi-official beloved, he was avidly chasing Mrs. Frances Stuart, the seventeen-year-old daughter of the Honorable Walter Stuart and one of the Queen's Maids of Honor. ("Mrs.", the common abbreviation of "Mistress," was the title given both married and unmarried women. A "miss" was either a very young girl or a kept woman.)

Frances Stuart was vain, empty-headed, and beautiful—so vain that on the least encouragement she would show her legs above the knee; so empty-headed that she loved childish romps and games, and courtiers amused her by building castles of cards; so beautiful that John Rotier, the famous engraver, used her as his model for Britannia on the King's new copper coins. She was tall, slender, graceful, and fair-haired, with large eyes and a "little Roman nose." For a while she put Lady Castlemaine's own excellent nose quite out of joint.

Amorous King Charles was so obsessed that whenever possible he would get Frances into a corner and "be with her half an hour together, kissing her to the observation of all the world." She accepted his gifts, permitted him many liberties with her person—and refused to sleep with him. One day he lost his temper and burst out with the hope that he might live to see her "ugly and willing." He even wrote her a love song which began,

> I pass all my hours in a shady old grove,
> But I live not the day when I see not my love;
> I survey every walk now my Phillis is gone,
> And I sigh when I think we were there all alone;
> O then, 'tis O then, that I think there's no hell
> Like loving, like loving too well.

One half the Court was convinced that Frances was already the King's mistress; the other half was equally certain that she soon would be. Both halves were wrong. To Frances Stuart goes a unique honor: her virtue was proof against the examples of her colleagues, the arguments of politicians who tried to "get" her for the King, and all the pleas, persuasions, and blandishments of her royal lover. She wanted a wedding ring.

King Charles set the standard of licentious conduct, and his servants, at Whitehall and in the theatres, did their best to better his instructions. To be sure, in the early days of the Restoration there were many honest and sober (but dull) men among the King's Cupbearers, Pages, Grooms and Gentlemen of the Bedchamber—the gentry and nobility who took turns waiting and sleeping in the royal ante-chamber, helping their master to dress and undress, serving him at table, and running errands. But as the years wore on the King surrounded himself more and more with men who also loved wine, wit, music, plays, poetry, and prostitutes. There were decent women at Court, too—even a few Maids of Honor who kept their precarious chastity—but many of the Queen's Ladies-in-Waiting had sold their virtue for their social preferment.

In a small way the theatres mirrored Whitehall. Some of the actors of the King's Company, Mohun and Lacy, for example, were men of dignity and moderation, who kept their sins well hidden. Thomas Betterton, leader of the Duke's Company, was an honorable gentleman, happily married and temperate in all his ways. But most of the actors were bawdy, dissolute fellows, much given to the obvious sins of drunkenness and lechery. Whatever their origins, they asserted their gentility and their right to wear swords off-stage, but they were sketchily educated, lacking in morals, and so prodigal that had they not been, as His Majesty's servants, immune to arrest for debt, they would have spent the best part of their lives in jail. As for their lechery, Thomas Killigrew once told Pepys that he was obliged "to keep a woman on purpose at 20s. a week to satisfy 8 or 10 of the young men of his house, whom till he did so he could never keep to their business, and now he do."

The women of the companies were little better than the men. They were not much given to wine, but with a few exceptions—such as Mrs. Betterton and Mrs. Shadwell at the Duke's House—they were notoriously short on virtue. However, it must be pleaded that they all worked hard for small pay, augmented only now and then by the profits from a benefit performance, or "women's day"; they had heavy expenses for the finery used on the stage, and they were constantly tempted by amorous gentry with well-filled purses. Following the style set by the King— one of whose earlier conquests was Elizabeth Weaver of the King's Company—dozens of titled rakes sought to increase their prestige by liaisons with actresses. It was the thing to do. Among the many successful gentlemen in the first decade of the Restoration were Prince Rupert, the Duke of Richmond, the Earls of Oxford and Rochester, Lord Buckhurst, Sir Charles Sedley, and Sir Robert Howard, to name only the well known. Attacked by such glittering men of property, many ladies of the theatre surrendered and became ladies of pleasure in their spare time or left the stage for lodgings in a fine quarter of the town.

In the winter of 1664-65 Nell was a tyro preparing for the competition on stage and in the greenroom. The three actor-managers, Hart, Mohun, and Lacy, kept her at bit parts and taught her the craft. She was not given a really good rôle until the following spring.

First of all, Nell had to get acquainted with the physical properties of the stage—she already knew the theatre. The outer platform of the stage extended into the pit, bringing the actors in close contact with the audience. Nell learned the knack of delivering an "aside" or a prologue, leaning forward over the lamps and taking the pit into her confidence. At the rear of the platform was the wide proscenium arch of the inner stage; scenes were changed by separating or bringing together painted flats which slid in grooves across the inner stage and met in the middle. Nell learned that actors "discovered" on the inner stage when flats were opened came forward to deliver their lines, and that those who "died" usually did so well within the arch so that at the end of the scene the flats could be closed in front of their bodies, with less work for the "bearers." On each side of the arch were three stage doors; above them were windows with balconies, used when characters were to appear "aloft." It was quite a trick to scramble down from one of these, fly around backstage to the proper door, and come on in time for a cue without being breathless. In fact, the whole business of acting was hard labor: the actors moved briskly on and off the stage and were on their feet practically all the time, unless they were flat on their backs on the floor, pretending to be dead.

Nell acquired a wardrobe and learned to wear fashionable clothes. The actors made few attempts at historical truth in scenes and costumes; richness and show were all they sought. Hamlet wandered through Denmark clad in Restoration garb—often a hand-me-down suit from a rich patron—flat-crowned, broad-brimmed hat sailing atop a monstrous periwig, lace-trimmed shirt of holland linen, close fitting long vest, loose surcoat reaching to the knees, full breeches, silk or worsted stockings, and shoes with ribbon bows. Ophelia was entrancing in a rich-colored French gown *à la mode* opened in front to display under-dress, flowered petticoats, and a good deal of Ophelia her-self—especially her breasts and shoulders rising from the lace-edged top of the linen smock or chemise. Sometimes this territory was covered by a lace collar or linen hand-kerchief. The company provided basic costumes for cer-tain special productions, but even then the actors provided their own swords, feathers, gloves, and shoes. Nell had to have not only dresses and petticoats but collars, necker-chiefs, gloves, fans, silk stockings, garters, and shoes trimmed with rosettes and ribbons. She learned to wear these things with the grace of a fine lady, to hold her body erect, walk with dainty steps, curtsy, wield her fan, and toss her curls.

The craft of the comedian was quickly mastered. Nell had only to be her own gay, giddy self, and to pick up a few tricks: the pouting lower lip and languishing cast of sleepy eyes denoting passion; the quick gesture or change of tone which emphasized the double meaning in a bawdy line; and the half-reluctant, half-inviting management of her body in scenes when an actor tried to lay hands on her. For the rest she made the most of her physical charms and to please the men in the front row danced a jig and, by whirling petticoats, gave them glimpses of "a neat silk leg and pair of holland thighs."

Although Nell was a natural comedian, the small re-

sources of the company could support no narrow special-
ists. She must be at least competent in serious parts. Trag-
edies were acted in a formal, highly artificial style. The
players strutted, bellowed, and intoned their lines of verse,
contorting their bodies in stylized gestures. They were
forever dropping to their knees, getting up, flinging themselves into somebody's arms (or "on his neck"), falling
back in alarm with faces averted, clapping hands to heart
or head, all according to rule. Dislike it as she might, Nell
had to become a tragedian. Among other skills she learned
how to die—in simulated agony as the result of drinking a
"bowl" of poison, or more commonly by the bloodier
way of sword or dagger, the sword blunted and taken between arm and side, the dagger a collapsible fake, the
blood real (fresh sheep's-blood) and applied to arm, neck,
or breast by a sponge tied in the palm of the victim's hand.
There was danger even in such mimic murder. Once Elizabeth Barry wielded a trick dagger so viciously in a scene
with Anne Boutel that "though the point of the dagger
was blunted, it made its way through Mrs. Boutel's stays
and entered about a quarter of an inch into the flesh."

At fifteen Nell was small and slender but well rounded.
She wore her bright chestnut hair in clusters of curls on
each side of her head. Her face was almost heart-shaped,
with a broad forehead, full cheeks, and a small, rounded
chin. Her wide, full-lipped mouth curled upward at the
corners, and her cheeks dimpled when she smiled. Her
nose was a bit on the blunt side, if not quite turned up, and
her eyes were hazel. She had "a foot the least of any woman
in England, which the merry Monarch is said often to
contemplate with great pleasure, in presence of his cour-

tiers"—an innocent cause of merriment. Because of her slenderness and gamin ways she was often called on to play the rôle of a woman disguised as a man and submit her well-turned legs to the critical inspection of the pit.

Typical of the small rôles she played that winter was a maid's part in Sir William Killigrew's *The Siege of Urbin*, produced early in 1665, a wild melodrama, full of plots, disguises, duels, battles, evil villains, and super-noble heroes. The heroine was tall, handsome Anne Marshall as Celestina, a lovelorn maiden who, to avoid a forced marriage, donned a man's periwig, coat, breeches, and sword and sallied forth to win battles and hearts. As Melina, her maid and confidant, likewise breeched and periwigged, Nell had a very thin part, with little to do but listen to her melancholy mistress, second her in her swashbuckling career as an epicene soldier, and show off her own legs. Neither of the young actresses could handle a sword. A stage direction explicitly ordered that "Florio[Anne] and Pedro[Nell] must not fight on the stage through the whole play." Sir William's dialogue was dreadfully dull.

Nevertheless Nell acquitted herself so well in this and in other, unrecorded, performances that in the next new play produced by the company, John Dryden's *The Indian Emperor* (March, 1665), she won the ingénue rôle of Cydaria, the emperor's innocent daughter. This rhymed heroic play, a sequel to *The Indian Queen* by Dryden and Sir Robert Howard, tells the story of the conquest of Mexico by stout Cortez (Charles Hart), who is conquered by Cydaria in turn. There are exciting complications, of course. For example, Montezuma (Mohun), a widower, sighs for wicked Almeria (Anne Marshall), who hates him and loves Cortez; Montezuma's two sons vie for the love of Almeria's sister, and Almeria's brother is contracted to Cydaria! There are the usual duels and battles, debates over love and honor, and scenes of lust and torture, but after much bloodshed all ends with love triumphant and Cydaria and Cortez united.

Dryden scored a great success with the play, and Nell scored a little one.

Picture the King's Theatre on an afternoon in early spring. It is the first performance of a play by a popular dramatist. Prices are doubled, but the theatre is crowded, and the élite of society are present. In a side-box on the right is the King, his sardonic face shadowed by his heavy black periwig, his eyes intent on Frances Stuart, beautiful in a red velvet gown. At his side is drab little Queen Catherine, showing her crooked teeth in a forced smile, and in the next box is Barbara, Countess of Castlemaine, looking out of sorts and sallow in white satin. Across the theatre sits long-faced James, Duke of York, the King's younger brother and heir-presumptive to the throne; with him is his plump duchess, Anne, daughter of Chancellor Clarendon.

In the pit Dryden's witty friends have gathered. There is the florid Duke of Buckingham, more interested in flirting with Anna-Maria, Countess of Shrewsbury, than in watching the play. There is moon-faced Lord Buckhurst who last winter while at sea with the fleet wrote the latest amusing song:

> To all you ladies now at land
> We men at sea indite,
> But first would have you understand
> How hard it is to write. . .

> Our paper, pen and ink, and we
> Roll up and down our ships at sea—
> With a fal, la, la, la, la!

There are Henry Killigrew; John Wilmot, the young
Earl of Rochester, with an angelic face and devilish morals;
stout Henry Savile, Groom to the Duke of York; fair
George Etherege, a budding playwright; and little Sir
Charles Sedley, still famous for an episode with Buckhurst
and Sir Thomas Ogle at the Cock Tavern when, in
drunken good humor, he showed himself nearly naked on
a balcony, preached a mock sermon, and threw bottles
("pist in") at the people of Covent Garden, "*contra pacem
and to the scandal of the government.*" The polite world is
present *en masse*.

Dressed in a flowered pink gown, with a profusion of
ribbons and lace and with plumes in her hair to suggest the
barbaric princess, Nell must compete with the leading lady,
Anne Marshall, for the attention of this sophisticated audience. We see her in her encounters with Cortez portraying
the growth of adolescent love—breast heaving with emotion, hands moving in formal gestures. We watch her in a
love-versus-honor debate with Cortez, and some cynic in
the pit, knowing of the affair between Hart and Nelly,
snickers at the incongruity. She is jealous of her rival,
Almeria, and registers anger; she detests her approved
suitor and registers scorn. Near the end of the play she
shrinks in fear from the furious dagger-wielding Almeria
and cries pitifully:

> Can you be so hard-hearted to destroy
> My ripening hopes that are so near to joy?

> I just approach to all I would possess;
> Death only stands 'twixt me and happiness!

Alas, she pleads in vain. The dagger flashes. Nell shrieks and staggers back, clutching at her bare arm and squeezing the bloody sponge tied to the inside of her middle finger. Cortez rescues her before further damage can be done; Almeria stabs herself and, dying, joins the lovers' hands and gives her blessing on their union. The scene closes on Almeria's prone body as the lovers go off-stage arm in arm, an actor dressed as Mercury comes on to deliver the epilogue, and the audience applauds.

The applause, of course, was chiefly for the brilliant acting of Anne Marshall and Charles Hart, but Nell had some share of it. She was adequate, if not sensational, and her personal charms made up in good measure for her lack of skill. The author of "A Panegyric" wrote:

> Fate now for her did its whole force engage,
> And from the pit she's mounted to the stage.
> There, in full lustre did her glories shine,
> And, long eclipsed, spread forth their light divine.

Nevertheless, her rise to fame was rapid if not meteoric. People began to take notice of her and to speak of her as "Nelly." Even Pepys, who had not seen *The Indian Emperor*, remarked her one day in April when she went on a busman's holiday to the rival theatre. He wrote in his diary, "All the pleasure of the play was, the King and my Lady Castlemaine were there; and pretty, witty Nell, at the King's House, and the younger Marshall [Rebecca] sat next us, which pleased me mightily."

Unfortunately Nell's shining glories were destined for

a new and lengthy eclipse. In the winter of 1664-65 the
commercial rivalry between England and Holland was
coming to a head. The nation of shopkeepers had reached
the decision that the world's trade was too small to be
shared with the Dutch, and Samuel Pepys, Clerk of the
Acts in the Navy Office, was frantically busy getting the
fleet ready for sea. War was formally declared in March,
1665, and throughout April and May the audiences at the
theatres grew daily thinner as patriotic young gentlemen
volunteered for naval service and timorous old gentlemen
took their families to their inland estates.

Moreover, an evil greater than war was creeping over
London with ominous speed. Bubonic plague, the dreaded
scourge of Europe, was returning in epidemic proportions
after lying almost dormant in England for sixteen years.
Beginning in the rat and flea infested areas about the docks,
it moved outward in waves toward the suburbs. Although
preferring those who lived in filth and poverty, the disease
played no favorites and struck alike at young and old,
great and small. Men walking in the streets staggered and
fell, stricken by dizziness and blinding headaches. When
the dreaded swellings, or buboes, appeared in groin or arm-
pit, many victims died of sheer fright. Whole families,
with one member ill, were left to die in locked and guarded
houses. There was no cure, no palliative drug, no help save
flight from those regions where house after house was
chalked with a red cross and the words "Lord have mercy
upon us."

By early May the scarlet tide was washing near Drury
Lane, and the fearful were fleeing from Covent Garden.
On June 5 the theatres were closed by royal order and

were destined to remain closed for the next eighteen months. The players were thrown upon their own resources. Some had savings, or other trades to which they could turn, and could ride out the storm in a village or town remote from plague-stricken London. Some could do no more than follow the Court as it fled from London to Hampton Court, then to Salisbury, and finally to Oxford. (After all, they were the King's servants, and King and Court were their best patrons and customers.) Some few stayed in London with other courageous souls. What Nell Gwyn did, no one knows. There are no records.

IV

"Pretty,
Witty Nell"

1 6 6 5 – 1 6 6 7

I V

WHILE GREAT EVENTS chased each other across the national stage, mere actors were small game and their doings went unrecorded. On June 3, 1665, the Battle of Southwold Bay resulted in an English victory, but both fleets were so badly battered that for the rest of the summer they remained in their home ports, licking their wounds. In London the numbers of the plague-stricken mounted daily; the rich fled to faraway havens and the poor moved out into the open fields for safety. On September 20, a total of 7,165 deaths was reported for the preceding week. "Lord!" wrote Pepys, "What a sad time it is to see no boats upon the river; and grass grows all up and down Whitehall Court, and nobody but poor wretches in the street."

The poor wretches—including Mr. Pepys—walked carefully, avoiding contacts with each other and even with buildings; the infection was everywhere. In their ears was the endless tolling of church bells and a constant low moaning compounded of the groans and wailings of the stricken. The swellings which were the fatal symptom of the plague were so exquisitely painful that the most stoic could not restrain their screams. Some victims shot themselves, some threw themselves from high windows, some ran naked through the streets to the river and plunged in.

Funerals were forbidden. By night bellmen went

53

through the streets, ringing their bells and calling, "Bring out your dead." Behind them came "dead-carts" into which the corpses were thrown, some wrapped decently in linen winding sheets, many stark naked, with stiff, angular limbs. The accumulated dead of a night were dumped into huge pits which served as communal graves, and over the decaying flesh soil was spread so thinly that the mounds were black with crows and ravens except when the gravediggers were at work near by.

Over the whole city hung a miasmic stench, strongest in the suburb slums where the nameless poor died in swarms. In all this horror devoted men continued to work—city magistrates, officers of the national administration, even a rare courtier or two, and many physicians. But the best the doctors could offer was a prophylactic of sage, rue, buttercup-root, angelica-root, snake-root, and saffron, infused in Malaga wine. Despite this witches' brew, by the end of the year nearly 70,000 Londoners had perished. "The plague defied all medicines," wrote Defoe, "the very physicians were seized with it, with their preservatives in their mouths; and men went about prescribing to others and telling them what to do, till the tokens were upon them and they dropped down dead, destroyed by that very enemy they directed others to oppose."

With the frosts of winter the weekly bills of mortality declined. Late in January, 1666, the King ventured back to Hampton Court and thence to Whitehall. His family and servants, who had been housed in the college halls at Oxford, followed him more timidly during the next two months. The dons were glad to see the last of the rude courtiers who were so careless of decorum that they used the fireplaces as privies. Lady Castlemaine had scandalously given birth to one of the King's bastards (her third) in the lodgings of a fellow of Merton College.

By March the numbers of deaths per week had fallen from the thousands into the low hundreds. Even in the midst of war and pestilence men began to hope for the old pleasant ways again. On March 19 Pepys visited the King's Theatre which was "all in dirt, they being altering of the stage to make it wider. But God knows when they will begin to act again." The starving players could echo his longing. They too were drifting back to town, but, except for rare performances at Court, there was no work for them until the following winter. In the obscurity hiding Nell there is only one rift: a royal warrant for granting liveries to actors, dated June 30, 1666, ordered that the usual four yards of bastard scarlet cloth and one quarter of a yard of velvet be delivered to each of eleven "women comedians in His Majesty's Theatre," among them "Ellen Gwyn." At least Nell was still a member of the company. She could spend her days looking at her livery, a scarlet cloak with a wide collar of crimson velvet.

The plague continued during the spring, although with diminishing fury; and the fleets prepared again for war. The Four Days Battle of the Channel (June 1-5) ended with terrible losses on both sides. Summer passed amid minor battles and threats of invasion by the Dutch. Slowly the plague faded away, but there was little heart for entertainment in the stricken city. Even the frivolous courtiers thought it "unseemly for them to be found playing and gaming as they used to be" and amused themselves innocently by lying long in bed.

Late in August things looked more hopeful, although the times were still hard for merchants, traders, actors, and courtiers. There had been some small successes at sea; the war seemed about to wear itself out; and the plague toll was down to three or four deaths a day. Amusement-hungry Londoners began to go to the Bear Garden on the Bankside to enjoy the "rude and nasty pleasure" of bull-baiting, or to Moorfields to see puppet shows. There were even rumors that the theatres were about to reopen.

But the gods had not finished with London. August was hot and tinder-dry; the old houses and shops in the City cracked in the sun, and the pitch melted in their seams. Early on Sunday morning, September 2, a fire started in a baker's shop in Pudding Lane, Fish Street, not far from the foot of London Bridge. It was out of hand almost at once. Fanned by a fresh gale from the east, by daybreak it had consumed over three hundred houses and was spreading westward at a gallop, scorning the efforts of amateur fire-men with their pickaxes, leather buckets, and primitive engines. When it came to the region between Thames Street and the river—crowded by warehouses filled with tar, oil, tallow, and spirits—the fire leaped into insane activity. That night thousands of watchers from the Bankside across the river saw the City "in a most horrid, malicious, bloody flame," with "one entire arch of fire" on both sides of the approach to London Bridge, "and in a bow up the hill for an arch of above a mile long." John Evelyn, an amateur scientist, thought that the heat, "with a long set of fair and warm weather, had even ignited the air, and prepared the materials to conceive the fire, which de-voured, after an incredible manner, houses, furniture, and everything." To distracted Londoners it seemed indeed that the Angel of God had come to scorch the earth with fire.

On Monday, while tired men labored vainly, pulling down houses in the westward path of the flames—which leaped contemptuously across the gaps—panic-stricken citizens loaded their goods on drays, carts, lighters, and boats for a universal exodus. The area of combustion grew steadily, creeping north and east, too, devouring Lombard Street, the Poultry, Cornhill, and the Royal Exchange, plus some forty churches. That night "all the sky was of a fiery aspect, like the top of a burning oven, and the light seen above forty miles round-about. The noise and cracking and thunder of the impetuous flames, the shrieking of women and children, the hurry of people, the fall of towers, houses, and churches, was like a hideous storm, and the air all about was so hot and inflamed that at the last one was not able to approach it." To add to the general consternation, rumors flew that the fire had been set by the French, and all the ancient English fears of Papist plots and foreign invasions came back with redoubled force.

Tuesday was the worst day. The fire engulfed St. Paul's Cathedral; the lead roof melted and poured like lava into the streets, and in the intense heat the very stones of the walls exploded and "flew like grenados." The Duke of York and his soldiers labored all around the perimeter of the area, blowing up houses with gunpowder, a device which stopped the flames toward the east just short of the Tower, but had little effect toward the west. But on Wednesday the wind died down; the blowing up of houses confined the fire more and more, and gradually it came under control and burned itself out.

In four short days a third of the old City was destroyed, from Tower Hill on the east almost to Chancery Lane on the west—short of the western suburbs—and in a semicircle north to Moorfields. Among the thousands of buildings consumed were the cathedral, the guild hall, and eighty-four churches. For weeks the waste of blackened rubble smouldered and smoked, and the ground was hot to the soles of wayfarers' shoes.

Although the theatres were not near the burned district they were still under an interdict. But after the first few stunned weeks, when the City had picked itself up and begun to rebuild, the actors fought for permission to resume playing. The bishops, who professed concern for public health, were their chief enemies. Near the end of November the actors bribed the church with promises to give a share of their profits to the poor and were allowed to play. Nell Gwyn reappeared out of darkness, having survived plague, war, fire, and Heaven knows what else.

Back again in her Drury Lane lodgings she took up the familiar routine of the theatre. She was now nearly seventeen, better developed in mind and body. Now she had her second chance at fame and fortune. She accepted, of course, whatever rôles were allotted her by the chief actors —and Charles Hart had reasons to favor her—but she could no longer be limited to playing maids and innocent young girls. There were comic parts to be cast, and Nell had

> . . . wit and sense,
> Beauty, and such a stock of impudence

that she could not be denied. Three months after the King's Theatre opened she was a star.

Her first known rôle in the new season was in a revival of James Howard's *The English Monsieur*, produced early in December. She had the female lead as Lady Wealthy, a rich young widow pursued by Welbred, a fortune hunter (Charles Hart), to whom she surrendered at last. Her part was not very long—most of the play was devoted to the antics of a group of bumpkins, fools, and fops—but she made the most of it, teasing, insulting, and railing at her blunt wooer with gusto. The comedy itself was rather a poor thing, but by the sparkle and snap of their delivery the actors made their lines sound very clever. The net result was, as Pepys put it, "very witty and pleasant." All the women did well, he added, "but above all, little Nelly." Nell had a good start on the road to fame.

Late in January, 1667, she played the important rôle of Celia in a revival of Fletcher's *The Humorous Lieutenant*. As the heroine of this bawdy comedy about the efforts of a king to seduce his son's low-born sweetheart, Nell had a rôle rich in opportunities to display her comic style. She insulted the bawds who brought her to court and dressed her in rich garments; fenced successfully with the lecherous king; and ridiculed her high-minded lover, Prince Demetrius (Charles Hart), who was convinced of her iniquity. The play ended happily when Demetrius, after a period of iambic agony, learned that Celia had been chased and not caught, and that she was really a virtuous princess in disguise. Joyfully he took her to his honorable bosom.

On January 23 Pepys took his wife and her maid to see the play. Afterwards his friend, Nell's colleague Mary

Knepp, took him and his family backstage "and brought to us Nelly, a most pretty woman, who acted the great part of Celia today very fine, and did it pretty well. I kissed her and so did my wife, and a mighty pretty soul she is." This was Pepys' first formal meeting with Nell. Following the easy custom of the day, when he was introduced he "saluted" her upon the lips—no mere peck but a hearty buss. He left the theatre much pleased by his trip backstage, "and specially kissing of Nell."

Two weeks later Nell had another fling at broad comic action in Fletcher's *The Chances*, altered by George Villiers, Duke of Buckingham. Playing the Second Constantia, a prostitute (not to be confused with the romantic heroine, a lost lady also named Constantia), she worked her wanton wiles on eager Don John (Charles Hart again), bringing him to such a pitch that he could hardly contain himself. The following dialogue was famous for its suggestive action; years later it was still remembered as the scene in which Don John was "pulling down" his breeches.

When Don John meets the Second Constantia she is wearing a mask.

> *Don John.* Come, pray unmask.
> *Constantia.* Then turn away your face; for I'm resolved you shall not see a bit of mine till I have set it in order, and then—
> *John.* What?
> *Const.* I'll strike you dead.
> *John.* [To the audience]. A mettled whore, I warrant her. Come, if she be now but young and have but a nose on her face, she'll be as good as her word. I'm e'en panting for breath already.

Const. Now stand your ground if you dare. [John looks at her and starts back in amazement].

John. [Aside]. By this light, a rare creature! Ten thousand times handsomer than her we seek for! This can be sure no common one. Pray heaven she be a whore!

Const. Well sir, what say ye now? [A passionate look].

John. Nothing. I'm so amazed I am not able to speak. [Aside]. I'd best fall to presently, though it be in the street, for fear of losing time.—Prithee, my dear, sweet creature, go with me into that corner that thou and I may talk a little in private.

Const. No sir, no private dealing, I beseech you.

John. [Aside]. 'Sheart, what shall I do? I'm out of my wits for her.—Hark ye, my dear soul, canst thou love me?

Const. [An inviting look]. If I could, what then?

John. Why, you know what then, and then should I be the happiest man alive.

Const. Ay, so you all say till you have your desires, and then you leave us.

John. But, my dear heart, I am not made like other men. I can never love heartily till I have—

Const. Got their maidenheads. But suppose now I should be no maid!

John. Prithee, suppose me nothing, but let me try— [He begins to undress].

Const. Nay, good sir, hold!

The comedy ended with the romantic lovers—Don Frederick and the First Constantia—planning a wedding, and the sophisticated couple eagerly preparing for a bedding. At the close Nell danced a jig, and when the applause died down the Epilogue played smartly on her growing reputation:

> . . . the author dreads the strut and mien
> Of new-praised poets, having often seen
> Some of his fellows who have writ before,
> When Nell has danced her jig, steal to the door,
> Hear the pit clap, and with conceit of that
> Swell, and believe themselves the Lord knows what!

"A good play I find it," commented Pepys, who had stolen an afternoon from his duties at the Navy Office, "and the actors most good in it."

Now a mature and experienced actress, in three short months Nell had risen almost to the top of her profession. She was "pretty, witty Nell" to the audience, and few bothered with her surname. Playwrights capitalized upon her impudence, writing parts, prologues and epilogues to fit her personality. She was a public figure, but for this year at least, her private life was still her own. Of course in the intimate world of the theatre a liaison with so prominent an actor as Hart could not pass unnoticed, but, in the main, the gossip was confined to the clan.

The players were gregarious people, and the well-behaved among them lived a pleasantly Bohemian life, gathering at each others' lodgings (or at the homes of certain favored laymen like Pepys) for supper parties with games, cards, singing, dancing, or the inevitable shop-talk which is always the best of conversations. Sometimes such parties lasted with "much mirth" until past one in the morning —a very late hour for a generation which often went to bed with the sun and rose long before dawn. Sometimes the mirth was not very innocent—the night, for example, when Mary Knepp, Nell's good friend, "fell a little ill," went to bed, and was waked later by the Clerk of the Acts of the Navy who "handled her breasts and did baiser la." And there were other furtive affairs.

Like other Londoners, on holidays the players made trips to see the sights: the freak shows of Holborn, the oddities of Bartholomew Fair, the drills of the trained bands in Artillery Fields, and the annual Lord Mayor's pageants. In fair weather they went boating on the Thames or resorted to the pleasure grounds of Vauxhall, Moorfields, or the Mulberry Gardens, where they strolled under trees and bought cheesecake, tarts, and syllabub; or they walked to the pond in St. James's Park to watch the King feed his ducks.

On Sundays, like everybody else—good and wicked alike—they went to church, sometimes to both morning and afternoon services. They were not very religious (although some of them had their honest faith), and it cannot be said that they attended with any sort of regularity. But church attendance was in some sort compulsory, although the laws were seldom enforced except against recusants—Roman Catholics who obstinately refused to attend the Church of England services. In the City, where the Sabbath was kept very strictly, there was not much else to do on Sunday, and besides, since everybody went, even the King and his ribald Court, it was the proper thing to do.

Nell belonged to St. Martin's Church, which was attended by numerous fine ladies and gentlemen who made a great show with their finery and new fashions. The successive rectors were always men of great learning and oratorical skill, who could hold their audiences spellbound with their sinewy arguments and fine passages of purple prose. Then there was organ music, a surpliced choir, the splendor of ritual and liturgy, and psalms in the metrical versions of Sternhold and Hopkins to be sung by the congregation. It was very satisfying, even to sinners.

Nell's private life was rich and full; new experiences and new friends crowded it. The wits of the Court and town —some of them successful playwrights—became her friends, and over the course of the years several of them were influential in determining her career. Even Lady Castlemaine took an interest in the little comedian.

The Duke of Buckingham, leader of the wits and reviser of *The Chances*—in which Nell had such success— was a gay, mercurial gentleman who, like Nell, had a talent for mimicry, a talent which had stood him in good stead throughout his chequered career. The King's constant companion and friend since their boyhood, he was forever getting into scrapes and forever winning his master's pardon by grace of his wit and ready humor. He was a tall, handsome man, now thirty-nine years old and showing in his puffy cheeks the effects of drink and dissipation. Vain, ambitious, versatile, he was "everything by starts, and nothing long." Above all he prided himself on his ability as a statesman, although he was too flighty ever to carry a project to a conclusion, too unprincipled to be respected, and too tactless for good diplomacy. He sought power and pleasure equally, wasted his enormous wealth on alchemists, projectors, politicians, musicians, and women, and would rather lose his friend than his jest.

In the winter of 1667 he was a very busy fellow. A leader of the "discontented members" of Parliament (the earliest version of the Country, or Whig, Party, with which Nell was to be identified later), he was working to oust Chancellor Clarendon and become chief minister himself. At the same time he had military, naval, and diplomatic ambitions; he was engaged in the manufacture of Venetian glass; he was producing his version of *The Chances* and working on a burlesque of heroic drama—and he was sleeping with Lady Shrewsbury, to the sour discontent not only of her husband but of Harry Killigrew, her jilted lover. Late in February, Buckingham—truly "not one, but all mankind's epitome"—was ordered under arrest for treasonable activities. He had engaged an astrologer to cast the King's nativity!

His mistress, Anna-Maria Brudenell, daughter of the Roman Catholic Earl of Cardigan, was a dark-eyed beauty with a voluptuous body and the grace of a panther. She had been married young to the middle-aged Francis Talbot, Earl of Shrewsbury (also a Roman Catholic), as his second wife. Anna-Maria had presented her husband with two sons in quick succession; then, brought to Court in 1661, she proceeded to enjoy life in a very hearty way. Her reputation as a heart breaker was made in 1662 when one Tom Howard slew Giles Rawlins and wounded Henry Jermyn in a duel over her favors. A year or so later she was kind to "Lying Harry" Killigrew (or so, at least, he boasted), and Killigrew described her intimate charms to his friend the Duke of Buckingham in so lively a manner that Buckingham's interest was aroused. He met the lady and promptly took her away from his friend. Anna-Maria was amorous, sensuous, emancipated, headstrong, vindictive, and pious—a fit mate for the Great Duke.

Among Nell's other witty friends at this time was the

Earl of Rochester (aged 20), whose short life was already replete with scandal and adventure. In 1665 he abducted an heiress, Elizabeth Malet (worth £2,500 a year), fled with her in his coach as far as Uxbridge, and was captured by the young lady's grandfather, Francis, Lord Hawley, Captain of the King's Guards. Rochester was sent to cool his heels in the Tower for a space, was released, joined the English fleet as a volunteer, and distinguished himself at the Battle of Bergen. On January 29, 1667, he married his faithful heiress who had persistently refused all other suitors, and became master of her broad acres in Somersetshire. These are the facts. The rumor mongers credited Rochester with continual drunkenness, amazing incontinence, and numerous cases of rape and seduction.

His close friend, Charles, Lord Buckhurst (aged 24), a tall, plumpish young man with slightly protuberant eyes, was too indolent to be a very successful rake. However, he had built himself a lively reputation. In 1661 he was one of five young men "apprehended for killing and robbing of a tanner," and in 1663 he was involved in Sir Charles Sedley's indecent escapade at the Cock Tavern. In spite of his lethargy, he was an amorous fellow who had had his share of mistresses; his affair with one Doll Chamberlain, a shopkeeper in the New Exchange, was satisfactorily scandalous. Withal, Buckhurst was something of a poet and translator, and a promising patron of the arts.

Among Buckhurst's protégés was the rosy-cheeked little poet, John Dryden, already famous for a number of occasional poems and three plays, two of which had been hits. Dryden's interest in Nell was largely professional; he was writing for her what proved to be her most successful rôle: Florimel, in *Secret Love; or, The Maiden Queen,* produced at the King's Theatre on March 2, 1667.

The play itself (a two-plot affair, one serious and one comic) was a great success, fortunately for the King's Company which badly needed a hit (Tom Killigrew lamented that the daily audience was "not above half so much as it used to be before the late fire"). For Nell the production was a personal triumph. The "mad girl" Florimel who tried to capture philandering Celadon (Charles Hart once more) was Nell Gwyn herself transposed to the stage. When Celadon first met Florimel she was masked.

Cel. Now I think on't, you must be handsome.
Flor. What kind of beauty do you like?
Cel. Just such a one as yours.
Flor. What's that?
Cel. [Peering]. Such an oval face, clear skin, hazel eyes, thick brown eyebrows, and hair as you have, for all the world. . . Then you have—let me see [Snatches at her mask].
Flor. I'll swear you shall not see.
Cel. [After a quick look]. A turned up nose that gives an air to your face.—Oh, I find I am more and more in love with you!—a full nether lip, an out-mouth that makes mine water at it; the bottoms of your cheeks a little blub, and two dimples when you smile. For your stature, 'tis well; and for your wit, 'twas given you by one that knew it had been thrown away upon an ill face.—Come, you're handsome, there's no denying it.

Certainly there's no denying this as a perfect description of Nell. Her portraits all show the "clear skin, hazel eyes, thick brown eyebrows," the full lower lip, the "out" (or more politely, generous) mouth, the "blub" (or rounded) cheeks, and the dimples. And of course the one who gave her the wit, knowing it would have been "thrown away upon an ill face," was Dryden himself.

As with appearance, so with behavior; like Nell herself Florimel was a complete madcap: impudent, brazen, and devastating in her mimicry. As the climax to the comic plot Nell donned the hat, periwig, coat, and breeches of a young gallant and came swaggering on stage to encounter Celadon with her two rivals for his fickle affections. Momentarily alone, she took the audience into her confidence:

> Yonder they are, and this way they must come. If clothes and a *bonne mine* will take 'em, I shall do't.—Save you, Monsieur Florimel! [Looking into a pocket glass]. Faith, methinks you are a very jaunty fellow, *poudré et ajusté* as well as the best of 'em. I can manage the little comb, set my hat, shake my garniture, toss about my empty noddle, walk with a courant slur, and at every step peck down my head. If I should be mistaken for some courtier now, pray where's the difference?

Of course she baffled her rivals and got Celadon for herself. The comedy closed with Nell dancing a jig in her masculine garb and then speaking the epilogue. Pepys was in ecstasies: "So great performance of a comical part was never, I believe, in the world before as Nell do this, both as a mad girl, then most and best of all when she comes in like a young gallant and hath the motions and carriage of a spark the most that ever I saw any man have. It makes me, I confess, admire her." He continued to admire her, seeing the play six times in the next two years and enjoying every performance. He had only one complaint: that Nell's dancing was not as good as that of Moll Davis at the Duke's Theatre.

The King was so pleased with *Secret Love* that he "graced it with the title of *his* play." On April 18 there was a command performance at Court with some costumes paid for by His Majesty, among them a man's suit of embroidered purple cloth, a flannel waistcoat, "Rhinegraves," and "other furniture for Mrs. Gwyn—£10.7s." Rhinegraves, fashionable at the time, were loose, very full-cut breeches (like wide shorts or divided kilts), open at the bottom and likely to fly up and show an expanse of thigh when the wearer danced. This was not the company's first visit to the Hall Theatre in the palace, but it was Nell's first appearance as the star of the show. It was a great event for her—the blaze of candlelight in the ornate theatre, the silks, satins, and gold and silver lace of the bejeweled, elegant audience, the King and Queen seated under a crimson velvet canopy on a dais raised above the pit—and impudent Nell from Covent Garden strutting the stage in a new purple suit.

This was success and preferment, and there was more to come. Meanwhile Nell continued on the public stage. After the run of *Secret Love* early in March she had something to do with a revival of Beaumont and Fletcher's *The Knight of the Burning Pestle*, which was altered to make it a burlesque of Dryden's play. When this was produced Nell spoke an epilogue written especially to capitalize on her insolent style:

> The prologue durst not tell, before 'twas seen,
> The plot we had to swinge *The Maiden Queen;*

For had we then discovered our intent,
The fop who writ it had not given consent,
Or the new peaching trick at least had shown,
And brought in others' faults to hide his own . . .
Thus our poor poet would have 'scaped today,
But from the herd I singled out his play.
Then heigh along with me—
Both great and small, you poets of the town,
And Nell will love you—for to run him down.

Dryden was a sensitive man, but he had no reason to complain; a burlesque of his play put on by his own company was good business.

Following this, Nell appeared as Samira in a revival of *The Surprisal*, a romantic melodrama by Sir Robert Howard, another of the "discontented members" of Parliament. (His wife, Lady Honora O'Brien, was discontented too; at the moment she was petitioning the King for relief from her husband's "ill usage.") *The Surprisal*, a worthless play full of windy rubbish, gave Nell no opportunities for comedy. More and more she was coming to dislike serious parts and to play them badly.

But play them she must. New plays, especially comedies, were rare, and the King's Company had to offer as its stock fare revivals of old plays, chiefly by Beaumont and Fletcher, Jonson, Massinger, Shirley, and others who flourished in the first half of the century. The actor-directors cast as well as they could with an eye to types and abilities. The leading rôle in a comedy now went, of course, to Nell. The lead in a tragedy went to one of the Marshall sisters, or to stately Anne Quinn, who joined the company early in 1667, and whose surname is often con-

fused with Nell's. A comic rôle in a tragi-comedy was
likely to go to Nell; otherwise she played, perforce, "out
of her calling, in a tragedy." And once she played a part
—however ill it suited her—it was hers for all subsequent
revivals. Occasionally there was no part at all for her, and
she took an enforced holiday.

In the spring of 1667, while Nell was playing a variety
of rôles in revivals, enjoying her successes as a comedian,
singing, dancing, jesting, and making friends, another act
in the national drama was unfolding. It was to have an
effect on her small career.

Still at war, but sunk in the lethargy of financial stagna-
tion, England was unable to prepare its fleet for sea. The
Dutch were in better condition; their fleet was ominously
ready. The King, forgetting for the moment the anguish
caused by pretty Frances Stuart's runaway match with the
Duke of Richmond, entered into secret negotiations for
peace. England was nearly ruined by war, plague, fire, and
loss of trade; prices were steadily rising, and only the
courtiers had money to spend. Even the weather was bad
that spring; it was so cold that in April hardly a tree was
in leaf.

In May the desperate King's Company had another hit,
James Howard's *All Mistaken; or, The Mad Couple*, a
tragi-comedy with a heroic, love-and-honor conflict for
the first plot, and a broad farce for the second. It was another triumph for Nell as sprightly Mirida in love with
mad Philidor (ubiquitous Charles Hart). Philidor boasted
of having deceived six ladies, who pursued him with demands that he keep his promises to marry them. (He must
have deceived three more, because he was pursued also by

three wet-nurses claiming payment for the care of his three bastards.) He was at least one up on Mirida, who could brag of having deceived only five men (and she had no bastards yet), but she was working hard to even the score, holding in play two suitors, a thin man and a fat one. She had promised to marry the first if he got fatter, and the second, Pinguister (John Lacy), if he got thinner. The action was a brisk medley of episodes and gross humors—particularly gross when Pinguister resorted to purges to melt away his fat. Hoyden Nell had the kind of rôle she loved, and of course she was given occasion to dance her famous jig.

Her best opportunity as a farceur came when little Nell, pretending she wished to console her fat lover, sat down on a stool and invited him to sit in her lap. Lacy was a big man and was well stuffed with cushions for his rôle. To add to the audience's delight in the scene, Nell's song was a parody of one sung at the Duke's Theatre by Moll Davis in a revival of Beaumont and Fletcher's *The Rivals* —"My lodging it is on the cold ground."

> *Mir.* Dear love, come sit thee in my lap, and let me see if I can enclose thy world of fat and love within these arms. [Pinguister sits down and leans against her.] See, I cannot nigh encompass my desires by a mile.
>
> *Ping.* [Cries]. How is my fat a rival to my joys! Sure, I shall weep it all away.
>
> *Mir.* Lie still, my babe, lie still and sleep;
> It grieves me sore to see thee weep.
> Wert thou but leaner, I were glad;
> Thy fatness makes thy dear love sad.
>
> *Ping.* Nay, if I had not taken all these courses to dissolve

myself into thy embraces, one would think my looking
on thee were enough; for I never see thee but I am like
a fat piece of beef roasting at the fire, continually
drop, drop, drop. There's ne'er a feature in thy face
or part about thee but has cost me many a pint of fat
with thinking on thee. And yet not to be lean enough
for thy husband—O Fate! O Fate! O Fate! O Fat!
[She lets him fall].

Mir. O Lord sir, I have let you fall, how shall I do to get
you up again?

Ping. Nay, that is more than all the world can tell.

Mir. I'll e'en lie down by thee then. [She lies down out
of his reach].

Ping. Nay, but prithee lie near me; thou hadst as good
lie a league off as at that distance.

Mir. Were I thy wife, fat love, I would.

She sings.

> My lodging it is on the cold boards,
> And wonderful hard is my fare,
> But that which troubles me most is
> The fatness of my dear;
> Yet still I cry, Oh, melt, love,
> And I prithee now melt apace,
> For thou art the man I should long for,
> If 'twere not for thy grease.

Unable to rise, helpless Pinguister begged her to lie still
on the stage while he rolled toward her. She agreed, but
teasingly rolled away from him as fast as he approached.
This horse-play went on until Mirida had rolled to one
side of the stage. Then she got up, laughed at Pinguister,
fought a mock duel with him (while he was still flat on his
back), declared she had no intention of marrying him, and

went off in wild good humor. Eventually the play came to an end with reconciliations and weddings for the stupid people in the heroic plot, but with Mirida and Philidor rejecting the ceremony in horror. They were perfectly willing to consummate, but they drew the line at committing matrimony.

In the audience was noble Lord Buckhurst, watching Nell with glistening eyes, according to the anonymous author of "The Lady of Pleasure." "He saw her roll the stage from side to side," and the portions of her anatomy revealed by her tumbled petticoats aroused a powerful emotion in him. Thereupon he sought out Nell's "keeper," Charles Hart, and begged her from him. Hart consented grudgingly:

> Take her, my lord, quoth Hart, since you're so mean
> To take a player's leavings for your quean,
> For though I love her well, yet as she's poor
> I'm well contented to prefer the whore.

So Hart and Buckhurst made a deal, and Nell was handed casually from one keeper to another. In the Restoration cloudland almost anything could happen. But before this remarkable transaction took place there was a significant event in the national drama and Nell was thrown out of a job.

In May, while she was rolling on the stage from side to side, the Dutch fleet was threatening the English shores. On June 12 it sailed up the Medway, broke a chain across the river at Chatham, captured a great warship, *The Royal Charles*, and burned a squadron of English men-of-war at anchor. (And that night, the King dined with my Lady

Castlemaine in the Duchess of Monmouth's apartments, "and they were all mad in hunting a poor moth.") London was thrown into a panic; people began fleeing to the country; there were fears of invasion, treason, and rebellion; and there were wild outcries against the King and his ministers. As usual at times of national crisis the theatres, already suffering from the hard times, were closed indefinitely. Once again Nell was thrown upon her own small resources.

But here at hand was Lord Buckhurst—Charles Sackville, eldest son of Richard, Earl of Dorset. Seven years older than Nell, Buckhurst was a wit, a writer of ironic little songs, a member of Parliament, colonel of a regiment of foot, and a deputy lieutenant of Kent. He took his duties lightly; he had little interest in fame or promotion. As the heir to great estates—the earldoms of Middlesex and Dorset —his prospects were magnificent.

For a while Buckhurst was elusive. He was too busy giving aid and comfort to his friend, the Duke of Buckingham, who in February had escaped the sergeant-at-arms sent to arrest him, and for three months had been skulking about London in disguise. Tiring of the game at last, Buckingham surrendered on June 28, but in a burst of bravado insisted upon dining publicly at the Sun Tavern with his allies, Lords Buckhurst and Vaughan, on his way to the Tower.

Early in July Pepys heard on good authority that Nell had gone off with Buckhurst and had "sent her parts to the house and will act no more." The young couple could hardly call it love, though at their age the hey-day in the blood was neither tame nor humble. It was a perfectly business-like arrangement: one hundred pounds a year (a fortune to Nell, especially in her jobless state) paid by Buckhurst for the right to have, hold, occupy, possess, and enjoy one tenement of clay.

It was very hot that July. The happy pair had fled from steaming, troubled London to the pleasant little spa of Epsom. Thither, quite by chance, Mr. and Mrs. Pepys followed them, stopping at the King's Head Inn. Pepys was surprised to learn that Nell and Buckhurst were lodged next door and that Sir Charles Sedley was with them, the three keeping "a merry house." Unctuously he commented, "Poor girl! I pity her; but more the loss of her at the King's House." There was no need to pity Nell; she had taken another step up in the world.

V

Summoned
by the
King

1 6 6 7 - 1 6 6 9

V

DURING THE SUMMER of 1667 the war clouds rumbled farther away, while at Breda the ambassadors of England, France and Holland dickered over a treaty of peace. In London the Duke of Buckingham proved himself innocent of treason, was released from the Tower, and taken back into favor again, largely because of the intervention of his cousin, Lady Castlemaine. While Buckhurst and Nell continued their illicit honeymoon, their friend, the great duke, had an encounter with Harry Killigrew which set all the gossips' tongues a-wag.

For some time Killigrew, Lady Shrewsbury's jilted lover, had been revenging himself by spreading abroad luscious stories and descriptions of her most intimate charms. Now at the reopening of the Duke's Theatre on July 20, he found himself seated next to a box occupied by Buckingham, his homely duchess (the blindly adoring Mary Fairfax), and Lady Shrewsbury herself. His bitterness boiling over, Killigrew "drolled with" the duke, "spake scurvy language at him," and at last struck him over the head with his sheathed sword and ran. Buckingham drew his own weapon and pursued the hero over boxes and forms, cut at him, knocked him down, and kicked him soundly, while Killigrew cried, "Good your grace, spare my life!" The theatre was in a turmoil;

Lady Shrewsbury was "hugely frighted," the duchess "swounded," and the duke lost his periwig.

The news that the players were acting again had its effect in the "merry house" at Epsom, where troubles were already brewing. Well-bred young sparks are sometimes pained to discover that an impudent, risqué actress is merely coarse and vulgar when taken away from the footlights, and the actress who listens to a gentleman's golden vows may be disappointed, too. Nell was an expensive plaything for a man of moderate income. Whatever happened between the two, in less than six weeks the summer idyl was over. There was only one place for Nell to go—back to the stage. By August 22 she was at the King's House playing her old rôle in *The Indian Emperor* ("most basely," quoth Pepys, although he was glad to see her again), and Orange Moll was spreading the report that Buckhurst had left her, that he was making sport of her and swearing that she had had "all she could get of him."

Nell had fallen from her step, and the bump was painful. In her indiscreet way she had let everyone know not only that she was quitting the stage to live with Buckhurst but even the annual wages of her sin. Now she had to return to the toil, uncertainty, and mere shillings per week of the theatre—a failure. She was very poor, said Orange Moll; Charles Hart, once her "great admirer," now hated her; Lady Castlemaine had withdrawn her patronage; and Nell was "neglected by them all." Not by the men, of course. She was shunned by the ladies of the stage, who prided themselves on maintaining their amateur standing —in public, at least.

For some weeks Nell had her troubles; there were quarrels with envious people who took advantage of her fall from grace. On one occasion that autumn, for example, Beck Marshall fell out with Nell and scornfully called her "my Lord Buckhurst's whore." As the story was told to Pepys, Nell replied, "I was but one man's whore, though I was brought up in a bawdy-house to fill strong waters to the guests; and you are a whore to three or four, though a Presbyter's praying daughter." Nell had not forgotten her liaison with Hart, but that had been an *affaire de coeur;* only with Buckhurst had she been a "whore." Score one for sharp-tongued Nell.

Within a month or two everything blew over, Nell's escapade was forgotten, and she was a member of the company in good standing. All her parts had been returned to her in August, and that autumn she played as usual in revivals of *The Indian Emperor, The Maiden Queen, The Surprisal,* and *The Mad Couple,* among others. Eventually she won her way back into Hart's good graces, if not into his bed, and he continued as her leading man. The following spring he consoled himself by an affair with Lady Castlemaine, with pious Beck Marshall acting as go-between.

In October Nell had a new rôle as Flora in a revival of Richard Rhodes' *Flora's Vagaries,* a romantic intrigue comedy, full of complications and confusion. It was, as Pepys pronounced it, "a very silly play." As Flora, a fairly lively character, Nell had some opportunities to be noisy and boisterous, but there was no real scope for her comic talents.

Pepys took his wife to the play on October 5. Since they were early, Mary Knepp took them upstairs "to the women's shift, where Nell was dressing herself, and was all unready, and is very pretty." Thence they went down into the scene room, and Pepys read the cues to Mrs. Knepp while she ran through her part in the play. Pepys' roving eyes missed nothing. It made him sick to see how both Knepp and Nell were painted, "and what base company of men comes among them, and how lewdly they talk! and how poor the men are in clothes, and yet what a show they make on the stage by candlelight. But to see how Nell cursed, for having so few people in the pit, was pretty!" As a hireling Nell had no financial interest in the size of the audience, but a poor pit usually meant rehearsals for another play in the morning. And sure enough, two days later Jonson's *Poetaster* was on the boards.

In November the company revived Beaumont and Fletcher's old melodrama *Philaster*. Hart had the name part, and Nell was Bellario, the love-sick girl who followed the hero disguised as a page-boy and was most unjustly accused of seducing the heroine. Originally intended to be played by a boy actor, Bellario was not a humorous character, but with an actress of Nell's talents such a "breeches part" was rich in comic, if not bawdy, possibilities. She and Hart became so identified with their rôles that twenty-five years later playgoers attending a performance of *Philaster* had their memories jogged by these lines in a new prologue:

> That good old play *Philaster* ne'er can fail,
> But we young actors, how shall we prevail?
> Philaster and Bellario, let me tell ye,
> For these bold parts we have no Hart, no Nelly,
> Those darlings of the stage that charmed you there.

That autumn and winter, while the theatres were profiting from the post-war rise in prosperity, the Duke of Buckingham and his "discontented" crew were laying their periwigs together in a scheme which was to affect the careers of two promising young players. Buckingham had plenty of time for plots. After the scandal in the theatre created by Harry Killigrew, Lady Shrewsbury, vowing mayhem and murder, had fled from England and was now hiding in a French nunnery. Killigrew fled to France also—but not to a monastery.

In the late summer Buckingham had formed an uneasy alliance with Lady Castlemaine to ruin Chancellor Clarendon. When their plot succeeded and Clarendon fell, on August 30, the cousins quarreled over the spoils of victory. Since Buckingham's enormous vanity could brook no rivals in his bid for power—indeed, he thought himself much better fitted to rule than his lazy friend Charles Stuart—he now plotted to destroy the countess via the backstairs. He "broke" with her, and "studied to take the King from her by new amours." Thinking that "gaiety of humor would take much with the King," he turned to the ladies of the stage, many of whom were gay, pretty, lively, and although a trifle shopworn, still young. The easygoing King rarely chose a mistress for himself, leaving that pleasant task to the Court favorites, who "managed" the new concubine to their own advantage.

Buckingham's chief aides were Colonel Thomas Howard and his brother Sir Robert Howard, the playwright. From the King's Company the conspirators chose Nell Gwyn, a noted comedian, experienced in love and well recommended. Then, on the principle that if one failed the other might succeed, from the Duke's Company they picked Moll Davis, an accomplished singer and dancer, and said to be a natural daughter of Colonel Howard himself.

Both ladies were approached at about the same time—late in November or early in December—and both, of course, responded eagerly. But for some reason Moll quickly took a commanding lead over her rival. On January 11, 1668, Mrs. Knepp told Pepys that "a good while ago" the King had summoned Nell to Whitehall a few times, that Nell had duly visited the monarch, but with what results in the way of lechery Mrs. Knepp did not know. But she knew very well what had happened to Moll Davis. Already the King had given Moll a ring worth £700, and now he was furnishing a house for her in Suffolk Street. Everybody knew that she was the King's newest mistress. She was behaving like an "impertinent slut," glorying in her elevation, and my Lady Castlemaine was melancholy.

What was wrong with Nell? She was every whit as pretty as Moll Davis, and if her singing and dancing were not up to the mark set by her rival, her wit was certainly better. Moreover she had Buckingham's backing. In the coarse terms of "The Lady of Pleasure," Buckingham is supposed to have said to the King, after scolding him for doting on Castlemaine,

> Permit me, sir, to help you to a whore . . .
> She'll fit you to a hair, all wit, all fire,
> And impudent to your own heart's desire,
> And more than this, sir, you'll save money by her.

Fictitious or not, the last argument was one to interest a king who was always short of funds. But Buckingham, Nell's "manager," made a serious blunder. As he told Bishop Burnet some years later, when Nell "was first brought to the King, she asked only five hundred pounds a year." *Only* five hundred pounds, an amount far out of line with all of Nell's previous experience! Yet to Buckingham, a wastrel who ran through one of the largest fortunes in England, it was no more than pin money. The King refused. He was always rich in promises, and sometimes he gave valuable presents, but he was understandably slow to settle large pensions on strolling players. Moll Davis, more wisely managed by Colonel Howard, accepted the King's gifts and throve.

However, although Nell failed of a full-time post, she was not dropped from the competition. "The wildest and indiscreetest creature that ever was in a court" could not easily be ignored. Buckingham was still her patron, and there were occasional bookings to be had as an entertainer at the King's private parties late at night. Sometimes she stayed on for more entertaining after the guests had departed.

It was not far from Nell's lodgings in Drury Lane to the palace—just a step to the Strand, then westward to Charing Cross and south in King Street—but socially it was a journey over a vast distance. Of course a pretty young actress would not be expected to trudge a-foot through the dark, dirty streets. One traveled in a sedan-chair, glittering with gold-leaf and glassed in against the weather; with two sturdy chairmen to carry the dainty conveyance, a link-boy to show the way with his flaring torch, and a footman, armed with a crab-tree cudgel, to bring up the rear. There were winding streets and sudden turns, then the sprawling mass of the palace with its courtyards and galleries and the passageway leading to the backstairs, Chiffinch's chambers, and the King's lodgings. . . . Fortune's door was open, and Nell had one foot over the sill.

Buckingham might have given her more help, but he rarely carried any of his projects to a conclusion. Anyway, Moll Davis had succeeded in diverting the King sufficiently; Castlemaine's power was waning and Buckingham's growing day by day. Moreover, he had troubles of his own. The Earl of Shrewsbury, pressed by his kinsmen to revenge his injured honor, at last and very reluctantly sent Buckingham a challenge. On January 17, 1668, a pitched battle was fought in a close at Barn Elms, with three men to a side. At the end Captain William Jenkins, one of Buckingham's seconds, lay dead on the field, and Shrewsbury was carried off, fatally wounded. He lingered for exactly two months, however. After his death the body was opened by a convocation of politic doctors who gravely pronounced that the wound "was perfectly healed."

For two months there were charges, petitions, appeals, and pardons, and Buckingham, for all that he put a brave face on the matter, even sitting openly in the pit of the Duke's Theatre with Buckhurst, Sedley, and Etherege, was a worried man. He had no time for Nell's affairs, and she was left to make her own way in the gallant world of Whitehall.

Her occasional visits to the palace were not allowed to interfere with her other profession. She continued on the

stage for nearly two years longer, performing in a variety
of rôles, gaining a few new laurels as a comedian, and in
serious rôles playing at best only adequately, at worst
"most basely." Pepys found it difficult to understand why
she performed in any serious part "just like a fool or a
changeling," and yet "in a mad part" played "beyond all
imitation almost."

On February 20, 1668, she played Maria in Sir Robert
Howard's new play, *The Duke of Lerma*. Maria was the
chaste daughter of a diabolical father, Lerma, who sought
to make her a king's mistress. In this serious rôle Nell
gained no particular fame. However, "Knepp and Nell
spoke the prologue most excellently," and Howard gave
Nell an epilogue which allowed her to speak her mind
about non-comic rôles:

> . . . I know you in your hearts
> Hate serious plays as I do serious parts—
> To trouble us with thoughts and state designs,
> A melancholy plot tied with strong lines!—
> I had not the least part today, you see;
> Troth, he has neither writ for you nor me.

A week later she had still another serious character to
play, a "breeches part" in a revival of Massinger's *The
Virgin Martyr*. As a member of the Heavenly Host sent to
earth disguised as a page-boy to watch over the soul of
Dorothea, the Virgin (Beck Marshall), Nell's chief function was to stand by and encourage the tried and tempted
heroine, pointing significantly to Heaven whenever she
seemed to weaken.

Largely because of its music and scenery the play was

popular and often performed. One night in May Pepys
went backstage just as the play was ended and saw Beck
Marshall come off-stage dressed in her white robe and the
gold crown of martyrdom, "mighty fine, and pretty, and
noble." With her came Nell as Angelo, the good angel,
"in her boy's clothes, mighty pretty." His bubble of illu-
sion was shattered at once. "Lord," he cried, "their confidence! and how many men do hover about them as
soon as they came off the stage, and how confident they
are in their talk!" It was enough to make a man "loath
them."

For the rest of the spring of 1668 new parts were few
and far between. Nell was ambitious, but the theatre had
little more to offer, and actresses rarely grew rich on their
salaries. In May pampered Moll Davis at last left the
Duke's Theatre for good, moving into her fine new house
and parading her glory in public. Nell was playing her
heart out on the stage, while at Whitehall Moll was getting
the curtain calls. Now and then Nell was summoned to
the palace, but her chances of preferment seemed slimmer
than ever. Lady Castlemaine was certainly fading, but
Moll Davis was just as certainly in full bloom, and now
Frances Stuart, Duchess of Richmond, still beautiful even
after an attack of small-pox, had been persuaded to return
to Whitehall while her husband was sent on convenient
missions abroad. There was no hope of help from Buckingham. That May the widowed Lady Shrewsbury returned to England. (Doggedly, Killigrew followed.)
When her family refused to receive her, Buckingham
took her to his own home. The meek Duchess of Buckingham objected that it was not seemly for wife and mistress

to live in the same house, whereupon the great duke replied, "Why, madam, I did think so, and therefore have ordered your coach to be ready to carry you to your father's." Thereafter he lived openly with his luscious Anna-Maria, to the scandal of the godly.

Dryden's new comedy, *An Evening's Love; or, The Mock Astrologer,* was produced on June 12 ("very smutty," said Mr. Pepys, "and nothing as good as his *Maiden Queen*"). His leading characters, Wildblood and Jacintha (Hart and Nelly) were modeled on his earlier creations, Celadon and Florimel, but his inventive powers had rusted. Again, however, Jacintha, another "mad girl," was designed to make the most of Nell's comic appeal. She flirted and bantered with her rakish lover, testing his constancy in a variety of ways—once she was disguised as a Moorish maid and once as a mulatto—and each time proving him fickle as a weathercock. Nevertheless she continued to love him and in due time accepted him with the usual quibbling provisos. Of course Nell had a chance to sing a couple of songs—one a mildly suggestive duet with Hart—and to dance her famous jig.

Dryden drew upon his knowledge of Nell and his familiarity with Court circles for one significant speech given to Jacintha. When Wildblood's passionate wooing was turned off with a quip, he asked, "Then what is a gentleman to hope from you?" Dreamily Jacintha answered, "To be admitted to pass my time with while a better comes; to be the lowest step in my staircase, for a knight to mount upon him, and a lord upon him, and a marquis upon him, and a duke upon him, till I get as high as I can climb." A dangerous speech, especially when the King—

the landing at the top of the stairs—was sitting in his usual side-box.

The theatre remained open during the heat of summer, playing to small audiences. Nell's life went on in its usual round. She was getting older, eighteen now—in the terms of her world almost an old maid—and she had neither husband nor keeper. Of course she had popular admiration a-plenty. On September 15 she played the rôle of Lysette, a witty waiting maid, in Richard Flecknoe's *Damoiselles à la Mode*, a comedy so bad that "when they came to say it would be acted again tomorrow, both he that said it, Beeson, and the pit fell a-laughing." Undaunted by failure, vain, foolish Flecknoe embalmed his admiration for Nell in deathless verse "On a Pretty Little Person":

> She is pretty, and she knows it;
> She is witty, and she shows it;
> And besides that she's so witty,
> And so little and so pretty,
> Sh'has a hundred other parts
> For to take and conquer hearts.
> 'Mongst the rest her air's so sprightful,
> And so pleasant and delightful,
> With such charms and such attractions
> In her words and in her actions,
> As whoe'er do hear and see,
> Say there's none do charm but she.
> But who have her in their arms,
> Say sh'has hundred other charms,
> And as many more attractions
> In her words and in her actions.
> But for that, suffice to tell ye,
> 'Tis the little pretty Nelly.

Such a glowing tribute was enough to sustain an actress through a whole winter of discontent.

On December 18 Ben Jonson's *Catiline* was performed by the King's Company in all the splendor of sixteen scarlet robes, paid for by the King. Nell had no part in the play, but there was a prologue for her "To be merrily spoke by Mrs. Nell, in an Amazonian habit"—a crested helmet, a belted tunic, cut short above her bare knees, buskins, and a bow and quiver full of arrows slung over one shoulder. It was the usual bantering, indelicate speech designed to put the audience in a good humor, making fun of the play and the playwright, who had a strange prejudice against women and wrote only to "poetic champions." The company, however, hoped more for the applause of those still in their "infancy of wit,"

> Which, if they prove the greatest number, then
> The House hath cause to thank Nell more than Ben;
> Our author might prefer your praise perhaps,
> We'd rather have your money than your claps.

The play was very popular, partly because Lady Castlemaine bribed Mrs. Corey, who had the rôle of the plotting busybody, Sempronia, to play her part as a take-off on Lady Elizabeth Harvey. Lady Elizabeth, wife of Sir Daniel Harvey who had recently been sent to Constantinople as ambassador to Turkey, was a notorious stateswoman. At the first performance, when the stage Cicero was asked, "But what will you do with Sempronia?" Castlemaine stood up in her box and bawled, "Send her to Constantinople!" The furious Lady Harvey had Mrs. Corey imprisoned. Lady Castlemaine had her released. At subsequent performances Lady Harvey hired men to hiss and fling oranges, and everybody came to see the fun.

On January 7, 1669, Pepys went to the King's House to see Fletcher's *The Island Princess*, in which there was no part for "the jade Nell." She chose instead to watch the play with a companion of hers from the Duke's Company. She sat in a box, "a bold, merry slut, who lay laughing there upon people," more interested in the audience than the performance.

A week later she was playing with Lacy in "a farce of several dances" between the acts of Katherine Phillips' *Horace*. Sometime in March or April she had another "breeches part" as Pulcheria, a lovelorn maiden, in a revival of Shirley's *The Sisters*. Other than these her performances that winter and spring were not memorable. A new play by Dryden had been scheduled for April, but troubles over the scenery forced its postponement until June. On May 18, Sir Charles Sedley's first comedy, *The Mulberry Garden*, was rather indifferently received; as usual the company fell back on its repertory of stock plays.

That month there was another episode in the Buckingham-Shrewsbury-Killigrew triangle. On the night of May 18, as Killigrew was riding in a hackney coach to his house in Turnham Green, he was set upon in the highway by four of Lady Shrewsbury's footmen. In the fight that followed Killigrew received "nine very desperate wounds," and was left for dead. During the fray Lady Shrewsbury watched happily from her coach. The next day she went into hiding, but, of course, no one identified the lady in the coach. Eventually Killigrew recovered, made his peace with Buckingham and the widow and was received again at Court.

Except that the principals were all her friends, the affair meant little to Nell, who was still only on the fringes of Court life. More important to her that month, because it reflected on her own unwanted state and at the same time gave her hopes, was the fact that fierce old Prince Rupert, the King's cousin, after dallying for at least two years with Nell's colleague, Margaret Hughes, finally took her from the stage as his acknowledged mistress. Thereafter (as Mrs. Hughes herself once said) "she and Prince Rupert were as constant to each other as any man and his wife were in England." (In 1673 their constancy was rewarded by the birth of a daughter, demurely named Ruperta.)

Dryden's long-delayed play, *Tyrannic Love; or, The Royal Martyr*, was finally produced late in June. The ingenious playwright had hit on a way to employ Nell's talents to their fullest in a tragedy. As Valeria, daughter of the cruel Emperor Maximin (persecutor of St. Catherine) Nell had little more to do in the play than wander about, bewailing her hopeless love for Porphyrius (Hart), and at last stabbing herself when it seemed that her stubborn beloved must die. He survived to marry Berenice (Beck Marshall). Nell's big moment came at the end of the play; this time she took care to die on the outer stage. The stretcher-bearers came out, lifted her onto their bier, and were about to carry her off when she sat up and called to the leader,

> Hold, are you mad! You damned, confounded dog!
> I am to rise and speak the epilogue.

Then she turned to the audience:

> I come, kind gentlemen, strange news to tell ye:
> I am the ghost of poor departed Nelly.
> Sweet ladies, be not frightened, I'll be civil;
> I'm what I was, a little harmless devil.
> For after death we sprites have just such natures
> We had, for all the world, when human creatures;
> And therefore I, that was an actress here,
> Play all my tricks in Hell—a goblin there!
> Gallants, look to't, you say there are no sprites,
> But I'll come dance about your beds at nights,
> And, faith, you'll be in a sweet kind of taking,
> When I surprise you between sleep and waking.
> To tell you true, I walk because I die
> Out of my calling, in a tragedy.
> O poet, damned dull poet, who could prove
> So senseless to make Nelly die for love!
> Nay, what's yet worse, to kill me in the prime
> Of Easter term, in tart and cheese-cake time!
> I'll fit the fop, for I'll not one word say
> T'excuse his godly, out-of-fashion play,
> A play, which if you dare but twice sit out,
> You'll all be slandered, and be thought devout!
> But farewell, gentlemen, make haste to me;
> I'm sure ere long to have your company.
> As for my epitaph when I am gone,
> I'll trust no poet, but will write my own:
> "Here Nelly lies, who, though she lived a slattern,
> "Yet died a princess, acting in Saint Cattern."

In a roar of applause Nell kissed her hand to the pit, sank back on the bier, folded her arms, and was carried off in triumph.

According to a pleasant tradition old enough to be respected, Nell "so captivated the King by the humorous turns" she gave to this epilogue that after the play His Majesty "went behind the scenes and carried her off to an entertainment that night." Of course, there were many kinds of entertainments. Sir Francis Fane tells of one kind which was not infrequent during the summer of 1669.

One night the King, who had lately taken to sleeping with his wife in hopes of an heir, pretended illness as an excuse for retiring to his own bedchamber. In the morning the simple Queen went in to see how he was. The King was almost surprised "between sleep and waking"; there was just enough warning for Nell to slip out of bed "in her nightgown and with one slipper on" and hide behind the hangings of the bed.

The Queen complimented the King on his apparent good health and turned to go. Charles thoughtlessly invited her to stay and sit down by him a while. Gratified at the small courtesy, the Queen was about to do so when she spied Nell's other slipper on the floor. She understood the situation at once and said quietly, "I will not stay for fear the pretty fool that owns that little slipper might take cold." Without a word of reproach she "went her way."

The King had no luck with his barren wife and all too much with his other bedfellows. By the end of the summer Nell was aware of a change in her condition. She continued on the stage as long as she could, but she found it increasingly difficult to play her favorite rôles, especially those in which she dressed as a boy. At last, late in the year, she gave up, left her lodgings in Drury Lane and moved to a house in Lincoln's Inn Fields. But she was still a member of the company. On October 2 her name was listed in another of the biennial warrants for liveries to actors: a quarter of a yard of velvet and "four yards of bastard scarlet cloth."

VI

Fruitful Interlude

1670

VI

THIS TIME there was a good chance that Nell's departure from the stage might be permanent. In the due course of nature she would bring forth a child in whose veins ran the royal blood of the Stuarts. She had every reason to hope that, as usual in such cases, his father would provide for him, and, of course, would shower the mother with wealth and honors. But no one could ever be sure about King Charles. Several years earlier there had been the affair of mysterious Mrs. Hazlerigg, another fertile beauty who had shared the regal bed. At the time everybody knew about "the King's new bastard by Mrs. Hazlerigg," but the child was never acknowledged and the mother dropped out of sight. Perhaps the infant died.

Anyway, the slow processes of gestation could not be altered by doubts or fears. Nell moved into her new place in Newman's Row, next to Whetstone Park—a street teeming with prostitutes—paid occasional visits to Whitehall and continued to contribute to the King's entertainment as best she could. Even the French Ambassador, Charles Colbert de Croissy, laughed at her "buffooneries," and told his master, Louis XIV, how much they amused the King of England.

Charles the Second, "by the Grace of God King of England, Scotland, France, and Ireland, Defender of the Faith," was now forty years old, a tall, dark man with a vigorous body, a saturnine face, and sensuous lips shadowed by a small black mustache. He had no faith in any sort of virtue, yet as kings go he was reasonably honest, often generous, and, in spite of his many sneers at religion, a secret Catholic. But his God was a gentleman who would never "make a man miserable only for taking a little pleasure out of the way."

Unfortunately it was more than just "a little pleasure." His more sober-minded courtiers often commented on "the wantonness of the Court and how it minds nothing else," and bewailed the shameless conduct of the King who, they said, spent most of his time with his mistresses, "feeling and kissing them naked." But Charles was no Nero given up to sloth, cruelty, and lust. He was annoyingly athletic, a lover of sports and games, good at bowls and tennis, devoted to hunting and fishing. He was versatile, subtle, and very clever; even Louis XIV, the "Grand Monarch" of France, was not his equal in diplomacy.

He had been a confirmed libertine for some twenty-four years. During the last eight of those years he had been a kindly if somewhat negligent husband. His wife, the dark-skinned, homely little Portuguese, Catherine of Braganza, had learned to endure her husband's infidelities and, lacking the comfort of children, had come to solace herself with masquerades, balls, fine clothes, and religion. She was a Roman Catholic, of course, but so were many of the English nobility. When the Countess of Castlemaine announced her own conversion to the faith hated so bitterly by all good Protestants, the King refused to interfere, remarking that he never meddled with the souls of his ladies.

Before Nell Gwyn came into Whitehall via the back-stairs, King Charles had meddled with the bodies of a large assortment of ladies, some of whom had presented him with new subjects, illegitimate, but cast in his image. By 1670 the roster of his known offspring was already size-able. During his exile in the Jersey Isles in 1646 he had become familiar with one Marguerite de Carteret. Her son grew up to become a Jesuit priest, known as James de la Cloche. In Holland, two years later, there was Lucy Walter, a bold, brunette beauty. Her son, James Scott, Duke of Monmouth, had luxurious apartments in White-hall and was his father's favorite. Some time in 1650, Eliza-beth, Lady Shannon (Tom Killigrew's sister) was kind to the exiled King and bore him a daughter, Charlotte Fitz-roy. Eleanor, Lady Byron, taken into keeping about 1652, was a disappointment. Catherine Pegge, later Lady Greene, gave the King two children: in 1657 a son, Charles Fitzcharles, Earl of Plymouth, and a year after-ward a daughter who either died in infancy or grew up to take the veil in a French nunnery.

Barbara Palmer, Countess of Castlemaine, chief mistress from 1660 to 1670, gave the King five children in that pe-riod: Anne in 1661, Charles in 1662, Henry in 1663, Char-lotte in 1664, and George, whose birth scandalized Ox-ford, in 1665. (After George there were seven lean years.) Strictly speaking, Castlemaine's progeny were not illegitimate. They were born in wedlock, although the lady's husband, Roger, Earl of Castlemaine, had stopped living with her in 1662 and had gone abroad, where he remained for the next fifteen years. But the children were all acknowledged by the King (with some doubts and hesitations) and given the common surname of Fitzroy. Charles now had a considerable family to care for: nine or ten children plus the mothers who were still alive.

He provided for them generously. Payments to the royal concubines were scaled according to their rank and the pressures they could bring to bear. A lady of gentle birth, even if she proved barren, was sure of some kind of a pension, a post at Court, or both. If she produced a child she had a permanent claim on the King's bounty and could look forward to at least a house in a genteel location near the palace—Pall Mall, for example, where Lady Greene lived—and an income befitting her creative talents. Lady Castlemaine, whose blue eyes, perfect features, five children, and furious temper gave her incredible power, was granted thousands of pounds worth of jewels, lands, and properties, and now had an income of £4,700 a year out of the Post Office revenues.

The King provided for his illegitimate brood by various devices. As rapidly as possible he raised his half-royal sons to the peerage, promoting them through the ranks to the very top. Eventually, counting those sons born after 1669, he had six dukes and one earl bearing his bar sinister on their shields. (If the Earl of Plymouth had not died in 1680 he would likely have been a duke too.) To get incomes for these ducal dignitaries the King levied on almost every branch and trickle of his hereditary revenue and kept an eagle-eyed watch for promising heiresses. He took care of his daughters economically enough by marrying them to scions of the nobility; thus in the course of

time the peerage was enriched by four half-royal coun-
tesses. (All told, Charles fathered—acknowledged—nine
sons and five daughters.)

In addition to the members of his large family there
were certain ladies who had claims on the King for services
rendered. There was Winifred Wells, one of the Queen's
Maids of Honor; Mary Knight, the famous singer, who,
like Lady Greene, had a house in Pall Mall; Jane Roberts,
said to be the daughter of a clergyman—and stolen from
the King by the angel-faced Earl of Rochester; and Mary,
the widowed Lady Falmouth, who in 1674 became the
first wife of Nell Gwyn's old lover, Lord Buckhurst.

There were many more, but most of them were not
ladies. One of the duties of William Chiffinch, Keeper of
the Privy Closet and Page of the Bedchamber, was to serve
as usher to various women of the night. The King's apartments overlooking the river connected with the rooms occupied by Chiffinch. These in turn opened onto a back
hallway which led in one direction to the backstairs and
so down to a courtyard, and in the other directly to the
Privy Stairs and the waterside. Across the hall, a little too
close for comfort, were the Queen's apartments. Most of
the King's nocturnal visitors came by boat from the City
and landed at the Privy Stairs, where Chiffinch took them
in charge. Chiffinch was also the King's private paymaster;
he received thousands of pounds from the Secret Service
funds "without account."

Many of this "numerous train of clean and unclean"
who went one by one into "William Chiffinch's ark" were
professionals; occasionally one was diseased and left a painful memorial of her visit. However, the Restoration atti-

tude toward "the pox" (a term applied without distinction
to both syphilis and gonorrhea) was pleasantly jocular.
The victim fluxed, took "diet-drink," went to a sweating-
house, or in extreme cases undertook the tedious mercury
treatment, much to the amusement of his more careful (or
fortunate) friends. Royal blood was not immune to bac-
teria.

For two years Nell Gwyn (like her predecessor and
fellow actress, Elizabeth Weaver) had been one of the
"numerous train"—a superior member, welcomed as much
for her wit and mimicry as for her sex, but nonetheless
only one of a common rout. Now, unable to work at
either of her trades, she was dependent on the King's
bounty as dispensed by Chiffinch's none too liberal hand.
If only the Duke of Buckingham could be persuaded to
help her she might yet displace Moll Davis and even rise
to challenge the great Lady Castlemaine. Nell was not pre-
sumptuous. She was an actress and therefore self-confident; more than that, she was impudent, ambitious, and
irrepressible.

But Buckingham, now all-powerful in the state, was
chasing down a new fantasy in the spring of 1670, a
scheme to ruin another of his enemies, the Duke of York,
heir-presumptive to the throne. The plot was beautifully
simple: to get the King a divorce from his barren wife and
to marry him to some more fruitful princess.

Although divorce had been practically impossible in
England since the time of Henry VIII, precedent was in
the making with the famous Roos case, now pending in
the House of Lords. Shortly after the Restoration, Lady
Anne Manners, wife of a country gentleman, John, Lord

Roos, deserted her husband's bed and, bored with life in the provinces, fled to London. After more than a year's absence she returned with proof that she had not wholly wasted her time. Within a few weeks she gave birth to a son. Since she herself could not recall the father's name, the child was aptly labeled Ignotus. Lord Roos, reluctant to have another man's son inherit his estates, asked the House of Lords for an act to illegitimize little Ignotus and any other infants produced by Lady Anne, who wilfully continued her errant ways. Meanwhile he sued in the ecclesiastical courts for a decree of separation.

After some years of litigation with testimony so lurid that even the bishops blushed, the House of Lords solemnly declared Ignotus a bastard, and the Court of the Arches granted Roos's suit for separation. But Roos was not content. He was the only surviving son and heir of the Earl of Rutland, and quite naturally he wanted a legitimate son to carry on his line. In March, 1670, he presented the House of Lords with a bill for a final decree of divorcement with permission to marry again.

While the King looked on with interest and some amusement Buckingham pushed the bill as hard as he could. The York faction, fearing the precedent—for if a wife's adultery could be grounds for divorce, so, perhaps, could her sterility—fought to defeat it. The watchful mistresses were not amused; Buckingham was working directly against their interests. Their hold on the King was mainly through their children, and a new Queen, bearing a succession of jolly little heirs, would ruin them as well as the Duke of York.

On April 12 the Roos bill was passed by a narrow margin. With indecent haste Buckingham was preparing a bill for the dissolution of the royal marriage when the King, with one of the sudden shifts for which he was famous, put a stop to the proceedings and declared that he would hang the man who so much as mentioned the Queen's infertility. Undaunted, Buckingham then proposed to abduct Catherine and send her overseas to a plantation "where she should be well and carefully looked to, but never heard of any more." Charles could then get a divorce on the ground of desertion. The horrified King refused. "He said it was a wicked thing to make a poor lady miserable only because she was his wife and had no children by him, which was no fault of hers."

Nell's condition was now obvious. She was finding it increasingly difficult to get about that April, and just as difficult to be her usual merry self. In seventeenth-century England childbirth was a heavy gamble with death. Women accepted the gamble as the way of life, and found harsh comfort in the Biblical injunction, "In sorrow thou shalt bring forth children." Men, as usual, took the matter more lightly, and even jested about their wives' "great bellies." A husband accepted the inevitable when his wife died in childbed. Sadly he said, "God's will be done," mourned briefly, and went forth to seek a new wife.

Nell was not alone in her tribulation. Somewhere in her shadowy background were her mother and sister and many friends. When her time came upon her she went through the customary procedure. An expectant mother "lay in" at home, in a room tightly closed against the dangers of fresh air and well filled with female friends and relatives. These took turns walking her up and down the room as long as she was able; the attending physician bled her at intervals; and the midwife made frequent use of glysters and syringes. Tough-fibred Nell endured this treatment and survived. On May 14 or 15 she was "brought to bed of a boy—the King's bastard." She named him Charles.

If the King was happy at the birth of his seventh illegitimate son he gave no sign of his pleasure. Of course his mind was on weighty affairs, and a new baby was hardly a novelty to him. From May 16 to June 2 he was at Dover whither he had posted to meet his beloved sister, Henrietta, Duchess of Orleans, whom he had not seen for nine years. Married to a half-impotent, jealous madman, poor Henrietta found little joy in her life, and the one brief trip to England, which she was permitted to make only because King Louis commanded, was the high point of her life. However, she had not come for pleasure only; she brought with her a treaty so secret that the noisy Duke of Buckingham, Chief Minister though he was, could not be trusted with its provisions.

King Louis XIV had long believed himself divinely appointed to rule all Europe, to colonize the new lands beyond the Atlantic, and to bring heretics back to the safety of the mother church. The Spanish Netherlands, owned by a rotting empire, were irresistibly tempting to his generals. He saw himself as the logical successor to the Spanish throne, ruling France, Spain, Flanders, and Holland. Only one obstacle kept him from realizing his dreams: stubborn, Protestant England and its slippery King.

Louis' foreign policy was always worked out with one eye cocked on King Charles. His ambassadors were instructed to omit no slightest item about the doings of the

English Court in their reports; Louis wanted to know all about his cousin's travels, dogs, horses, mistresses, and servants. Every possible way of influencing Charles was tried, from bribing his councillors to managing his mistresses. The King of England must be persuaded either to stay out of continental affairs, leaving France with a free hand, or to join with France and share the loot.

It was with alacrity, then, that Louis adopted Henrietta's "grand design." The duchess, a sincere Catholic and a loving sister, desired above all things to bring her brother Charles into the Catholic fold (James, Duke of York, had long been a Catholic) and to see an enduring alliance between England and France. The cynical Kings used her as their innocent mediary; Louis seeking to further his own grand design of conquest, Charles, in desperate need of money, as usual, wanting to line his pockets with French gold. The duchess had her idealistic triumph; Charles got his money; and Louis was left holding the empty bag. On May 22, Charles signed a document in which he promised, first, to join France in a war against Holland, receiving a subsidy of some £225,000 a year while hostilities lasted, and, second, to declare himself a Roman Catholic whenever the time seemed ripe. For carrying out this promise he was to get £150,000. The propitious moment never came. But war with Holland was already in the air; Charles knew quite well that his imperious Parliament would insist on it; he would have to pay the cost; and Louis' subsidy would be a very handy aid.

While Nell was nursing her first-born and finding every day new resemblances to his father, the royal sire was happily flirting with one of his sister's Maids of Honor,

Louise de Perroncour de Keroualle, daughter of a poor but noble Breton cavalier. Twenty-one years old (a year older than Nell), Louise was a baby-faced brunette with an air of surprised innocence. Originally placed in the duchess's household by her family in hopes that King Louis might take a liking to her, she was outshone by a colleague, Louise de la Vallière, who became the King's mistress. Disappointed, de Keroualle engaged in an intrigue with the Comte de Sault, an affair which tarnished her reputation but had no effect on her look of innocence. When the duchess was preparing to return to France, King Charles suggested that he leave the gentle Breton with him as a "jewel" for remembrance. Louise blushed prettily, but the duchess refused; she was responsible, she said, to the girl's parents.

Three weeks later the duchess died suddenly at Paris. King Charles was not the only one stricken with grief. For years Buckingham had adored the duchess with one segment of his highly divisible heart. Partly to console him, partly to keep him out of mischief, the King sent him on a mission of condolence to Henrietta's husband, the Duke of Orleans, and threw dust in his eyes with the details of another secret treaty which Buckingham could negotiate all by himself—a fake designed to conceal the real treaty signed at Dover. Buckingham set forth in July accompanied by Buckhurst, Sedley, and other wits well qualified to "instruct and civilize fair France."

The great duke carried out his missions with his usual flamboyance, and on September 15, leaving France much improved, he started his return trip. With him he carried many rich presents from King Louis—including a pension

for his mistress, Lady Shrewsbury—and Louise de Keroualle, picked up he never quite knew how. (It was
French Ambassador Colbert's idea.) The flighty duke got
his charge safely to Dieppe, but he promptly forgot her
and took ship, leaving her to chew her fingernails for the
next ten days. Then Ralph Montagu, the English ambassador, forwarded her to England where she was promptly
registered among the Queen's Maids of Honor. She never
forgave Buckingham.

Meanwhile very little had happened to Nell. Sometime
that summer, the King, moved by her pleadings or by his
own impulse, set her up in a small house near the eastern
end of Pall Mall, just a few doors from Suffolk Street
where Moll Davis lived. Nell's was one of the poorest
dwellings on the street, rated at only sixteen shillings a
year taxes. When someone asked her why she moved from
her "good apartment in Lincoln's Inn Fields to worse near
Whitehall," she replied with typical impudence that "she
had but one good friend in the world and she loved to get
as near him as she could." Her good friend did nothing
more for her. She lived in a rented house and her living
costs were paid; his generosity went no further.

In all the tangle of intrigue about the throne there was
no place for Nell. Lady Castlemaine, no longer the King's
bed-mate, was amusing herself with a succession of lovers.
Henry Jermyn, a courtier (1668), had been succeeded by
Charles Hart, the actor (1669), who in turn had given
way to Jacob Hall, a rope-dancer (1670). But in spite of
her known infidelities, Castlemaine was rich, imperious,
and so powerful with the King that on August 23 he had
created her Baroness Nonsuch, Countess of Southampton,

and Duchess of Cleveland. Then there was Moll Davis, still childless but beautiful and promising, with her fine house, jewels, and her own coach. And now came the new pretender, Louise de Keroualle, with apartments in White-hall where the King visited her daily. She had been told that "the more a woman pretended to virtue and chastity" the more the King's heart would be inflamed. Therefore she appeared "with so much seeming modesty that the fond King believed her an angel."

Nell was not being treated like the others "with the decencies of a mistress," but rather as if she were only a common prostitute—stuck off in a corner of Pall Mall and ignored. She wanted her son acknowledged, and she craved dignities and pensions for herself. But the King did nothing.

No one doubted that little Charles was his son. Nell was always a one-man woman; she had taken her lovers in series, never in multiple. But all the King's other children were half-royal, half-gentle. The fact that young Charles, begotten on a commoner, was half-royal, half-base, posed an interesting problem. Moreover, it was the King's na-ture to avoid commitments, to put off decisions with kind words and vague promises, to move only when compelled. Lady Castlemaine could bring all kinds of pressures to bear; Moll Davis had behind her the power of Colonel Howard and his numerous brothers, sons of the Earl of Berkshire; Louise de Keroualle was backed by the French ambassador, the French faction at Court, and King Louis himself. Nell Gwyn had only her infant son.

She had advisers in her dilemma, such friends, for ex-ample, as the Earl of Rochester, who proved himself to be (in his own words) "a good pimp." But she had only two alternatives worth considering. One, to stay where she was, live on crumbs dropped from the tables of more successful courtesans, and patiently plead her cause, was utterly foreign to her head-long nature. The other was to put pressure on the King in the only way she could. In December she did something for which there was no precedent among royal mistresses—she went back to work.

VII

A Lady

of

Pleasure

1 6 7 0 - 1 6 7 1

VII

Nell's SECOND RETURN to the King's Company was much happier than her first. This time she was heartily welcome; the players could profit from her notoriety as the mother of a royal bastard. Although she was totally unsuited for the part, they promptly assigned her the leading rôle in Dryden's new two-part play, *The Conquest of Granada*, then in rehearsal, and the playwright whipped up a boldly topical epilogue, apologizing for the delay of his long-promised drama and ending with an indelicate reference to Nell:

> Think him not duller for the year's delay;
> He was prepared, the women were away,
> And men without their parts can seldom play.
> If *they* through sickness seldom did appear,
> Pity the virgins of each theatre,
> For at both houses 'twas a sickly year.
> And pity us, your servants, to whose cost
> In one such sickness nine whole months were lost!

In addition Dryden wrote a prologue designed to make the most of Nell's small stature and her skill at mimicking the "motions and carriage of a spark." Eight months earlier the Duke's Company had presented a comedy before the King, the Duchess of Orleans, and their followers at Dover. The low comedian, Nokes, poked fun at the extreme French fashions by wearing a remarkable broad-brimmed hat, an abbreviated coat, and a very wide belt; he looked like a dressed-up ape. The joke had proved so successful that Nokes had repeated it several times.

When the first part of *The Conquest of Granada* was presented late in December, Nell swaggered on the stage in boy's clothes, wearing a hat the circumference of a cartwheel, a short coat, and a very wide belt. The audience roared with laughter and applause. Then said Nell,

> This jest was first of t'other house's making,
> And, five times tried, has never failed of taking;
> For 'twere a shame a poet should be killed
> Under the shelter of so broad a shield.
> This is that hat whose very sight did win ye
> To laugh and clap as though the devil were in ye.
> As then for Nokes, so now I hope you'll be
> So dull to laugh once more for love of me.

The audience had to be content with one laugh; there was no intentional comedy in the play and no scope for Nell's talents—no wit-combats, horseplay, songs, or dances for her. She played Almahide, the chaste, high-minded heroine who loved the hero Almanzor (Charles Hart again), yet, true to her promise and the dictates of honor, married King Boabdelin at last. In the second part of the play (presented on January 9, 1671), Almahide was the very spirit of honor. Loving Almanzor passionately, she resisted his absent-minded attempts at seduction and refused even to think of crowning his joys until after her husband was slain, at the end of the play. Then she insisted on a year of decent widowhood. No, Almahide was not exactly Nell's type.

The Conquest of Granada was played at Court on February 10 and 11. Shortly thereafter Nell left the stage for good. King Charles was not a sensitive man, and certainly he was not niggardly with his mistresses, but no one enjoys questioning glances, lifted eyebrows, and sly allusions. It was incredible that the mother of a royal bastard would return to the stage—actually work for a living—of her own accord!

The good-natured King made his usual large promises for the future, but this time, as earnest of his intentions, he started negotiations for the leasehold of the house Nell was to live in for the rest of her life. This one was also in Pall Mall, on the south side of the street, a quarter of a mile west of the mean little place in which she had been living, and very close to St. James's Palace, the Duke of York's residence. At its western end Pall Mall was a wide, dignified street, shaded by elm trees and bordered by handsome brick dwellings. No one could ask for a more aristocratic location.

In effect, Nell was now an acknowledged mistress. Young Charles was not yet legally recognized as the King's son, and she herself still had no source of income save the elastic and often thin purse held by Chiffinch. But now she had learned how to squeeze that purse, which, for all she knew, was inexhaustible. Her future was tinged with gold. At the moment, however, she needed (and got) new furniture to fill the spacious rooms she was about to acquire.

The new house was fine enough for an earl—in fact, an earl had been living in it. It was a three-story brick mansion with a frontage of thirty-three and a half feet on Pall Mall. At the back its grounds extended south to the wall of St. James's Park. From the rear windows or from a terrace against the garden wall, one could look down into the Royal Gardens, watch "the King walking in the Park with a great crowd of his idle people about him," and, through the green mist of trees, catch glimpses of the towers and gables of Whitehall, half a mile away. Originally built by the Earl of St. Albans, a right noble promoter who developed the entire section north of the Park, the house was leased by the King for a term of forty-nine years at the cost of some £1,400. That is to say, the rent was paid in advance; after forty-nine years the house returned to its owner; meanwhile the leaseholder was to keep it in repair at his own cost. Nell moved into the mansion some time in February, but the formal transfer of title did not take place until April 1, when the latest leaseholder, Nicolas Leake, Earl of Scarsdale, assigned the property to the King's agent, George Hewitt, who in turn assigned it to Nell.

On March 2 the King strolled through St. James's Park with precise Mr. Evelyn and stopped in the Royal Gardens for a chat with his new neighbor. Evelyn's face burned as he was forced to listen to "a very familiar discourse between [the King] and Mrs. Nelly, as they called an impudent comedian, she looking out of her garden on a terrace at the top of the wall, and [His Majesty] standing on the green walk under it." He was "heartily sorry at this scene." He was sorrier still when the King sauntered on to visit the Duchess of Cleveland (at Berkshire House, across Pall Mall from St. James's Palace), "another lady of pleasure and curse of our nation."

The opinions of John Evelyn and his ilk mattered nothing to Nell. When she took possession of her new property she moved a large step up in the social world. Except to prigs and precisions she was no longer "an impudent comedian"; to her friends she was "Mrs. Nelly," to all others, "Madam Gwyn." Tradesmen doffed caps and besought her custom, knowing that the King would pay. Minor officials fawned upon her, and even great lords put on a measure of compelled politeness. The King's favor was a magic cloak about her slender shoulders.

Not content with the original, now living in Pall Mall, the King ordered a facsimile of Nell to hang among his trophies. Some time that spring she sat for the fashionable portrait painter, Sir Peter Lely, "naked, leaning on a bed with her child." While she posed, the King made frequent visits to the artist's studio, where Nell "was naked on purpose." The portrait remained in the royal collection until the flight of James II in 1689, when John Sheffield, Earl of Mulgrave, took it for his own delectation and managed to conceal it from posterity.

Nell was quick to make friends with her neighbors in Pall Mall and in the still newer residential section to the north, St. James's Square. Some of them were her professional colleagues—"great men's misses"—Cleveland, Lady Greene, and Mary Knight, for example, and the Countess of Shrewsbury, who now lived in King Street, just off St. James's Square. (Four years later Moll Davis moved to a house in the square itself.) Nell's immediate neighbors were Edward Griffin on the west, a Groom of the Bedchamber to the Duke of York, and on the east the widowed Frances Weston, Countess of Portland.

In general Nell was accepted by the rank and file of the

Court. When she strolled across the Park to Whitehall and entered the Palace gates where the yeomen of the guard stood sentinel in their scarlet coats, breeches, and velvet bonnets, there were many courtiers who greeted her with pleasure. Her wild humor and unfailing good spirits made her a host of friends. After all, there was not much difference between the people she had known in Covent Garden and the habitués of Whitehall. The gentry bathed oftener (sometimes as much as twice a year) and used perfume freely between times; their manners were more polished, but their morals were somewhat worse than those of Covent Garden; their speech was more grammatical, but it was often larded with oaths and obscenities worthy of rogues in a bawdyhouse. Nell was quite at home with them.

There were, of course, certain sour politicians who refused to accept her. One of the King's ministers, the Earl of Arlington, told the French ambassador that "it was well for the King's good servants that his Majesty should have a fancy for Mademoiselle Keroualle, who was not of an evil disposition and was a lady. It was better to have dealings with her than with lewd and bouncing orange-girls and actresses, of whom no man could take the measure." Some elegant ladies, too, were offended by the admission of an ex-orange-girl into their society. Mary Villiers, Dowager Duchess of Richmond (Buckingham's sister), complained to the King that "she could not abide to converse with Nell and the rest of that gang." The King retorted that "those he lay with were fit company for the greatest woman in the land." Usually the *grandes dames* talked about Nell behind her back; remarks made to her face were returned with interest. Once Mrs. Kirke, wife of George Kirke, Keeper of Whitehall Palace, called Nell "whore" to her face. Nell replied that if anyone else had called her so she would not have minded, but "it afflicted her to be called so" by one who had been "an old notorious whore even before whoring was in fashion."

Certainly Nell never pretended to be anything else, and one famous story about her, although it rests on no reliable authority, is at least in character. "The famous Nell Gwyn, stepping one day, from a house where she had made a short visit, into her coach, saw a great mob assembled, and her footman all bloody and dirty. The fellow, being asked by his mistress the reason of his being in that condition, answered, 'I have been fighting, madam, with an impudent rascal who called your ladyship a whore.' 'You blockhead,' replied Mrs. Gwyn, 'at this rate you must fight every day of your life. Why, you fool, all the world knows it.' 'Do they?' cried the fellow in a muttering voice, after he had shut the coach-door; 'they shant call me a whore's footman for all that.' "

Even with her friends Nell was blunt. In May she gave a birthday party for the King. Lady Shrewsbury heard of it and hinted to the King that she would like to be invited. Charles passed the request on to Nell, who refused it, saying, "one whore at a time was enough for His Majesty."

That spring and summer Nell alone seemed to be "enough for His Majesty." The Duchess of Cleveland—the former Lady Castlemaine—had been given her release by the King with only one condition: "live so for the future as to make the least noise you can, and I care not who you love." She took him at his word. After her affair

with Jacob Hall, the rope dancer, she became the mistress
of handsome Will Wycherley, whose first play, *Love in
a Wood*, was produced in March, 1671. One of Wycherley's songs in the play ended with the interesting assertion,

> Great wits and great braves
> Have always a punk to their mother!

Playing delicately on this axiom, the duchess first attracted
Wycherley by calling to him as she drove by in her coach,
"You, Wycherley, are a son of a whore," at the same time
laughing heartily. The flattered "great wit" fell in love
with her on the spot.

Some time during Lent word was brought to the King
that the Duchess of Cleveland was sleeping with Wycherley at the Pall Mall house of Mary Knight. Concerned
about possible scandal, the King walked in one morning
unannounced, climbed the stairs, and on the landing met
Wycherley, "muffled in his cloak." The two passed each
other without a word. Finding the duchess in bed, the
King demanded an explanation. "It is the beginning of
Lent," said the duchess, "and I retired hither to perform
my devotions." "Very likely," said Charles, "and that was
your confessor I met on the stairs."

If Cleveland was no more to Charles than the remembrance of things past, Keroualle was the tantalizing promise of things to come. She was playing a clever game with
him, but her continued coyness was driving him frantic.
She had no intention of yielding her precious virginity
until she had the King safely and permanently in her toils.
At one time she would listen to his wooing in a melting
mood, at another she would coldly remind him that he was

a married man, and urge him to remain true to his vows. The anxious French ambassador pleaded with her to give in. King Louis wanted to know how long the "childish-looking girl" would continue to hold out. King Charles redoubled his amorous efforts.

For the moment Nell Gwyn was the substance of things present. It was a relief for the King to turn from the prudish Keroualle to the frankly wanton Nell, who stimulated his lechery and satisfied it too. Moll Davis had some share of the monarch's attentions, but in a conflict between the two actresses, Nell always won. Watching the unequal contests, the gossips explained Nell's success by a wild story. Once (they said) when it was Moll's "turn to lie with the King," Nell invited her to supper and put a powerful purgative in her food—with results inhibitory to Eros.

But Nell had no need for drugs or charms. For some six months she was, more truly than any of her competitors, the King's mistress. After years of slow climbing, the triumphant little comedian had reached the heights, and now lay basking in the royal sunshine. In his own strange way the King loved her (even while pursuing Keroualle), and she gave him her heart without reserve. Now, in the halcyon days, Nell bloomed with the coming of spring—and by summer she was fruitful, too.

In these days she could well afford to be friendly and sympathetic with Lady Shrewsbury. Early in March Buckingham's mistress had borne him a son, her third—she had two by her husband—but Buckingham's first. (Buckingham's duchess, like the Queen, was barren). The great duke was wild with happiness; in a foolish attempt to legitimize the infant he gave it a family title, Earl of Oxford.

A few days later the child died, and Buckingham, extravagant in his grief as in his joy, buried his son in Westminster Abbey with almost royal pomp and ceremony. Even the most hardened libertines were affronted, not by his immorality but by his public defiance of good form.

Although Nell was acceptable enough to courtiers, to the commonalty she was just another grievance. In December, 1670, a proposal had been made in Parliament to levy taxes on the theatres. When the Court party opposed the motion on the ground that "the players were the King's servants and a part of his pleasure," Sir John Coventry, a grim member of the opposition, rose to inquire "whether the King's pleasure lay among the men or the women that acted?" "Was it not known," he continued, "that the King had two stage harlots, Nell Gwyn and Moll Davis, in keeping?"

Such impertinence could not go unpunished. Some of the gentlemen of the King's Guards (a select company commanded by the Duke of Monmouth) decided to play a little joke on Coventry by way of avenging the insult to the King. On the night of December 21 they waylaid him near his house in Suffolk Street, fell upon him in a body, wrapped him tightly in his own cloak, and slit his nose. The House of Commons, officially notified of the affair on January 9, 1671, failed to appreciate the humor and for two months vainly sought to bring the pranksters to justice. The only result of their fury was the so-called "Coventry Act" against cutting and maiming.

For some reason Nell was blamed as the instigator of the attack. The anonymous author of a broadside satire, "The Haymarket Hectors" (1671), asserted that Nell, angered by Coventry's insult, had borrowed the King's Guards for her instruments of vengeance. The poet warned:

Beware, all ye Parliamenteers,
How each of his voice disposes,
    Bab May in the Commons, C. Rex in the Peers,
Sit telling your fates on your noses,
And decree, at the mention of every slut,
Whose nose shall continue, and whose shall be cut.
If the sister of Rose   [Nell Gwyn]
Be a whore so anointed
    That the Parliament's nose
Must for her be disjointed,
Then should you but name the prerogative
                    whore,   [Cleveland]
How the bullets would whistle, the cannons would roar!

The many-headed multitude had nothing against Nell as a personality or because of her unconventional way of life. But she was known now as the King's mistress—it was to "Nelly" that he sauntered, when he "should be at prayers"—and to the popular mind she was another symbol of the waste, extravagance, and mismanagement of the Stuart reign. For a year or two she bore the brunt of the libellous attacks. (Retiring Moll Davis was little known, and coy Keroualle was to get her share later.) A satire published in May, 1671, "Upon the Proroguing of Parliament," was in part a jibe at Nell's second pregnancy—Dame Rumor had quick ears—and a lamentation over the vast sums supposedly spent on the "dunghill wench."

"Nell's in again, we hear," wrote the poet, speaking as a member of Parliament. "Methinks we might have met again," at least to provide funds for baby clothes, for

> our wont has been
> Never to miss a sessions 'gainst lying-in.

At such times, he claimed, rumors of war were always raised, and Parliament was asked to vote money for defense, money which was diverted "to keep the jade."

> And ten to one, before the spring be over,
> Our cavalry must march again to Dover,
> To guard the shore against the Dutch and French,
> When all this means but new supplies for wench.

The barrage continued well into the following years. After a young actor, Richard Bell, lost his life in the burning of the King's Theatre on January 25, 1672, a ballad writer (or his printer) reflected on Nell with the couplet,

> He cries just judgment, and wishes when poor Bell
> Rung out his last, 't had been the stage's kNell.

And later that year a prose satire, "Questions and Answers from Garroway's Coffee-House," under the heading "Advertisement for a sale of choice goods," offered "Twenty-four ells of Nell Gwyn's virginity in three pieces, 1 yellow, 2 black, full yard broad and a little better, at 3 s. per yard, to advance 2 d. each bidding." French yellow was the color of passion; black, of course, was the symbol of sin.

As an experienced actress Nell was used to insults, and now she could well afford to overlook them. Unofficially she was a member of the King's Court, serenely superior to the yapping of journalists and politicians. Early in the summer of 1671 the King took his Court (including the Queen, the moral Keroualle, and a host of Maids of Honor) to the old medieval castle and town of Windsor, twenty miles up the river from London. He installed Nell and little Charles in a convenient town house just a step from the castle.

At Windsor Nell had a happy reunion with her old friend and colleague, Margaret Hughes, whose lover, Prince Rupert, lived in the castle as its constable, spending his days in chemical and metallurgical research. Unfortunately for the peace of the town, there were too many hotheaded young men with too little to do. One June night Mrs. Hughes' brother and one of the King's servants disputed "whether Mrs. Nelly or Mrs. Hughes was the handsomer now at Windsor." Tempers flared, swords were drawn, and Mr. Hughes was neatly and fatally perforated. No blame attached to Nell, of course, and both Prince Rupert and his mistress remained her good friends.

Except for this episode it was a happy summer for Nell, in some ways the peak of the year. There was beautiful forest land to ride in, the cool river for boating and fishing parties, and evenings of jollity with friends. Often the King dropped in after a day's hunting or a trip to London, and stayed after the other guests had departed. Nell knew, of course, about his infatuation for Keroualle, but she was supremely self-confident.

Her confidence was justified that summer when a new candidate for the King's bed came out of Ireland. Lady Alice Clanbrassil, the beautiful young wife of Henry Hamilton, Earl of Clanbrassil, gained her experience as the mistress of John, Lord Berkeley of Stratton, Lord Lieutenant of Ireland from 1670 to 1672. The liaison was known to everybody, including her complacent husband. In the spring of 1671, Lords Berkeley and Arran, con-

spiring with a number of Irish gentry, decided to send the
seductive countess to England, there "to catch His Majesty" and engage him for the Irish interest. On June 10 the
Berkeleys and Clanbrassils arrived in London.

Unfortunately for the plot, immediately upon his arrival
Lord Berkeley was mixed up in a quarrel with another
nobleman, and in the resultant confusion mismanaged
"Lady Clanbra's" affairs. For three months she shuttled
back and forth between London, Windsor and Newmarket, hoping for a chance "to trip up Nell Gwyn's
heels," but the King was preoccupied with Keroualle and
satisfied with Nell, and the lady's unskilful managers had
small influence at Court. She herself cared little; dazzled
by the delights of London she pursued a number of eligible
gallants and even became involved for a time with that
wildest of rakes, Harry Killigrew. Early in October the
disgruntled Irish went back to Dublin, dragging reluctant
"Lady Clanbra" along.

The Court returned to London toward the end of July,
and the King rode off on a series of progresses or official
tours in the eastern counties. In September he went as
usual to Newmarket, the little racing town on the wind-
swept heath sixty miles north of London, where the stables
were all "wainscotted and sculptured and the horses fed
on new-laid eggs and Spanish wine." All the jolly courtiers
descended on the town and spent their days and nights
(said Evelyn) "racing, dancing, feasting, and revelling,
more resembling a luxurious and abandoned rout than a
Christian Court." Nell Gwyn was there, of course, and
the Duke of Buckingham, who had brought along "that
impudent woman, the Countess of Shrewsbury, and his

band of fiddlers, &c." Everybody but Evelyn had a good time.

The center of interest at Newmarket was the now-famous Louise de Keroualle, who arrived on October 4 in the King's own coach, attended by Lord Arlington and the impatient French ambassador. She was received "in great state" and taken to Arlington's great country mansion, Euston, near Newmarket. The King was Arlington's guest nearly every day and often spent the night. Now was the time for Keroualle's triumph; she had gradually reduced the King to such a state that he was willing to promise anything. One night in the middle of October, after Keroualle had spent the whole day in "an undress" (without stays and in négligée), and Charles had lavished a world of "fondness and toying" on her, she went to bed with him. The result was apparent in just nine months.

All the good gossips but Evelyn (who was also a guest at Euston) agreed that the bedding was preceded by a mock marriage; that five or six people took the couple into a room "where one in the habit of a priest mumbled over something," and that afterwards the King and his new mistress were put to bed with the usual improper ceremonies. One gossip who wrote a "Secret History" of Charles's reign argued that the marriage was valid because "the law allows all men one wife, and therefore a king, who is above law, may surely have two." He asserted that Keroualle considered herself married and that some time later, "upon some discourse that brought it out," she cried, "Me no whore! If me thought me were a whore me would cut mine throat." It is certainly true that after that night at Euston Keroualle *behaved* like a wife, but she was never foolish enough to mistake a mock ceremony for the reality.

The French faction at Court was jubilant. Ambassador Colbert promptly sent a courier with the good news to Louis XIV, who in reply ordered him to present the royal congratulations to Mademoiselle de Keroualle. "There is every prospect," wrote Colbert, "that she will hold long what she has conquered." He was an excellent prophet.

When the Court returned to Whitehall in November, the besotted King continued to revel in the charms of his newest mistress, and his other ladies were forgotten. So long as her income continued, the Duchess of Cleveland cared not a particle. She had not yet discarded Wycherley, but she was acquiring a new gallant, young Jack Churchill, the future great Duke of Marlborough. Moll Davis merely settled farther back into quiet obscurity. The Queen gave up the struggle for good and moved to Somerset House on the bank of the Thames a mile to the east, coming less and less often to Whitehall.

On Christmas Day, 1671, in her house in Pall Mall, Nell gave birth to her second son. She named him James in compliment to the Duke of York. There were no bonfires to celebrate the birth of the King's eighth illegitimate son.

VIII

The

Rival

Ladies

1 6 7 2 – 1 6 7 4

VIII

THE NEW YEAR came in with feasts and revels at Whitehall, even though at the Navy Office preparations for war with the Dutch went on at high speed. This time there would be no inconclusive treaties of peace; Holland was to be overrun and wiped out of existence. According to plan France prepared an army of 120,000 men for invasion by land. England's task was to destroy the Dutch fleet and land an expeditionary force in the Lowlands. Caught between the jaws of the pincers, Holland could not long resist. The allies gloated as they contemplated the spoils. France was to get the lion's share of territory; England was to have four islands, the town of Sluys, and all of Holland's fishing rights and overseas trade. It was a thoroughly piratical project and the two cynical kings carried it out with the Jolly Roger flying high. They made impossible demands upon the Dutch, refused even to wait for replies, and finally made war without excuse or overt cause.

But these were matters for ministers and rulers; on the surface life was peaceful and little men went their daily rounds. When Nell came back to Court in January she found everyone in high spirits. The Duke of Buckingham's burlesque of heroic plays, *The Rehearsal* (first produced on December 7, 1671), was still a popular subject of conversation. Lacy's imitation of John Dryden—as

"Poet Bayes," the villain of the piece—was something to remember. Buckingham had coached Lacy in Dryden's hesitating speech and had dressed him in Dryden's clothes. Then (said the gossips) he and his cronies had escorted Dryden to the theatre and had sat with him in a box so they could watch him squirm. The farce was a huge success. Its fame even reached France, and King Louis hinted to Ambassador Colbert that to be in fashion he too should write a play.

As usual, the brilliant Buckingham, who,

> in the course of one revolving moon,
> Was chemist, fiddler, statesman, and buffoon,

was also "all for women." Catching Nell alone one day in a private room at Whitehall, he made violent love to her. She had no objection to being kissed, but when he tried to take certain other liberties and rumpled her lace collar, she boxed his ears.

Buckingham was at his zenith as a statesman at this time. As leader of the "Cabal" of ministers—so-called because of their initials: Clifford, Lord Treasurer; Arlington, Chief Secretary of State; Buckingham, Master of the Horse; Ashley (the famous Earl of Shaftesbury), Lord Chancellor; and Lauderdale, Secretary for Scotland—he was, in effect, Prime Minister. Of course he had not yet come in conflict with Louise de Keroualle—"Carwell" to the irreverent—who was willing to let him have his way so long as his policies agreed with the French interest. But she had no love for him; she had never forgotten her ten days of agonized waiting at Dieppe. She was "infinitely in favor" and rapidly becoming "prime mistress."

The Duchess of Cleveland had lost all interest in politics. By bullying the King she continued to amass wealth, and she drove about the streets of dazzled London in a magnificent coach with eight horses. Ensign Churchill was still her lover, and there was evidence that she was "with child by him." As a reward she laid the foundation of his fortune with a handsome cornerstone of £5,000. However, she was already casting amorous leers at another ambitious young man, John Sheffield, Earl of Mulgrave.

Keroualle's hold over the King was not due to her beauty; her eyes were small and slightly a-squint, and her "baby-face" was marred by a look of petulance. Moreover she was not, like Lady Cleveland, skilled in "all the tricks of Aretin . . . to give pleasure," or, like Nell Gwyn, humorous and frankly sensual. In fact she had no humor at all, and *au fond* she was frigid. But she was a very cunning young woman who had studied her captive monarch and knew his every mood and fancy; she knew when to offer intelligent conversation on subjects political, economic and artistic (she was well schooled by the French Ambassador), and when to offer herself. She was a master at dissembling, and she had very distinguished manners.

Although Nell was barely twenty-two, still fresh and attractive, she had two small babies to handicap her, and unfortunately she could not compare in education, polish, or craft with the cultured Keroualle. But she had no lack of friends to advise her. A small group of courtiers who were "the King's companions at most suppers in the week" —he dined in public state at high noon and supped in private at night—were Nell's friends, and their meeting place was often her house in Pall Mall. Among them were her old friends Harry Killigrew (sometimes known as "lying Killigrew"), Henry Savile, groom to the Duke of York, Henry Guy (Beck Marshall's whilom keeper), Cup-bearer to the Queen, Baptist May, Keeper of the Privy Purse, Lord Buckhurst and a recent protégé, ribald Fleet-wood Shepherd, the Earls of Rochester and Mulgrave, and the Duke of Buckingham, three Gentlemen of the Bed-chamber to the King.

Rochester was her most valued adviser. He and Nell were alike in their love of pleasure, and they were both interested in the stage. In 1672 Rochester was schooling his young mistress of the moment, Elizabeth Barry, not only in "the tricks of Aretin" of which he too was a master, but also in the formal gestures and tones of trage-dy. She became Nell's protégé also, and a highly successful tragedian in spite of her mentors.

Easily the leader of the Court wits, Rochester knew Whitehall inside and out, and he had a practical under-standing of the ways of men and women. He employed a footman who knew all the Court, equipped him with a sentinel's red coat and musket, and stationed him every night at the door of a different lady in Whitehall to see "who walked about and visited at forbidden hours." When he was well supplied with gossip, Rochester would retire to the country (where he kept his wife and chil-dren) and write vicious little satires. His philosophy was completely cynical. He believed, as he wrote, that

> Those creatures are the wisest who attain
> By surest means the ends at which they aim.

His advice to Nell followed with perfect logic: "Take your measures just contrary to your rivals, live in peace with all the world, and easily with the King. Never be so ill-natured to stir up his anger against others, but let him forget the use of a passion [anger] which is never to do you good. Cherish his love wherever it inclines, and be assured you can't commit greater folly than pretending to be jealous, but on the contrary, with hand, body, head, heart, and all the faculties you have, contribute to his pleasure all you can and comply with his desires throughout. And for new intrigues, so you be at one end, 'tis no matter which; make sport when you can, at other times help it."

The pale, handsome young earl was very much in earnest, and in the main Nell took his precepts to heart, although she was too impulsive and scatterbrained to adhere to a rigid plan. She supplied what Keroualle could not: good humor, broad jests, and bawdy entertainment. It was not long before the King was making his regular trips to Pall Mall again. As the author of "The Lady of Pleasure" wrote, Nell's function was to drive away the King's melancholy:

When he was dumpish, she would still be jocund,
And chuck the royal chin of Charles the Second.

Her success was attested by Bishop Burnet: "She acted all persons in so lively a manner and was such a constant diversion to the King that even a new mistress could not drive her away."

But Nell could never resist an opportunity to poke fun at Keroualle, even at the risk of stirring up the King's anger, and ambition drove her to take the same measures as her rivals did. They all fought—with the King and each other—for wealth and honors for their children and themselves. In this battle-royal Nell was hampered by the one fact which even the King found it difficult to overlook: no matter how much she put on "the lady of quality," she was base-born.

Like any great lady she had her portrait painted that winter in the prevailing Arcadian mode, as a shepherdess. She wore a lace-edged smock, opened to show her left breast. A length of light-brown taffeta was draped over one shoulder and down across her lap. Lely painted her in a conventional pose, fondling the ear of a stuffed lamb with her left hand, while with her right she offered it a spray of flowers. She was still young looking and unmatronly, with the "blub" cheeks, full mouth, and small chin of Dryden's description. There was mischief in her eyes.

War with Holland was declared on March 17, 1672. For a while it was a popular move in spite of the press gangs which roamed the streets seizing men for the Fleet. The destruction of its great rival would give England control of the seas and their rich trade lanes; everybody wanted to die for Lombard Street. The King's favorite son, the Duke of Monmouth, went abroad to help the French army, incidentally taking along a regiment of regulars. An army of volunteers prepared to invade Holland by sea (it never left England), and such periwigged fops as Lord Mulgrave became knights in shining armor. Buckingham, yearning to add to his many-leaved laurels, wanted to be commander-in-chief. His request was refused on the excellent ground that Lady Shrewsbury would be unhappy if he was long absent.

After the bloody and indecisive battle of Southwold Bay on May 28 (when Henry Savile was listed among the dead and deflated the rumor by publishing his eye-witness account of the fight) the pro-war sentiment ebbed rapidly. The armies of Louis XIV (aided by Monmouth) were rolling over the Netherlands with such ridiculous ease that Englishmen—even Buckingham—fretted and wondered if they were on the right side. The power of Catholic France began to look dangerous, and the Dutch were at least Protestants. By autumn, when the Dutch had opened their water-gates and let the sea in upon their land, resolving to "die in the last dyke," France and the war were alike unpopular—except at Whitehall which flourished under warm showers of French gold.

Intrigues and scandals went on at Whitehall, untouched by war. On July 16, 1672, the Duchess of Cleveland gave birth to a daughter, Barbara—not a Fitzroy. Even the great lady lacked the cheek to father her sixth opus on the King. On July 29 Louise de Keroualle gave birth to a son, another Charles, and no one could doubt his paternity. Now the King had four sons named Charles; on occasion he was mildly confused. Keroualle pressed to have her boy acknowledged. She even argued that the King should legitimize him by marrying her. She saw no reason, she said, why the King, who was "Defender of the Faith" and head of the church, could not give himself a dispensation "to have two or three wives at once."

But at Whitehall as in the English Channel, victory went

to the ships with the greatest weight of metal; the Duchess of Cleveland had all the weaker vessels outgunned. In August her second son, nine-year-old Henry, was boosted to the peerage as Earl of Euston and immediately married to Lord Arlington's daughter, a five-year-old heiress. Cleveland's first son, Charles, was already Earl of Southampton; her third was now called by courtesy Lord George Fitzroy. Within a few months she persuaded the King to grant "his dear and natural daughters, the Ladies Anne and Charlotte Fitzroy," the right to bear the royal arms "in lozenge with a baton sinister ermine." Of course the duchess got new properties and pensions for herself. In the absence of Churchill, who had followed the heroic Duke of Monmouth to Flanders, she consoled herself with Lord Mulgrave. A year later it was falsely reported that she was "with child" by him.

Although Nell could do nothing for her sons this year, she managed to get a pension of £100 a year for her sister Rose and her husband, Captain Cassels, and by her friendship with the King's ministers she was able to do a small favor for her neighbor, the Countess of Portland—"she procured her £1,000 out of the Exchequer." Keroualle prospered financially, but before she could have the full benefit of all the "gifts and honors" which King Charles was panting to bestow on her, she had to have King Louis' leave to become a British subject. This procedure took time. Meanwhile, in the heart of the winter of 1672-3, Queen Catherine was seriously ill, and Keroualle dreamed of wearing the crown. From morning till night she talked hopefully about the Queen's ailments.

In the spring of 1673 English republicanism perked up

its head, began to ask nasty questions about France and
popery, and to cry out against arbitrary power. Parliament worked off its wrath by passing the Test Act
(March 29) which made it impossible for Roman Catholics
to hold public office. Although the King jested that "he
would purge his Court from all Catholics except his barber, whom he meant to keep in despite of all their bills,
for he was so well accustomed to his hand," he managed
to get a special dispensation for the Queen to keep her
Catholic ladies-in-waiting, among them Cleveland and
Keroualle.

Protestant Nell was not disturbed by the Test Act, of
course, but certain changes resulting from it affected her
in time. For example, the Catholic Duke of York had to
resign as Lord High Admiral; the admiralty was put into
the hands of commissioners, and her old friend Samuel
Pepys was made secretary. More important, the Cabal
cracked wide open when Lord Treasurer Clifford gave
up his post for his faith. (A few months later he committed suicide.) In June a protégé of Buckingham's, Sir
Thomas Osborne, was appointed treasurer and vigorously
set about reforming the royal budget.

The mistresses worked harder than ever to line their
purses before Osborne's new system could put an end to
the old, profitable chaos. Much to the amusement of the
Court, they fought each other tooth and nail. In July "a
pleasant ridiculous story" was circulated—false, as it proved
—that Cleveland and Keroualle, believing that the King
had given Nell Gwyn £20,000, had invited her to supper
at Berkshire House and, while "they were drinking," had
suddenly choked Nell with a napkin, "of which she is

since dead." Fortunately the narrator could nail the lie; he had seen Mrs. Gwyn only "yester night in the Park."

There was no reason for Keroualle to resort to violence. On July 25, 1673, the King gave her a thundering roll of honors, climaxed by the ducal coronet; she became at one stroke Baroness Petersfield, Countess of Farnham, and Duchess of Portsmouth. She celebrated her strawberry leaves with a ball and supper for the whole Court at Barn Elms, and for the next two weeks there were almost nightly festivities and "treats" in her honor.

Nell Gwyn was furious. She complained to the King about her own miserable state: her sons were unrecognized and had not even a surname; she herself had no title and no house of her own; the Pall Mall mansion was only a leasehold. Charles made his usual large promises: everything would be taken care of in due time, she would be a countess as soon as he could see "how the people will relish it"—carelessly he even specified a possible title, Countess of Plymouth. Nell was not appeased. Forgetting Rochester's good advice and thinking to force the King's hand, she "got a patent drawn to be Countess of Plymouth" and took it to the Lord Keeper to be sealed. That official refused the patent and asked the King, who weakly admitted that he had been "but in jest" with Nell. Democratic as he was, it was hard for the King to take Nell's pretensions seriously. To add insult to injury, the very title she sought was granted that summer to Lady Greene's son, Charles, who became Earl of Plymouth. Nell remained a houseless commoner with two surnameless little boys.

She had her small revenge on the new Duchess of Portsmouth. One day Nell appeared at Whitehall dressed in "an exceeding rich suit of clothes." The duchess said smugly, "Nelly, you are grown rich, I believe, by your dress; why, woman, you are fine enough to be a queen." "You are entirely right, madam," said Nell, "and I am whore enough to be a duchess."

Nell's angry mood continued into the autumn. Since the French subsidies proved wholly inadequate to pay for a costly war, the King's finances were in bad shape that year. He compensated his "chargeable ladies" by giving them warrants for goods out of ships captured from the Dutch. In September the new treasurer (Osborne, now Earl of Danby) put a stop to the practise, and "neither Madam Kerwell's nor the Duchess of Cleveland's nor Nell Gwyn's warrants would be accepted." The loss to the Duchess of Portsmouth was some £30,000, but King Louis came to her aid with the offer of his share in the next East India ship to be captured. Hopefully Nell asked King Charles for money. He replied quite honestly that he had none to give. "I will tell you how you shall never want," said the impudent comedian, "send the French into France again, set me on the stage again, and lock up your own cod-piece."

It was sound advice; with a flash of wisdom Nell had hit off the sentiments of some millions of good citizens. Feeling against the Court was running high that autumn. To the popular mind the King, his ministers, and his mistresses were idle folk who delighted in rapes, riots, and Romanism. The honest English looked upon Whitehall as a gilded brothel, and took Keroualle's promotion to the peerage as a personal insult. On October 19 they had a new scandal to rage at when Moll Davis gave birth to a girl, Mary, the fourteenth and last of the King's natural children. It was even "a matter of some talk" later that month when Nell was visiting Chiffinch at his country house, Filberts, and the King chanced to dine there one day. There was widespread discontent with the government, and the Country (or Whig) Party in Parliament—republican, anti-French, and anti-Catholic—made political capital of every peccadillo.

The King needed money to pay for more than mistresses; unless he was voted a subsidy by his faithful Commons he would be forced to withdraw from the war. But the Commons were in a truculent mood when Parliament met on October 20. Led by the Country Party, they began by passing a resolution against Catholic Mary of Modena, the Duke of York's second wife, whom he had recently married by proxy. Then they fell upon the alliance with France, debated the iniquity of a standing army, railed at the growth of popery, moved against the King's ministers, and refused to even consider money bills until all their grievances had been righted. King Charles, still hoping for an appropriation which would free him from dependence on Louis XIV, was reluctant to prorogue Parliament, but the French Ambassador wanted a prorogation above all things. If the francophobes in Parliament were not silenced, England might be swung from its alliance with France. At this juncture (according to a most remarkable fable) the Duchess of Portsmouth went into action.

One night (says her anonymous biographer) she invited the King to "a costly banquet . . . with divers sorts of music and variety of liquors. The persons who composed the company had screwed their mirth and wit to the highest pitch; all care and anxious thoughts were banished, and the night entirely dedicated to Bacchus and Venus." It was nearly dawn when the party ended, but the duchess refused to let the King go. She retired with him and "two other great ladies" into a private room. After a little dalliance, the three ladies, complaining of the heat, disrobed, the King assisting in the process. "Not unlike the three goddesses, Juno, Pallas, and Venus before Paris, did those three naked ladies stand before the King, who was ravished with the sight, and examined every part about them with his own hands and eyes, with all imaginable curiosity."

When his visual and tactile senses were sated, the four —with the ladies still draped only in their modesty—fell to playing Questions and Commands. "When it came to the ladies' turn to command, they commonly would impose upon the King the drinking of a glass of wine to each of their healths, to bear up his spirits." At last it became Portsmouth's turn after several rounds—His Majesty was now in a malleable condition. To her first Question— "Whether he would not be glad to govern absolutely without Parliament?"—there could be only one answer, yes. To her second—"Whom he thought the happiest monarch in the world?"—there could also be only one answer, Louis XIV, an absolute monarch. Thereupon, as her Command, Portsmouth ordered him to prorogue Parliament, and the very next morning he did so. It was really very simple.

The truth of the matter was that the King had to act quickly in order to save his ministry. On November 4, just as the House of Commons was proceeding to impeach the Earl of Lauderdale, King Charles prorogued Parliament until January. But he was too late for one minister. The shifty Earl of Shaftesbury, long ago infected by the heresy of political dissent, was too far gone to be of further use. For some time, as the King well knew, he had been negotiating with the Country Party. On November 9 King Charles dismissed him from his post as Lord Chancellor; grimly Shaftesbury put off his judge's gown and took up the sword of opposition. Now only three of the old Cabal were left.

As far as the House of Commons was concerned, Buckingham was the prime target. All through the rest of the year, the Country Party labored at preparing its case against him. In those critical months Nell Gwyn was loyal to the great duke and brought her small influence to his aid. Her friendship was not without self-interest, of course; so long as the Duchess of Portsmouth ruled at Whitehall, the chances of the King making her a peer were very slim. But either Buckingham—if he remained in power—or the Lord Treasurer, Danby (who was see-sawing between his old alliance with Buckingham and a new league with Portsmouth), could easily make her a countess. Nevertheless, her most important reason was friendship.

In November and December Nell attended many little supper-parties at which all kinds of wild political schemes were discussed. But it was Buckingham's nature always to make light of trouble—even now, when he faced the greatest fight of his career. Once Edward, Lord Conway, was invited to Lady Shrewsbury's house and found there "my Lord Treasurer [Danby], Nell Gwyn, the Duke of Buckingham, and Mr. Speaker [Seymour]." They all "went to supper, were very merry, and drank smartly."

When Parliament convened again in early January, 1674, Buckingham's enemies used a new weapon. For six years Lady Shrewsbury's two sons had been wards of her dead husband's family. Now, speaking in behalf of the older boy, the young Earl of Shrewsbury, these guardians petitioned the House of Lords to do something about "the wicked and scandalous life" of his mother and her ducal lover. The honest petitioners would not have complained, they said, "had the offenders employed the usual care to cover their guilt and shame," but they persisted in their course publicly, "in defiance of the laws of God and man, having caused a base son of theirs to be buried in the abbey church at Westminster with all solemnities . . ." Buckingham's insult to the aristocracy was the one unforgivable sin.

Attacked in both houses at once, Buckingham waged a bitter defensive war, in the Commons laying the blame for all unpopular policies on Arlington and the dead Clifford, and in the Lords denying, extenuating, and finally admitting his guilt and begging "pardon of God and the House." The Commons voted an address for his removal as minister; the House of Lords, which could have invoked the ecclesiastical laws against adultery, was more merciful. It forbade the guilty pair to cohabit again, under penalty of forfeiting bonds for £10,000 which each was required to execute. The middle-aged Antony (he was forty-six) and his plump Cleopatra agreed and signed. Lady Shrewsbury fled to a nunnery in France, whence, after a time, came word that she was making "strong resol-

utions" and had "great faith." Buckingham, dismissed
from all his offices, went penitently to church with his
faithful wife. Then he followed Lord Shaftesbury into
the arms of the Country Party. He continued to be a frequent and welcome guest at Nell Gwyn's house in Pall
Mall. Fallen statesmen could rise again; anyway, Buckingham was her friend.

It was no more difficult for Buckingham to turn his coat
and adopt a brand new set of principles than it had been
for Shaftesbury. Both men were opportunists, willing to
ignore ideals, principles, and personal animus in their pursuit of power. Now Buckingham made friends with the
Mammon of republicanism, allowed himself to be argued
out of his Anglican views by nonconformist fanatics, and
made overtures to the very enemies who had brought
about his downfall. Shaftesbury had quickly become the
acknowledged leader of the Country Party; within a year
Buckingham was his closest rival and lieutenant. The two
politicians were never really friends, and neither quite
trusted the other (Shaftesbury thought Buckingham was
"inconstant and giddy"), but they learned to work well
together as leaders of the opposition and built up a ruth-
less, powerful, party organization.

With Buckingham's defeat, the wise Earl of Danby allied himself with the Duchess of Portsmouth and became
the King's chief minister. King Charles got no money
from Parliament and no new subsidies from Louis XIV.
Without funds to set forth his fleet again, with dissension
and clamor against Papists and standing armies at home,
and the fortunes of the allies failing on land and sea, there
was nothing to do but withdraw from the French alliance

and—in spite of his solemn promises—make a separate peace with Holland. On February 9 a treaty was concluded. Charles apologized profusely to the French Ambassador and saved face by leaving several English regiments (among them that in which Nell's brother-in-law was a captain) in the service and pay of the French army.

It was time for England to save itself. In Holland's day of peril young William of Orange (King Charles's nephew) had been made general of the small Dutch army and emerged as the savior of the Netherlands. A man of small body but resolute mind, by his military skill he succeeded in blunting the French sword driving into the heart of Holland. Moreover, he proved himself an able diplomat, drawing into the war against France the German Emperor, the King of Spain, and the Elector of Brandenburg. Against this coalition even the mighty French army could not prevail. For four more years it marched across northern Europe, besieging towns, fighting bloody battles, dying for the glory of "His Most Christian Majesty," Louis XIV—and achieving nothing. England was at peace, traded with both sides, and prospered.

With the war ended for England in the spring of 1674, Whitehall returned to normal. In April the Duchess of Cleveland turned Lord Mulgrave out to grass, with the blazing star of the Garter pinned to his coat, granted for his "faithful services and great abilities." In one of his satires Lord Rochester accused the Duchess of Cleveland of wearing out six courtiers in succession: the Duke of Monmouth, the Earl of Cavendish, Sir Carr Scroope, and Messrs. Henningham, Villiers, and Newport; but this was a base libel—Rochester had no sentry at the doors of Berkshire House. The duchess took on only one new lover this year, Henry Savile, now a Groom of the Bedchamber to the King.

Savile, a big, blunt, hearty Yorkshireman, was a new type to the Duchess of Cleveland. Paradoxically, he was an honest courtier and diplomat. Younger brother to the Earl of Halifax, he had early made up his mind to rise in the world by Court favor, and philosophically accepted servility and attendance as his lot in life. Although he claimed to be "the laziest man alive," he was industrious and able, and his personal and diplomatic letters were often brilliantly penned. On occasion he acted with remarkable rashness, and in his cups he was given to blurting out the truth, much to the chagrin of his superiors.

His rashness is well illustrated by an episode of some three years earlier than this time. Among those present at a house party at Althorp, country home of the Sunderland family, were Savile and the young and recently widowed Countess Northumberland, upon whose virtue (or property, said to be worth £10,000 a year) Savile had designs. In the dead of night, clad only in his shirt, Savile crept into the countess's chamber, "having the day before stole away the bolt so that there was nothing but a latch to lift." The countess woke up, Savile plumped to his knees and poured forth protestations of love. The frightened lady, caught naked in her bed, instinctively pulled the bell-rope—a step, said the gossips, which she would never have taken had the lover done more and said less. The house was roused; Savile fled betimes and was pursued to London by stern male relatives with swords drawn and honor to avenge. A duel was prevented partly by the

King's amused intervention, partly by Savile's hurried departure for France. As usual, he apologized to all concerned and was forgiven. There was something engagingly boyish about Henry Savile. He was the Earl of Rochester's intimate friend, and Nell Gwyn was very fond of him.

During the spring and summer of 1674 the Duchess of Portsmouth was out of the amatory competition. While Buckingham was defending himself against charges of adultery in the House of Lords, King Charles was contracting "the pox" from a careless wench brought to his chamber by way of the Privy Stairs. The King recovered after the normal period of treatment, but before he knew he had the disease he gave it to Portsmouth. Although she was consoled in her misery by Louis XIV's gifts of a pearl necklace and a valuable diamond she was in wretched health for nearly eight months, traveling to Bath and Tunbridge Wells for the waters, and trying one physician after another.

Nell escaped infection and spent a happy summer with the King and her children at Windsor. A few of Chiffinch's accounts for the period May 19 to August 1 show that she lived comfortably at the King's expense, with considerable expenditures for "diet" for herself and her family, for "oranges, lemons, etc.," for the feeding and care of her horses, the carriage of her goods, manure for her garden, and even "£30. 12s. 8d. for building a pump" for her small house at Windsor. Nell bought as she pleased, and the bills were submitted to Thomas Groundes, her steward, who turned them over to Chiffinch for payment. It was not a bad arrangement for Nell, but it was hard on the tradesmen who often waited months for their money.

Late in August the whole Court was present at a sham battle representing the siege of Maestricht in Holland. A year earlier the gaudy Duke of Monmouth had been the hero of that battle: slightly hampered by a few thousand French soldiers and some English volunteers, he had captured a strategic counter-scarp. Now, in a meadow below Windsor Castle, "bastions, bulwarks, ramparts, palisadoes, graffs, horn-works, counter-scarps, etc., were constructed." There was all the pomp and circumstance of a formal siege; great guns were fired, "grenadoes" shot off, and mines sprung; prisoners were taken and exchanged; soldiers fell wounded and lay twitching on the field. It was very pretty, and, "being night, it made a formidable show." The battle ended with the capture of the famous counter-scarp by Monmouth, sword in hand, while the spectators rent the skies with their applause.

In the autumn of the year the Duchess of Portsmouth returned to command again at Whitehall. By now, partly because national prosperity had brought a large increase in his revenues, partly because the brilliant Lord Danby had brought order out of chaos, the King was able to consolidate his casual gifts and "bounties" into regular annuities for his ladies. Of course Cleveland got the lioness's share, with £6,000 a year for herself and £3,000 for each of her sons—£15,000 in all. At the same time her third son, Lord George, was created Earl of Northumberland. Portsmouth was second with £8,600 for herself and her son, "for her natural life and one year after her decease." As usual Nell was third with only £4,000 (roughly $80,-

ooo) a year for herself and her two boys; significantly the pension was not for Nell's life but only during the King's "pleasure"—that is, it could be stopped whenever he chose, and it ended with his death. Of course, over and above these annuities, all three ladies had other sources of income: gifts from the King, lands in England and Ireland, receipts from minor taxes, fees from offices, and the like. There was no pension for retiring Moll Davis.

That autumn was a busy and exciting time for Nell, with all sorts of things stirring. The best event was her new pension; the worst was the news that her brother-in-law, Captain Cassels, whose regiment had been loaned to the French king, had been killed in Holland. When it became necessary to send an agent overseas to attend to Cassels' affairs, the Secretary of the Navy, Mr. Samuel Pepys, placed a yacht at Nell's disposal to convey "Mr. Philip Pigeare" to Dieppe and back. Only a week before that time another friend, Lord Mulgrave, had been seriously wounded in a duel over the possession of wanton Mall Kirke, whose mother, Mrs. Mary Kirke, had been so quick to call Nell "whore" three years earlier. Then toward the end of October Henry Killigrew was promoted to the post of Groom of the Bedchamber to the King, and Lord Buckhurst announced his marriage to Lady Falmouth; at the same time, by the death of an uncle, Buckhurst became Earl of Middlesex. Finally, in November the Court was a-stir with preparations for a new masque, *Calisto*, by John Crowne. Moll Davis was coming out of retirement to personate the river Thames; Mary Knight was to sing the rôle of Peace; and Lady Mary Mordaunt, another of Nell's friends, was to have the rôle of an envious nymph, Psecas. In a serious masque there was no part for Nell the comedian, but she was consoled by the dedication of Thomas Duffett's new play, *The Spanish Rogue*, in which the impartial poet described her as "the greatest goodness in the world," "free from sullen pride and affected stateliness," and "the most perfect beauty" of the age. Truly "Madam Ellen Gwyn" was now a great lady.

Her "goodness" did not include charity to the Duchess of Portsmouth; she never missed a chance to ridicule her rival. Sometime that autumn Portsmouth had herself painted in an elaborate lace smock, with one breast bare. Seated against a background of rich draperies, she held a dove in her hands as if defending it against her two-year-old son, pictured as a Cupid. Nell went to the same painter, wore the same smock or a duplicate, with a like degree of nudity, and had herself painted reclining on a bed of flowers against the identical background of draperies. Her two sons were shown hovering near as Cupids, the older pulling back the curtains to disclose his mother, the younger flying toward her from the right with an impish look on his face, a bow in one hand and a flaming torch in the other. To complete the picture a regal figure in the right distance personated the King. The torch, of course, symbolized his burning love for Nell. It was a nice painting to hang in one's drawing-room and show off to guests.

Again, early in December, when word came from France that the famous Chevalier de Rohan had died, Portsmouth went into deep mourning, "as being, forsooth, of kin to that family." Not to be outdone, the next day Nell too donned black, claiming that she was mourning for the recently deceased Cham of Tartary, who bore just the same relationship to her as de Rohan to Portsmouth.

It was very good fun but unprofitable. Young Charles was now four, James was nearly three, and the King gave no sign of keeping his promises. Sadly Nell told her boys that they "were princes by their father for their elevation, but they had a whore to their mother for their humiliation."

IX

"Madam
Ellen Gwyn"

1 6 7 5

EXCEPT for her failure to get her sons acknowledged, there was no reason for Nell to bewail her origin and occupation. At twenty-five there was little of Covent Garden left in her. Madam Ellen Gwyn was accepted as a friend by the blue-bloods of the Court circle, and—except for occasional lapses into profanity when her temper flared—she was a complete lady in speech, dress, and manner. She lived in "high equipage" with her mansion, a sedan-chair, a coach and horses, a retinue of servants, and an assured income—at least during the King's pleasure. By various tricks and cajolings she managed to add considerably to that income.

For example, on December 5, 1674, the King gave her £500 for hangings for her house. On February 18, 1675, he gave her another £500 which was "not to be accounted any part of her allowance." These sums were charged against the Treasury. In addition, between December 31, 1674, and April 30, 1675, he gave her a total of £2,500 from the Secret Service funds as "bounty." Now all of these payments were over and above her regular annuity, which was supposed to be paid quarterly but was usually a month or so in arrears. During 1675 the Treasury paid only £3,500 of her pension. From the end of 1674 to the end of 1675 her total income, then, was £7,000—roughly equivalent to $140,000 (the pound of that time being approximately equal to $20 in our values). Of course her rivals, the Duchesses of Cleveland and Portsmouth, were paid even larger sums, but after all they were ladies by birth and had to be more heavily compensated for their descent into trade.

Nell was not a thrifty person; the more she got, the more she spent, and she was rarely solvent. By happy accident a number of her receipted bills for 1675, some of them complete, some only mutilated and tantalizing fragments, have survived the dangers of fire, mold, mice, and manuscript collectors to tell us something about her way of living and its cost.

The taxes on her home were trivial by comparison with her income. Although there are no bills for hearth money, church rates, subsidies voted by Parliament, or special assessments (all of which usually came to about £20 a year for well-to-do people) we know that Nell paid £2. 12s. a year for the poor of St. Martin's Parish, £3. for water (piped to her house from a wooden conduit maintained by the parish), and £1. for scavenger service. The cost of keeping her house in good repair is not indicated. There is one fragmentary bill from her plumber, John Chennet, for "solder used about the mount" (of her pump?) and for "labor for that and the balcony," but the charge is missing. The only item that might be considered a part of the regular overhead for her house is a bill for fuel in August: £13. 13s. for twenty-one "loads of coals"—a load was usually a chaldron, or thirty-two bushels.

Nell had at least eight servants. The cheapest of these was the "maid wench," the cook's helper, who was paid the magnificent sum of 1s. a week (plus, of course, her keep). The costliest was Thomas Groundes, her steward and man of business. Good majordomos were paid salaries ranging as high as £100 a year, but they did not live in the house. A cook and a nursemaid could be hired for £4 each a year, with board and lodging. A footman, a porter, and a coachman were paid each £6 to £10, plus liveries, board, and some kind of a hole to sleep in (the coachman usually lived at the stables where the horses were kept). A personal maid—a woman of some refinement and education, able to act as Nell's amanuensis at need—cost £12 or £15 a year, plus the usual board and lodging.

Although Nell owned her own sedan-chair, she hired professional carriers by the week. On October 13, 1675, William Calow and his partner submitted a bill for £1. 11s. 6d. for carrying Nell at various times to visit her sister, Mrs. Cassels, her friends, Mary Knight, Arabella Churchill (the Duke of York's mistress), Madam Mary Young (the King's seamstress), and "waiting," once for four hours, once for seven. They charged also for carrying another friend, Lady Lucy Sandys, "to the play at Whitehall and waiting," and for carrying Nell to an unstated destination "and waiting eleven hours." The two chairmen set a low valuation on their time, about 6d. an hour for each.

Of course Nell owned a "French coach" (with glass windows), emblazoned with her monogram in gold. For this she had to have at least six good horses which were kept in rented stables and fed richly. One of John Topham's bills for "horsemeat" covered supplies of hay, oats, beans, and straw from July 6 to August 8, 1675, at a cost of £21. 1s. Her coachman, John Cooke, kept an itemized list of his expenditures whenever Nell took a trip to Windsor or Newmarket. He was reimbursed for stabling, "horsemeat," "greasing the coach," the fee of a farrier who bled one of the horses, and even for alms given to "a poor man."

What with herself, her two sons, her servants, and her mother who was living with her in 1675, Nell had a large number of mouths to fill at every meal. Then, too, she often had guests for dinners, suppers, or "collations" late at night. The eating habits of the time were based on the touching faith that health and strength came from large quantities of solid food and strong drink, particularly the latter. Breakfast for almost everybody consisted of a "morning draught" of ale or beer, with bread and butter or something savory: radishes, anchovies, or pickled oysters. Dinner at noon was the heaviest meal of the day with roasts of beef and mutton, meat pies, fish, fowl, bread, cheese, an occasional salad or a vegetable, fruits in their season, tarts, and sweets—all on the table at once. Supper was only a smaller version of dinner, eaten at any odd hour of the evening. At a formal dinner Nell's guests sat on armless chairs around a long table loaded with steaming dishes. The gentlemen wore their hats except when a toast was proposed. Those who were very mannerly were careful not to fill their mouths too full, not to belch publicly, not to pick their teeth with their forks, and not to break bones with their hands and suck the marrow noisily.

Meat was the staple food. On January 26, 1675, Nell's cook submitted for the week past a carefully itemized bill which included "4 stone & pound of beef," 13 pounds of mutton, a leg and a loin of pork, and a leg of veal—roughly 120 pounds of meat costing £1. 6s. 10d. In addition the cook spent 14s. 2d. on oysters, salt fish, gudgeons, smelts, salmon, shrimps, and "hogs sweet-breads," and 7s. 8d. for eggs, a pullet, "a chick," and "a hen with eggs." Against a total of £2. 8s. 8d. for flesh she spent only 6d. for barley and rice, 1s. 3d. for "half a peck of flour," 1s. 6d. for "small bread" (rolls), 5s. for "household bread," 1s. for "half a hundred turnips," and 4s. 3d. for currants, raisins, oranges, and "golden pippins"—a total of 13s. 8d.

The total expended for the week was £4. 5s. 9d. (about $85). This covered also such odd items as milk (1s. 8d.), a cheese (2s. 8d.), a custard and a cheese-cake (6d.), a bottle of sack for cooking (2s.), "blacking and whiting and soap" (3d.), a week's pay for the "maid wench," and half a crown for the chairman who brought Master Charles home one day. It did not include, of course, the cost of beer, ale, wine, and brandy. When Nell gave a party the cook's account nearly doubled; a fragmentary bill for only three days came to a total of £3. 9s. 3d. That a party was in preparation is shown by the listing of such delicacies as two pigeons (3s. 4d.), four chickens (6s.), a neck of veal (5s.), a shoulder of mutton (3s.), "2 lb of dou clarified sugar" (2s. 8d.), five pounds of butter (3s. 2d.), and quantities of cream, cloves, currants, raisins, and pastries.

The English nation of five million people consumed annually some twelve million barrels of beer and ale. Nell's household did its best to raise the national average. A bill for a six month's supply of malt beverages covered nine kilderkins, or half-barrels (totalling 144 gallons), of ale and twenty-three and a half barrels (856 gallons) of small beer—"eight-shilling beer." The cost was £14. 3s. The small beer was for the servants and the children; the ale— strong or "ordinary"—was for the mistress and her guests (for old Madam Gwyn there was brandy). No one, not even the children, drank water except as a desperate last resort. If the household followed the national pattern it consumed also very large quantities of wine. A gentleman did not sip claret or burgundy from a dainty little glass; when he drank a health he emptied a goblet—a "brimmer" —at a draught, turning the empty glass "supernaculum," upside down against his thumb nail, to show that not a drop was left. At a formal dinner the host walked about the table proposing a toast to each guest in turn and lead- ing the liquid chorus. The ladies managed to hold their own on such occasions.

Nell's household suffered from the usual ailments: colds, catarrhs, fevers, and the digestive distress caused by a too- heavy diet. A dilapidated apothecary's bill from July, 1675, to November, 1676, totalled £45. 14s. 9d. for drugs, medical supplies, and treatments. (Nell still owed £81. 3s. 9d. on a "former bill which was delivered to Mr. Chif- finch.") Since the medical axiom was that all diseases could be alleviated, if not cured, by evacuation, the commonest charges were for a "glyster" (an enema given by the apothe- cary), for the instruments used, "an ivory pipe and blad- der," and for purges and emetics.

From July through December, 1675, there were charges for "cordial mixtures," "glysters," and "ointments" for old Mrs. Gwyn. In addition she took "plague water" at the rate of a quart a week—at 8s. 4d. a quart. "Plague water," a very popular tonic, was brandy flavored with herbs. Old

Madam Gwyn was well fortified against the now almost non-existent plague. The nostrum helped her dipsomania, too. In 1676 she moved to a house in Chelsea and her name disappeared from the apothecary's list.

As usual, sturdy Nell enjoyed good health, but she bought a number of cosmetics: "Queen of Hungary's water" (a popular toilet preparation), "oil of white lilies and oil of roses" (supposed to be good for the eyes), "rose water," and other "waters for the face." Her children suffered from ordinary colds, colics, and stomach-aches. "Pectoral syrup," plasters, and sugar candy were prescribed for their coughs. The heroic (and circular) nature of the remedies is shown by entries for "two blistering plasters" followed at once by "plasters to dress the blisters." Master Charles, now five, was a healthy lad, although in October, 1675, a delicious and effective "cordial julep with pearls" was prescribed for him. In April, 1676, Master James had a siege which called for a plaster, three doses of "purging powder," a "cordial," and "two ounces of diascordium"——a witches brew of herbs. The servants, too, had their ailments. John Cooke was ill for two weeks in March, 1676, requiring a "sudorific potion," six glysters, and several quarts of cordials. Like the other patients, he survived.

Fuel, food, drink, and drugs were the mundane necessities for any large household; buying them gave Nell no pleasure. As a matter of fact, she had little or nothing to do with ordering or paying for such everyday things. Thomas Groundes, her faithful steward, took care of the household routine and saw to it that the larder and cellar were stocked, the horses groomed, and the house kept in repair. He scrutinized all bills for services and supplies, objecting to excessive charges, and sometimes refusing to pay until a bill was reduced. He was careful to have every tradesman sign a receipt according to a conventional formula: "Received then of Madam Ellen Gwyn at the hands of Thomas Groundes the sum of —— in payment of this bill and all other demands to date." Sometimes when Groundes (because of Nell's extravagance) was short of cash, he had to stall off a creditor with a payment "on account."

Unfortunately Nell was often too extravagant for Mr. Groundes' peace of mind. She denied herself nothing and ran up accounts everywhere, confident that the bills would be paid. She even charged the cost of her amusements. Two or three times a week she went to the theatre with at least one companion and sometimes with two or three guests, sitting always in the best seats. Late in 1676 the Duke's Theatre presented a bill for performances she attended from September, 1674, to June, 1676, casually putting the charges "on the cuff" until the total came to £35. 19s. Nell played cards at the Groom Porters, and bet on horses and gamecocks—quick ways to the poorhouse. She entertained lavishly, bought clothing, jewels, silver, and furnishings without counting the cost. As a result she was always short of cash and forever seeking additions to her income.

As the King's mistress her credit was excellent, and it was fun to shop at the fashionable New Exchange, an arcade in the Strand with rows of shops along double galleries of black stone. Here the displays of modish linens, laces, hats, shoes, and gloves were presided over by bold-eyed young women who were famous for their wares and notorious for their private lives. There were jewelers', silversmiths', hosiers', perfumers', booksellers', and fruiterers' shops, and of a morning the Exchange was crowded with "persons of quality." Nell's coach took her to the Exchange in jolting state; then, followed by a footman to carry her purchases, she wandered through the galleries, stopping now and then to chat with a friend or to finger a fine fabric.

She bought recklessly, not only fine clothing for her children—"2 white sarcenet [silk] hoods with scarfs to um" and "a doz of childrens white gloves"—but lavish and expensive ready-made articles for herself, shoes, materials, and particularly the garish laces used to trim and decorate her petticoats. (Over-dresses were opened down the skirt in front and drawn back to show off the petticoats in all their glory.) For example, on June 18, 1675, Henry Robins sent her a bill for fifty-three and a half yards of black, green, gold, and silver lace, the total coming to £17. 8s. 2d. On July 17 Richard Howe's bill for £12. 10s. was for three white satin under-petticoats and three night gowns (dressing gowns), one of white satin. On July 30 Henry Roberts' bill for shoes bought since the last of February came to £14. 5s. This covered ten pairs for Nell and five pairs for the children. Nell's shoes and slippers were made of cloth-of-silver, or of green, gold, scarlet, or "sky-colored" satin. Master Charles had a pair of "satin shoes laced over gold"—trimmed with gold braid.

That summer the widowed Rose Cassels, a careful and thrifty shopper, did some sewing for her sister, submitting bills for only the materials used. (In the autumn Nell managed to get Rose's pension increased to £200.) One of Rose's statements added up to £5. 18s. 6d. for ribbons, pins, knots, shoestrings, and "colbertine" and other laces for a rich petticoat. Another bill for materials for a gown and petticoat came to £14. 12s. 4d., but it included also "a fine landskip fan." At the bottom of one bill for ribbons and laces, some "narrow to ruffle," some "broad for the body" of a petticoat, Rose wrote to her sister, "I have sent you the rest of the ribbon and lace that was left. I was in twenty shops looking for cheaper but could not [find any] for my life." Certainly Rose was no spend-thrift.

Nell's love of finery and show was not solely the result of her vulgar background. It was a gaudy age. The most genteel courtiers vied with each other in costly and elab-orate clothes, rococco decorations and furnishings, gilded and laquered sedan-chairs and coaches. Two years earlier the refined Duchess of Portsmouth had had "the famousest chair making that ever was seen, beyond the King's or Queen's by far." Now, with her own almost unlimited credit, it was only natural that Nell should go her rival one better. Her new sedan-chair, delivered on June 17, 1675, was a splendid example of the joiner's craft. It was lined with serge, covered on the outside with "the best neat's leather" over canvas, studded with thousands of gold-headed nails, and gilded liberally on windowframes and iron-work. Thomas Groundes objected to the bill for £34. 11s., and Mr. Wright, the joiner, accepted £30 "in full discharge."

Nell's expenditures for clothing, shoes, a sedan-chair, and household furnishings (for example, £60 for "a doz

of silver trencher plates") were small by comparison with
what she spent this year on improvements in her bedroom
—where she did her important entertaining. The work
was started in May, 1674, when a woodcarver, a joiner,
and an upholsterer combined their skills in "Stuff and work
done for Madam Gwyn's bedroom." The results of their
collaboration were satin window curtains set in richly
carved frames, two "wainscot seats with compass ends,"
carved and embellished with Nell's monogram (a chaste
"E.G."), and various minor repairs and improvements to
the tune of £23. 19s. 8d. (The bill, trimmed by Groundes
to £20. 10s., was not paid until August 25, 1675.)

With £500 worth of hangings (brocade or tapestry
drapes covering most of the wall space) Nell had a splendid background for the baroque silver bedstead designed
and executed by John Coques, silversmith. His labor and
materials cost approximately £1,100. The basic structure
of the canopied bed was carved wood, but the headboard
and the posts which supported the canopy were decorated
with silver crowns, eagles, cupids, a head of the King, and
a miniature figure of the Duchess of Cleveland's ex-lover,
"Jacob Hall dancing upon the rope of wire work." (This
was a nice touch of humor. It was the duchess's infatuation
with Jacob Hall in 1670 which finally broke up her carnal
relations with King Charles and left the field clear for Nell
and other competitors.) Coques' total bill was £1,135. 3s.
1d., but this included the cost of mending "the great
silver andirons" and "the gold hour glass," cleaning and
burnishing "a sugar box, a pepper pot, a mustard pot, and
two cruses," and making and delivering two silver bottles.

All of this work—window-curtains, seats, hangings, and bed—was finished by August, 1675. Now, to complete the bedroom and let the light of day gleam upon its splendors, Nell had all her old, dingy, discolored windows reglazed. Edward Traherne "sold and delivered" £61. 7s. 8d. worth of Normandy glass—the best and clearest obtainable— "diamond cut" from handmade rounds into small panes and puttied "into the shapes." The price was exorbitant, of course, and Groundes could pay only £40 on account, but no matter; Nell's bedroom was now completely refurbished at a cost of some £1,700. It was a rich setting for a lovely jade.

Some time that autumn, in all the luxury of her fine house, rich furnishings, and beautiful clothes, Nell gave a party. She invited the King, the Duke of York, and a few of her intimates to a "concert of music" in her drawing-room. Candlelight glowed on satins and lace and gleamed on burnished silver. The company sat in cushioned chairs while young Bowman from the King's Theatre sang of the joys of love to the soft strains of fiddle, theorbo, and lute. The evening was a great success, and Madam Ellen Gwyn was the *grande dame* in the height of her wealth and beauty.

At the close of the performance, the King—the source of all her riches—thanked the musicians (his usual phrase was "I thank you heartily, again and again") and expressed his pleasure in high terms. "Then, sir," said Nell, "to show you don't speak like a courtier, I hope you'll make the performers a handsome present." The King fumbled in his pockets, admitted with some embarrassment that he had no money, and asked the Duke if he had any. "I believe, sir," said the Duke, "not above a guinea or two." Suddenly Nell was struck by the irony of the situation. Turning to her other guests and borrowing the King's pet oath she cried, "Od's fish! What company am I got into?"

X

The

Triple

Combats

1 6 7 5 – 1 6 7 6

X

FOR AT LEAST six years after the defeat of Buckingham, Nell was in politics up to her elbows. The leaders of
the Country Party were often at her house, took her at
least part way into their confidence, and tried to influence
the King through her. Pale, long-faced Shaftesbury, always tortured by the suppurating ulcer in his side, and
Buckingham, as blustering as ever, talked in flaming words
about liberty, conscience, toleration, the rights of the
people, and such tiresome stuff. To protect themselves
against possible arrest, the two leaders had taken residences
within the old liberties of London: Shaftesbury in Alders-
gate Street and Buckingham in Dowgate—the King sar-
castically called Buckingham "Alderman George." Nell's
home was a kind of neutral ground, and not infrequently
the King, who wanted to know what his enemies were
thinking, met and talked with them there. Nell's own reasons for being in politics were entirely personal: the politicians were her friends, and she wanted wealth and honors
for herself and her sons. The fundamental conflict between
the Court and Country Parties meant so little to her that
sometimes she worked innocently against her own best
interests.

However confused the political details seemed, the real
issue was clear enough. The King and his party were determined to preserve all the ancient rights of the Crown; the

Country Party was bent on setting up Parliament as the real governing power. Both sides had their principles; both were in the right, and neither would compromise. Charles refused to be dictated to on his foreign policy or his choice of ministers; whereupon Parliament refused to vote him money. It was a beautiful impasse.

Shaftesbury, the acknowledged leader of the Country Party, was a curious blend of patriotism, duplicity, and megalomania. Had he been born a king, he would have set out to conquer the world, trusting in his stars and convinced that what he did was for the good of humanity. He was learned, brilliant, industrious, and sometimes honest. Dryden, in his "Absolom and Achitophel" (1681), pictured him as a man fitted "for close designs and crooked counsels," sagacious, bold, restless, dissatisfied whether in or out of power,

> In friendship false, implacable in hate,
> Resolved to ruin or to rule the state.

As a statesman, Shaftesbury was

> A daring pilot in extremity,
> Pleased with the danger, when the waves went high
> He sought the storms, but, for a calm unfit,
> Would steer too nigh the sands, to boast his wit.
> Great wits are sure to madness near allied,
> And thin partitions do their bounds divide.

There were times in Shaftesbury's turbulent career when it seemed that the thin partitions had broken down.

Political parties, particularly when out of power, tend to draw together numbers of irreconcilable elements, united only by their common desire to gain power. The Country Party was no exception. There were honest patriots among its members, men like Algernon Sidney and Lord William Russell, who (again according to Dryden) "thought the power of monarchy too much," and sought to limit and control it. More numerous were the opportunists, dissatisfied place-hunters like Buckingham, Ralph Montagu, and the Earl of Sunderland, who "for interest sought t'embroil the state." But the bulk of the rank and file were fanatics—old-line Presbyterians and Puritans, haters of popery and prelacy; republicans, Cromwellians, and theocrats, "Of the true old enthusiastic breed;" and the London citizenry who were

> well versed of old
> In Godly faction, and in treason bold;
> Cowering and quaking at a conqueror's sword,
> But lofty to a lawful prince restored.

And, finally, there was the mob (the word was just being coined),

> the herd of such
> Who think too little and who talk too much.

Only a political genius could weld together and use such a miscellany of types, and Shaftesbury was a political genius of the first order. But so was King Charles.

In 1675 the government was almost a one-man ministry. Lord Treasurer Danby had succeeded Buckingham as chief minister and towered head and shoulders above his colleagues. Of course the Duchess of Portsmouth, the King's French mistress (charged by Louis XIV with the duty of looking after the French interest) was a kind of minister *ex officio.* Lord Arlington, formerly Secretary of State, had been demoted to futility as Lord Chamberlain of the Household. The uncouth old Scotsman, John Maitland, Duke of Lauderdale, the only one of the Cabal still in power, was now High Commissioner for Scotland, but he devoted his time to oppressing his countrymen. All the other ministers were nonentities. To oppose the growing strength of the Country Party, Danby built up the Court Party—largely by gifts of places, pensions, and cash—and sought to revive the absolutism of Charles I's reign. Old Puritans had long called the anniversary of Charles I's execution "Calf's Head day;" now they applied the bovine epithet to Danby.

One day in March, 1675, a few weeks before Parliament was due to meet, the King was complaining to a group of Nell's guests about his lack of money. Boldly Nell suggested that "if he would take her advice she doubted not that His Majesty should be supplied." The King asked, "Which way?" Nell replied that when Parliament sat "he should treat them with a French ragou, Scotts collops, and a calf's head." The King laughed and seemed "well pleased." Viciously Nell added, "Hang up the Scotch dog and the French bitch."

She was well informed on Parliament's mood. In the session of April 13 to June 9 the Commons did their best to impeach Danby and voted an address to the King praying him to remove Lauderdale "from his presence, his counsels, and all employments." They could do nothing to show their hatred of Portsmouth and had to take it out in talk. Four months earlier Portsmouth had made her younger sister, Henriette de Keroualle, a countess by marrying her to Philip Herbert, Earl of Pembroke, a noble brute with a flair for homicide. (The marriage had been delayed several months while Pembroke recovered from an attack of pox.) Now in May, 1675, when the Sieur de Keroualle came to England to visit his daughters, the "angry Parliament men" said bitterly that they expected to see him "an earl, at least, if not a knight of the garter too, in a very little time." Against the onslaughts of the Country Party Danby countered with a bill for a new Test Act which would have forced office-holders to take an oath of non-resistance to the Crown. The session broke up in confusion; nothing was done and the King got no money.

And that year Nell had no honors for herself or her sons and no increase in wealth. In part she was herself to blame. The good-natured King never resented her barbed remarks; in his ironic fashion he was merely amused. But Lord Danby, who controlled the finances and the seals required for patents of nobility, was not so tolerant. He was a proud, harsh man; he had no love for the little comedian who was giving aid to his enemies, and he had a good memory for insults. Nell's pointed witticisms were often ill-timed, to say the least. Once, for example, she called on the Duchess of Cleveland and, thinking that the great lady was a trifle cool to her, Nell "clapped her on the shoulder and said she presumed that persons of one trade loved not one another!" There was no malice in such remarks; Nell honestly tried to follow Rochester's dictum: "Live in peace with all the world and easily with the King." She merely spoke whatever came into her giddy head.

In Midsummer the two duchesses, Cleveland and Portsmouth, launched a new drive for honors for their offspring, and Rochester was not on hand to counsel Nell. One night in June he and his friends, Harry Savile, Lord Middleton, and Lord Sussex had been "drinking and roistering all night with the King." As the young men left Whitehall at dawn "they came to the great dial in the Privy Garden and said, 'Kings and kingdoms tumble down and so shalt thou,' and took it in their arms and flung it down." The King was not amused at the loss of his sundial —an elaborate confection of glass spheres, "the rarest in Europe"—and the vandals were banished from Court for a time. Rochester had no sooner returned than he fell under the Duchess of Portsmouth's displeasure for something he was supposed to have written about her, and he was banished for nearly a year to the horrors of the country and the society of his own wife. He denied that he had ever offended the duchess "in thought, word, or deed," but some poet—rumor said Rochester—had stuck a paper on her chamber door with the couplet,

> Within this place a bed's appointed
> For a French bitch and God's anointed.

The Duchess of Cleveland was out to get her first and second sons created dukes of Southampton and Grafton respectively. Portsmouth chose the title Duke of Richmond (vacated by the death of Frances Stuart's husband) for her son. Hearing the thunder of the guns, Nell threw herself into the fray, unsupported. Within a few weeks reports came in that her older son was to be made "Earl of March to pacify her a little and to ease her in some measure of the mighty disquiets" aroused by news of the other proposals. But a mere earldom was not enough to content the embattled mother, "she looking upon her son [to be] as fit to be made a duke as any of the others."

Her protests were fruitless; the clamorous duchesses simply ignored her and the battle of the Titans rolled on. Cleveland wanted her patents passed first, so that her boys would have precedence over the "French hussy's brat." Portsmouth was equally determined that her son should have precedence. The easy King tried to solve the problem by having all three patents passed at the same time, but Portsmouth got her son's documents to the complaisant Lord Treasurer well ahead of her rival. By August the battle was over. Portsmouth's son—by the name of Charles Richmond—was created Baron of Settrington, Earl (ironically!) of March, and Duke of Lennox and Richmond. Quickly thereafter Charles Fitzroy became Duke of Southampton and George Fitzroy became Duke of Grafton. In her defeat poor Nelly was only partly consoled by an appointment as a Lady of the Privy Chamber to the Queen, a post within the gift of kind-hearted Queen Catherine and not subject to Danby's veto. At least Nell was now officially a lady.

There was nothing she could do about the long-established Duchess of Cleveland, who had not been her amatory rival since the days of Jacob Hall, but she refused to concede the victory to Portsmouth and continued to argue her case. Aristocratic observers across the channel were smugly amused by Nell's constant skirmishes with Portsmouth. For the moment they saw the duchess as the winner. The King slept with her almost every night; she had a son by him, now acknowledged and presented with two duchies; she was heaping up wealth and making herself feared and respected. But she had been unable to get rid of Nell Gwyn, by whom the King was "bewitched." He divided "his care, his time, and his health" between the two. Nell continued to insult Portsmouth, make faces at her, steal the King from her, and boast of his preference for herself. She was "young, wanton, brazen, debauched, and humorous," and she plied her trade "with a will."

The French courtiers were not fond of the upstart Duchess of Portsmouth, and they quoted Nell's arguments with approval. "This duchess pretends to be a person of quality," Nell said. "She claims that everyone in France is her relation; the moment some great one dies she puts on mourning. Well! If she is of such high quality, why does she play the whore? She ought to die of shame. As for me, it's my profession; I do not pretend to anything else. The King keeps me, and I am constant to him at present. He has given me a son; I claim he ought to acknowledge him and I am sure he will, for he loves me as much as his Portsmouth." The wiseacres nodded happily and predicted more troubles for Portsmouth at the hands of this "creature."

Parliament met again on October 13, and took up the same old weary round. The opposing parties were so evenly matched that nothing could be done. Buckingham and Shaftesbury called for a dissolution to be followed by a general election, but Danby preferred the known to the unknown evil. On November 16 both Houses were prorogued again. No money worth counting had been voted, and Danby immediately began a vigorous retrenchment, cutting down on Court tables, "board wages, pensions, salaries, gifts, and what not."

To the Duchess of Cleveland his action was the final straw. For some time she had been planning on going to France, ostensibly for the education of her children, actually so that she could live in greater splendor on her income. Now that Danby was growling before the doors of the treasury and there was no hope for further gifts, she decided to go at once—an elastic term with her, since it took her three months to get ready. On March 13, 1676, she embarked with a retinue of forty people, with coaches, horses, and baggage.

She had another reason for leaving. Following her annual custom she had separated amicably from her latest lover, Harry Savile, and welcomed to her bed Ralph Montagu, Ambassador to France. She was too fond of Montagu to languish in England while he labored in France. Montagu was married to Elizabeth, Countess of Northumberland, the beautiful heiress whom Savile had once failed to seduce. Savile's new mistress was witty Lady Mary Scroope, widowed mother of the courtier-poet Sir Carr Scroope, who had himself once been in love with Cleveland. It was all in the family.

Cleveland's imminent departure made little difference to Nell, but Portsmouth was delighted. With the retirement of her senior colleague she could get what merchandise she would of the King. Already her splendid apartments in Whitehall were stocked with "massy pieces of plate," and "whole tables and stands of incredible value," furnishings ten times richer and more glorious than the Queen's. Portsmouth saw nothing inappropriate in such a display. She was reported as telling her servants that "she was just as much the King's wife as the Queen, only she was not married by a bishop." As a wife by the left hand she claimed her rights in the King's worldly goods.

But while she was happily planning new ways to evade the treasury's watchdog, her enemies were preparing an unpleasant surprise. Late in December, 1675, a cavalier came riding up the road from Torbay, attended by a well-mounted troop: five menservants, two women, and a small blackamoor. The little company clattered through the streets of London to Lady Elizabeth Harvey's house in Covent Garden; the cavalier dismounted, threw off muddy greatcoat, hat, and periwig, and disclosed the classic face and midnight-black hair of Hortense Mancini, Duchess of Mazarin. Another beauty had come to flutter the King's harem.

Hortense was thirty years old (five years older than Nell and middle-aged by Restoration standards) but her beauty was the kind which age could not wither nor debauchery stale. She was the youngest daughter of a noble Italian, Lorenzo Mancini, and favorite niece of the great Cardinal Mazarin (once Chief Minister of France), who left her a fortune on his death. At sixteen she was married to a peer of France, Armand Charles de la Ponte, Marquis de Meilleraye, who was created a duke and took the surname Mazarin, without the customary "de." It was not a happy marriage. Not only was Duke Mazarin incredibly jealous of his wife, he was also a religious bigot whose prudery amounted to mania. He destroyed nude statues with a hammer, defaced nude paintings, and even considered it wildly indelicate for his maidservants to milk cows.

After six years of misery with her husband and four children (begotten in his lucid intervals) Hortense applied to King Louis for a separation and fled to a nunnery. She passed the next eight years either in convents (which she corrupted) or at small Italian courts where she became proficient in every known vice—and Italy was the seat of all knowledge. Quick-witted, well-read, and an intelligent conversationalist, she was also sensuous, unscrupulous, and completely amoral. Her most recent haven was the Duchy of Savoy, where she had created so much scandal by an open affair with César Vichaud, Abbé de Saint-Real, that she was politely asked to leave. Now she had come to England, sure of a welcome from King Charles—who had made love to her in the days of his exile—and hopeful that there was an ember of his former fire still glowing. There was.

The coffeehouse gossips had a new topic of conversation. They agreed that it would be "more honorable for Great Britain to have its monarch subdued by a famous Roman dame than by an obscure damsel of Little Britain or by a frisking comedian." Since the romantic Mazarin was supposed to be immensely wealthy, it would be much cheaper too. Here the gossips were sadly mistaken. The Duke Mazarin demanded restoration of his conjugal rights and kept a firm grip on his wife's dowry, allowing her only about £400 a year. Eventually King Charles had to give her an allowance.

The Duchess of Mazarin was managed by Lady Harvey (*vice* her scheming brother, Ralph Montagu), Lord Arlington, now the Duchess of Portsmouth's bitter enemy, and the French diplomat, Philiberte, Comte de Grammont (destined to become the hero of a famous memoir). The King was obviously infatuated with the Italian beauty and promptly set her up in apartments in St. James's Palace, but she was coy with him for some months—until she was sure that her husband would not increase her allowance. During those months the Court watched with joy the conflict between the two established mistresses and the new pretender. The courtly old poet Edmund Waller, a friend to all three ladies, celebrated the rivalry in a mock-heroic poem, "The Triple Combat." Here was "fair Mazarine," a new invader of the British Isles, hoping to make them yield again to Roman arms as they once had to Julius Caesar. Here was Portsmouth, heir to the power of Brittany, which had also conquered England in the remote past.

> Legions of Cupids to the battle come,
> For Little Brittain these, and those for Rome.
> Dressed to advantage, this illustrious pair,
> Arrived, for combat in the lists appear.
> What may the Fates design? For never yet
> From distant regions two such beauties met.

Over the camp the Goddess of Victory hovered "with doubtful wings" until she spied Nell Gwyn, "the lovely Chloris," representative of the English forces, who

> well attended came.
> A thousand Graces waited on the dame;
> Her matchless form made all the English glad,
> And foreign beauties less assurance had.
> Yet, like the three on Ida's top, they all
> Pretend alike, contesting for the ball.

What indeed, did the Fates design? Although Waller displayed his insularity by his implied preference for Nell, he refused to prophesy, preferring a well-drawn battle.

Another poet, an anonymous political satirist who was no gentleman, dealt with the whole matter more coarsely:

> Since Cleveland is fled till she's brought to bed,
>   And Nelly is quite forgotten,
> And Mazarine is as old as the Queen,
>   And Portsmouth, the young whore, is rotten,
>
> Since women at helm have ruined the realm,
>   And statesmen have lost their anchors,
> The Lords and the Commons know what will come on us,
>   But the kingdom must break like the bankers.

The politicians had reason to be disgruntled. After the prorogation of Parliament in November, 1675, the King had decided to do without the law-makers for a while and get along on his regular revenues, even though the trade boom had broken and his fixed income was falling. He was helped out by a gift of £100,000 from King Louis as a reward for keeping England out of the continental alliance against France.

In the first quarter of 1676, while King Charles pursued the blushing Mazarin and Portsmouth went into a decline —her melancholy "increased by discontent at somebody's visiting the Duchess Mazarine at my Lady Harvey's"— Nell gradually withdrew from the competition to a neutral corner. Finally she was learning the full wisdom of Rochester's advice. She would "make sport" while she could; at other times she would "help it." Mazarin was far less dangerous to her than to Portsmouth. Let Charles have his

fling with the lush adventuress; he would always return to
Nell for fun and frolics.

Portsmouth's winter of discontent became a springtide
of sickness. News of her condition reached Rochester in
exile, and with true Christian charity he wrote to Savile,
"I am sorry for the declining duchess and would have you
generous to her at this time, for that is true pride, and I
delight in it." However his charity did not restrain him
from joining in the poetic chorus. He sent his friends an
obscene little squib, a "Dialogue," in which first Nell and
then Portsmouth were made to boast of their orgiastic
accomplishments and to cry damnation on that "great
whore Mazarine" (tallest of all the mistresses). Then the
King was allowed to speak of the joys of his harem and
of how pleasant it was to make his heaven in a lady's lap
while Mary Knight sang "her bawdy song." Finally the
"People" cried out for Providence to protect their "faith's
defender" from "Paris plots,"

> From Mazarine, that new pretender,
> And from that politic Grammont.

In May the Duchess of Portsmouth journeyed to Bath,
recovering her health slowly through June and early July.
On her return to London she had a chilly reception from
the King when she stopped to dine with him at Windsor.
Since she was not invited to stay she had to drive on to
London that night. She was thin and worn after her long
illness. To make matters worse she had somehow hurt one
eye, which remained swollen and black for days. The
Court jesters accused her of trying to transform herself
into a brunette like the Duchess of Mazarin. Convinced

that the King was through with her, she wept almost constantly. One day Nell appeared in deep mourning for (she said) the discarded duchess and her dead hopes.

Through the winter and spring Nell had been working quietly behind the scenes to improve her position. In February, 1676, she succeeded in getting a promise that the next Registrar in Chancery, an officer who enjoyed an income of £1500 a year, would be either her oldest son or his agent. (The office, then held by Baptist May, did not revert to Nell's son until 1697.) At about the same time the King gave her the "grant of the logwood," a hereditary duty on all logs exported from the kingdom. These gifts were not finally official until November 24, when the King ordered the Secret Service to give Nell "£200 for horses and £162. 5s. od. for passing the patent of the grant of the logwood and the grant of the office of Registrar in Chancery in reversion." The grant of the logwood began producing at once. It was "demised" by the King to one of Nell's friends, Lawrence Hyde, as her trustee, for the nominal fee of £5 a year. Hyde in turn "farmed" the tax (leased it to speculators who did the actual collecting) for an annual rent of £500, which the "farmers" paid to Nell.

For the second half of the year Nell was practically the reigning mistress. The Duchess of Mazarin (the only one of the mistresses who owned and read books) was cultured, witty, and beautiful, but she lacked ambition and cared as much for the society of the handsome Prince of Monaco, the exiled old philosopher St. Evremonde (keeper of the King's ducks!), or Cleveland's daughter, the young Countess of Sussex, as for that of the King himself.

Charles came to treat her as only an occasional light-of-love. In the autumn and winter he visited Portsmouth often by day, and he was always friendly toward her, but the worried French Ambassador, Honoré Courtin, discovered that he passed his nights most often with Nell. In December the Ambassador wrote sadly to King Louis that Charles had angered Portsmouth by "drinking twice in twenty-four hours to the health of Nell Gwyn" with whom he supped regularly, and who "still made the Duchess of Portsmouth the butt of her tickling sarcasms." The French interest was suffering.

During these months Nell worked hard on her main problem: recognition for her two sons. The matter was getting desperate. Young Charles was now six years old. At that age a well-bred boy was already started on his education, with masters to teach him dancing and deportment, and the household chaplain or a neighboring vicar for reading, writing, and the elements of Latin grammar. But if Nell ever wanted to enter her boy at one of the schools for sons of the gentry—Eton or Westminster, for example—he would not even have a surname under which to register. "Master Charles" was all very well for a child's name, but a six-year-old in a time when boys went to the universities at twelve and took degrees at sixteen was something more than a child.

The situation in the autumn of 1676 was favorable. Nell had many friends to help her, including the now restored Earl of Rochester. Cleveland and her noble brood were safely in France. Not only was Portsmouth's son, the Duke of Richmond, well taken care of (he was Master of the Horse at the tender age of four), but the French mistress, who might have frustrated Nell's plans through sheer malice, was temporarily powerless. Quiet Moll Davis, installed in a new house in St. James's Square, made no audible demands for herself and her daughter.

That gossip, Tradition, has handed down two delightful (and contradictory) fables about the means Nell used to get her son a peerage. According to one of these, the King was coming up a garden path to visit Nell when she appeared at an upper window with the boy in her arms and threatened to throw him out unless he was ennobled at once. With remarkable presence of mind the King cried, "God save the Earl of Burford!" According to the second fable, one day in the King's presence Nell called to young Charles, "Come hither, you little bastard." When the King gently reproved her for her language, she replied that "she had no better name to call him by." His Majesty took the hint and provided the child with a whole string of aristocratic names!

The truth of the matter is that King Charles had always intended to acknowledge Nell's children, in spite of their half-base blood. He was an indolent man who needed constant prodding, but he was also patient; he knew how to wait and mature his plans slowly. Everything he had done for Nell so far—her house, her pension, her place in the Queen's Privy Chamber, and the two new grants to her that year—had prepared the way for the next step. Now the time seemed ripe. Parliament was not in session to cry out; the grandees of the Court had become so accustomed to Nell that they were not likely to complain at the elevation of a commoner's children; and Danby had his hands full preparing for the next meeting of Parliament.

Sometime in November Nell's constant pleading combined with circumstances to bring about the King's decision. In that month he started the legal mills grinding on three projects at once: a patent creating young Charles an earl, a grant of £1,000 a year as his allowance, and—to make some provision for little James—a scheme to buy the freehold of Nell's house and deed it to her, with inheritance and remainder secured for James.

The first of these projects was the first completed. On December 21, 1676, a warrant was passed for "a grant to Charles Beauclerc, the King's natural son, and to the heirs male of his body, of the dignities of Baron of Heddington, co.Oxford, and Earl of Burford in the same county, with remainder to his brother, James Beauclerc, and the heirs male of his body." The surname, Beauclerc, was a meaningless invention. The titles were the names of two Oxfordshire towns; Burford was the scene of a famous horserace, held annually. To make his acknowledgement complete, a few weeks later the King granted both children the usual right to wear the royal arms crossed with a bar sinister, and to James (as an earl's younger brother and heir-presumptive) he gave "the title of Lord Beauclerc, with the place and precedence of the eldest son of an earl."

The other two projects, which involved money and real estate, naturally took longer. The £1,000 pension for Lord Burford was not finally settled upon him until April 9, 1677; the money, of course, was paid to Nell as his guardian. The real estate deal was set in motion as early as December 1, 1676, when by an elaborate deed under the Privy Seal the King gave the Earl of St. Albans, builder and owner of Nell's house, three and a half acres of land near Soho in exchange for his equity. But there were so many claims, leases, and half-rights in the Pall Mall property that the whole business was not finally settled until April 6, 1677. Then a whole bundle of deeds, abstracts, and a great "Indenture Tripartite" were signed, and out of the sea of parchment Nell emerged triumphant, with the rights to "have, hold, occupy, possess, and enjoy" her house, "peaceably and quietly" for the rest of her life. The inheritance was vested in Nell's younger son, "the Right Honorable James, Lord Beauclerc," and in the event of his death without heirs, in his brother Charles.

Here now were riches and security for Nell and her sons. But her heart was never so full as on that cold, snowy day just before the Christmas of 1676, when she was handed her son's patent as Earl of Burford—the culmination of six years of plotting, pleading, and wheedling. At last her first-born was an earl, a peer of the realm with a seat in the House of Lords when he reached his majority, as much a gentleman as any of the royal bastards. By virtue of his elevation Nell herself was now the equal of the Court ladies who had once complained that they "could not abide to converse" with her, or had called her "whore" to her face. It was a wonderful feeling. For the next few weeks she continued to receive the congratulations of friends and acquaintances—even the Duchess of Mazarin sent her compliments.

Nell, the ex-barmaid, should have been satisfied; Fortune had been more than bountiful. But she was still ambitious; her son was "as fit to be made a duke as any of the others." Moreover, what of her second son, a lord only by a technicality? Two of Cleveland's sons were dukes and the third was an earl. Were her boys any better than Nell's? Finally, and by no means hopelessly, Nell still pursued the beckoning vision of a coronet for herself. Countess of something-or-other she would be, or know the reason why!

XI

Intrigues
and
Politics

1 6 7 7 - 1 6 7 8

X I

ONE OF Nell's pleasanter duties was to dress up of an afternoon in her best gown with a mantle and hood and call on her feminine friends. She visited all sorts and conditions of ladies: Mary Knight, the Countess of Portland, Arabella Churchill, Lady Harvey, Mrs. Frances Jennings (mother of the future Duchess of Marlborough), Lady Mary Mordaunt, Lady Susan Williams, and her old friend Lady Shrewsbury, who was now shriven of her sins and very acceptable at Court. Early in the new year Nell was kept happily at work calling on the many ladies who had sent their congratulations on her son's advancement.

One winter day Ambassador Courtin, an amiable little man, was visiting the Duchess of Mazarin at her apartments in St. James's Palace when the Duchess of Portsmouth was ushered in. Hardly had the newcomer been greeted than Lady Harvey sailed in, towing Nell Gwyn, who had come to thank the Duchess of Mazarin for her compliments. There was a moment of awkward silence; then the Italian duchess took command, and soon all four ladies were chatting gaily with only a hint of the feline in their perfect manners.

Portsmouth was the first to go. She had hardly left the room than Nell turned upon the nervous ambassador and boldly demanded why the King of France "did not send presents to her instead of to the weeping willow who had

just gone out?" Before Courtin could answer she swept
on in her impetuous style: it would be to France's profit
to send her gifts; King Charles liked her better than he
did Portsmouth; indeed, he slept with her almost every
night. Modest little Courtin shuddered, cringed, and temporized; he hardly knew how to answer this indelicate bid
for bribes. Madame Mazarin adroitly turned the conversation. She had heard stories about Nell's luxurious under-
garments, she said. Could she be permitted to see them with
her own eyes? Flattered, Nell stood up, and the two other
ladies raised her petticoats one by one, exclaiming with
delight at the laces and fine linens. Courtin was not em-
barrassed by a display of this kind. He wrote to Louvois,
the grim French Minister of State, "I never in all my life
saw such thorough cleanliness, neatness, and sumptuosity.
I should speak of other things that all were shown . . .
but with you I must be grave and proper!"

Usually when Nell and Portsmouth were thrown together at social functions, Nell observed the amenities. In
smaller gatherings she delighted in annoying "the weeping
willow" in every possible way. One night, so the story
goes, when Nell, the duchess, and the King were supping
together, there were two boiled chickens on the table. In
a flippant moment, Portsmouth claimed that she could
make three out of the two. " 'That cannot be,' says Nell.
'Why,' says Portsmouth, 'there's one, and there's two, and
one and two makes three.' 'Yes,' says Nell, 'so they do,'
and putting one on the King's plate and another on her
own, bid Portsmouth take the third for her pains."

Since there were still honors to be gained for their sons
and money for themselves, the rivalry between the two

mistresses was as intense as ever. The happy hunting ground for courtesans was Ireland, where, as the result of war, rebellion, and Cromwell's colonizing, there were many estates with clouded titles. Guided by an informer (who took a percentage of the profits) one of the King's favorites could put in a claim for a property, push it through the Irish Court of Claims with the King's warrants as levers, and dispossess and beggar the nominal owner. Such actions were legal, and therefore moral. Equally legal, if somewhat ghoulish, was a practice much favored by the Duchess of Portsmouth: getting the King to grant her the forfeited estates of suicides and executed criminals.

Early in the spring of 1677 Nell tried a cast in the Irish fishpond. The King granted her a warrant for certain disputed lands, and, with the Earl of Rochester as her trustee for greater prestige, she submitted her claim to the Lord Lieutenant of Ireland. After the issue had lagged for three months in the Court of Claims, Nell, working through Secretary Coventry, tried to get the King to put pressure on the Court. Drily commenting that "women seldom understood their own business," His Majesty refused. There could be only one outcome, of course, but it took time for the obliging Irish officials to browbeat other suitors and persuade them to withdraw their claims. In November the properties were granted to Nell. They were "farmed" for her benefit by her then trustees, Charles (Buckhurst), Earl of Middlesex, and Thomas Felton, one of the Duke of York's gentlemen. On November 26 her old friend Sir Robert Howard (now Auditor of the Exchequer) wrote to thank Lord Lieutenant Ormonde in Nell's name. "She vows she loves you entirely," he concluded. She had reason: her annual income was increased by £800.

For Nell this was only a lucrative sideshow; the main events of her year were political. Early in 1677 she had come to Lord Treasurer Danby with an appeal that he "strive to make her a countess." Upon his flat refusal she became more closely allied than ever with his bitter enemies, the leaders of the Country Party.

When Parliament met on February 15 after a recess of fourteen months, Shaftesbury and his colleagues played a legal quibble as a trump card, moving that, since an act of Edward III requiring annual sessions had been violated, Parliament was automatically dissolved. There had been no general election since 1661. The Country members were eager for a dissolution, sure that the consequent new election would result in greatly increasing their now slim majority in the House of Commons. (The members of the House of Lords, of course, did not stand for election.) On the other hand, the Court members dreaded a new election and fought bitterly against every move for dissolution. Now, with a clear majority in the House of Lords, they took the trick by first voting down the motion, then ordering the mutineers—Shaftesbury, Buckingham, Salisbury, and Wharton—to apologize, and finally, when they refused, clapping them in the Tower. There they were to stay until they recanted their heresy and apologized to the King and the House. Deprived of their leaders and fearful of a war with France, the Country Party in the House of Commons found a last refuge in patriotism and voted the King £600,000 to build warships.

All through the spring and summer the four stubborn

lords languished in durance which was irksome if not vile.
They were not allowed to confer together, and no one
could visit them without permission from the King or the
House of Lords. But they had comfortable apartments,
their own servants, and everything they wanted except
their liberty. After a futile attempt to gain his freedom by
a *habeas corpus*, Shaftesbury turned his fiery mind to the
study of literature and geography. Buckingham set up a
laboratory in his chamber and amused himself with
chemistry.

His friends of "the merry gang" (as Andrew Marvell
called them)—Nell, Lords Rochester and Middlesex,
Savile, Bab May, and others—did what they could for
Buckingham at some danger to themselves. They were all
placeholders at the King's pleasure, and the men were
technically members of the Court Party—Savile, the last
of them to enter Parliament, was elected a member from
Newark in April, 1677. Nevertheless, that May the Earl
of Middlesex dared royal disfavor by presenting the King
with a petition from Buckingham. Charles refused it, saying grimly that "though there was great humility to himself, there was none to the Lords." Danby would have
been only too happy to keep his enemies locked up
forever.

While Buckingham fumed behind bars, Louis XIV
continued to win victories in Europe; King Charles, taking money from France to keep out of continental affairs,
prepared to double-cross his royal cousin by marrying the
Duke of York's oldest daughter, Princess Mary, to William of Orange; the Duchess of Cleveland came back to
England briefly to marry her daughter Charlotte to the

Earl of Lichfield, Lord Rochester's nephew, and then returned to France to strike up an alliance with a new *bon ami*, Alexis Henry, Marquis de Châtillon; Nell Gwyn finally got her house free and clear of all encumbrance; Lady Shrewsbury married George Rodney Bridges, a wit noted for heavy-headed reveling; and on May 28 Parliament was prorogued. The merry gang trimmed their sails on a new tack.

It was safe enough for Nell to visit Buckingham. One day early in June she drove to the Tower armed with a note to the duke from Lord Middlesex: "The best woman in the world brings you this paper and at this time the discreetest"—a significant comment! "Pray, my lord, resign your understanding and your interest wholly to her conduct; mankind is to be redeemed by Eve. With as much honor as the thing will admit of, separate your concern from your fellow-prisoners; then an expedient handsome enough and secret enough to disengage yourself [will be found]. Obey and you are happy."

The mouse would free the elephant, perhaps even get him restored to favor. Nell told Buckingham that King Charles was secretly well-disposed toward him and would be glad to set him free without formal apologies, but that he disliked opposing Danby, Portsmouth, and the Duke of York. But with some more cloak-and-dagger stuff and a personal appeal to the King, Buckingham's old friend and comrade-in-arms, much might be done. Between them, Nell and Buckingham drew up a letter to the King which began, "I am so surprised with what Mrs. Nelly has told me that I know not in the world what to say." At some length, then, Buckingham described his grief at the supposed loss of His Majesty's favor and his joy at the news that some affection for him still lingered in the royal bosom.

The groundwork was prepared; now the ministers of pleasure proceeded with their "expedient." A few days later Buckingham wrote again, begging the King for an interview. To blind his enemies he proposed a few days' liberty for the avowed purpose of visiting the mansion he was building at Cliveden. On June 21 his request was granted. Accompanied by his jailer, the lieutenant of the Tower, he set forth, but (according to plan) so late in the day that he got no farther than his house in Dowgate, where he spent the night. There were mysterious doings that night: coaches drove up to his door and gossips hinted that among the cloaked visitors was a tall man with a regal bearing. The next day Buckingham and his guards posted fifty-two miles to and from Cliveden and were back in the Tower by dusk. That night, with his missions accomplished, Buckingham wrote cheerfully to Middlesex, "My lord, I am now very busy drinking your lordship's health, and shall very shortly have the honor to receive your and Mrs. Nelly's commands."

His next step was a petition for "a month's air" to counteract the effect of "several indispositions" resulting from his imprisonment. At their end the ministers of pleasure wheedled and coaxed to good purpose; early in July Buckingham was granted a leave which soon became "an entire liberty." Instead of returning to his house in Dowgate, he went to stay with Lord Rochester in Whitehall, where he led his usual carefree life. At about the same time Lords Salisbury and Wharton were released upon their abject submission. Only Shaftesbury remained in the Tower, hugging his chains and his principles.

The ministers of state were very uneasy that summer; there were too many occasions when Buckingham and the King were "very merry" together in Rochester's lodgings, and there was talk that Buckingham might be given a place at Court as Lord Steward of the Household. Danby, Portsmouth, and York lectured the King on the "indecency" of Buckingham's conduct and argued that the royal authority was being flouted. In August the King gave way and ordered the duke to leave Whitehall. Placidly he moved across the Park to Pall Mall, where he spent the rest of the summer as Nell's guest. For the ministers of state this was even worse. The King went almost daily to visit Nell, and the ministers of pleasure had a free hand. One of Buckingham's favorite tricks was to mimic the dignity of Lord Danby, while Nell burlesqued the treasurer's pompous wife. The King looked on "with great delight", and the politicians fretted lest the trifling jest portend Danby's fall.

To Danby himself it seemed that Nell was the key to the whole situation. From Newmarket he wrote to his wife on September 28, ordering her to visit the young Earl of Burford "without any message to Nelly"—thus indicating Danby's disapproval. "And when Mrs. Turner [the boy's governess] is with you, bid her tell Nelly you wonder she should be your lord's enemy that has always been so kind to her, but you wonder much more to find her supporting only those who are known to be the King's enemies, for in that you are sure she does ill."

Nell was not to be moved by smooth talk. She wanted

only one thing from the Lord Treasurer—a patent of nobility—and failing that she remained "at perfect defiance with him." She continued to support the Country Party that autumn, and often had its leaders to sup with His Majesty. The new French Ambassador, Barillon, worried almost as much over the goings-on in Pall Mall as over the marriage of William of Orange and Princess Mary (on November 4). Since it was essential to keep England neutral while France pursued its conquests, Barillon poured out bribes to all parties with a lavish hand.

Of course, not all of Nell's guests were politicians. She loved people and collected all kinds. There was Sir Carr Scroope, for example, a queer little fellow, half courtier and half poet, dubbed the "ugly beau-garçon" by Lord Rochester, with whom he was carrying on a poetical war. Nell amused herself by letting Sir Carr make love to her in her idle moments. She became quite fond of him. Another oddity was William Fanshaw, a lean, poverty-stricken courtier who held the small office of Master of Requests and boasted of the fact that his wife, Mary (Lucy Walter's daughter by the Earl of Carlingford), was the Duke of Monmouth's half-sister, and therefore flavored with royalty. That autumn Fanshaw became a father, and Nell, his great friend, advised him not to spend his small stock of money on a pompous christening, but to "reserve himself a little to buy him new shoes that he might not dirty her rooms, and a new periwig that she might not smell him stink two stories high" when he knocked at her door.

Another frequent guest was the actress Elizabeth Barry, whose long commerce with Lord Rochester bore fruit early in December. Savile wrote to his lordship in the country the news that he had a daughter "borne of the body of Mrs. Barry." He quoted Nell, the lady's "friend and protectrice . . . in the Mall" as lamenting Elizabeth's poverty and the fact that she "lay in" without the usual show and finery appropriate to parturition. Nell had made some sharp remarks about Rochester's "want either of generosity or bowels" toward a lady who had permitted him the full enjoyment of her charms. Rochester was seriously ill at the time, but Nell's reproaches stirred him to action. He demonstrated his "bowels" by sending Elizabeth a box of clothing and money, and by writing to her of his satisfaction at her safe delivery and his pleasure that the child was of "the soft sex" he loved.

Then, as usual, there was mad Harry Killigrew, the unpredictable. In November Nell condoled with him when his wife died and he lamented not only her loss but also the fact that he was now free to "play the fool again" and remarry. A month later he made her the butt of a stupid joke. Early in December the Duchess of Portsmouth was so seriously ill that her death was anticipated by a number of hopeful Court ladies. Suddenly she took a turn for the better. At four o'clock one morning, Killigrew, soundly drunk, hammered on Nell's door, and when she thrust her night-capped head out of an upstairs window he announced that he had come "to acquaint her with the good news of the Duchess of Portsmouth's recovery." After that he "rallied her with his abusive tongue extremely." This was too much even for good-natured Nell; she complained to the King, and Killigrew was banished for a period of penitence.

It was truly a miscellany of people who came to Nell's house bent on business or pleasure—rich lords and ladies, politicians, tradesmen, actresses, minor officials, poets, and the undefinable Killigrew. One among them was either a souvenir hunter or a thief. In the *London Gazette* for January 3, 1678, Nell advertised the loss of a small piece of plate, "marked with the cipher E.G., flourished, weighing about 18 ounces," and offered a reward for the capture of the thief.

The year 1677 ended with Portsmouth relapsing and proving Killigrew a liar. Although she promised her confessor that "in case of recovery she should have no commerce with that known enemy to virginity and chastity, the monarch of Great Britain," and would enter a nunnery, she continued seriously ill throughout the winter. Even from her sickbed, where, crucifix in hand, she lectured the King on his evil ways, she was still a power in the state. When Parliament convened on January 28, 1678, the leaders of the Country Party—including Shaftesbury who had wasted a year in prison—recanted, apologized, and were restored to the seats of the mighty. Buckingham had high hopes of returning to the ministry, but Danby, his fell and mighty opposite, was a shrewd leader, and back of Danby were the wiles of Portsmouth. Only Nell Gwyn supported Buckingham. His friends of the Country Party rightly feared his motives, and although the King turned readily to Nell and Buckingham for amusement, he took his advice from Danby and Portsmouth. Buckingham was limited to aiding Shaftesbury in his rule-or-ruin tactics: urging war with France while denying the King funds for an army and navy. The spring of 1678 was a time of troubles, plots, intrigues, and confusion.

In the boiling turmoil about the throne it was a case of every man for himself, and friendships fell before self-interest. Ralph Montagu, Ambassador to France and a very charming scoundrel, wanted to be Secretary of State in the place of Henry Coventry, who was preparing to retire. Portsmouth, who had fully recovered by April (and the devil a nun was she), professed friendship for Montagu. So did Lord Danby, Lawrence Hyde, Henry Savile, and Nell Gwyn. But the moment Coventry announced his willingness to resign, knives flashed and the battle was on.

Montagu learned that Coventry, Buckingham, Hyde, Savile, and Nell had formed a "cabal." Coventry offered his place to Hyde for £10,000 plus Hyde's promise to sell his place as Master of the Robes to Savile (Coventry's nephew). Needing money to pay for the new post, Savile asked the Duchess of Cleveland to get him the King's permission to sell his present post as Groom of the Bedchamber to still another party. Somehow, in this game of musical chairs, Buckingham was to become a Gentleman of the Bedchamber again. Nell's interest in the plot was double: to help her own friends, and to see that "no friend of my Lord Treasurer's" became Secretary of State.

Complaining that it was not "very well in Mr. Savile . . . to manage such an affair underhand," Montagu turned to his supposed allies for help and found that Portsmouth (who had never forgiven him for "managing" the Duchess of Mazarin) would not stir in his behalf, and that Danby was already "engaged" for the secretaryship to Sir

William Temple. Hurt but undaunted, from across the
channel Montagu conducted his campaign according to
the honorable rules of backstairs war. To destroy Cleveland's influence over the King and keep her from aiding
Savile, he intercepted some of her torrid letters to her
latest lover, the Marquis de Châtillon, and sent them to
King Charles. To ruin both Portsmouth and Nell at one
sweep he instructed his sister, Lady Harvey (one of Nell's
best friends), to angle for the King's favor with a new
mistress as bait. To injure Buckingham he collected and
sent to Danby all the damaging information he could find
about the duke's activities. Meanwhile he carefully saved
Lord Danby's private letters as possible weapons for the
future.

Although Nell was in the center of this sticky maze,
she never quite knew what was going on. Everybody (except, of course, Portsmouth and Danby) was her friend,
and everybody used her for his own ends. Warm-hearted,
indiscreet, and trustful, Nell moved according to impulse
and mood; she was incapable of sustained plotting. Her
few letters are perfect mirrors of her mind.

Early in May, 1678, Nell sent a gossipy little note
(dictated to an amanuensis) to Lawrence Hyde, who was
then at Nimuegen as one of the negotiators for a peace
treaty between Holland and France. It was a pleasant,
frank letter, dealing chiefly with trivia, and written with
blithe unconcern for the spinning web of Court intrigues.
She began by apologizing for her long silence, the result,
she said, of a three months' illness—not serious enough to
keep her from good company where she had never failed
to drink Hyde's health. Skimming off the first subject that

floated to the top of her mind she complained that Pall Mall was a dismal place now since she had "utterly lost Sir Carr Scroope, never to be recovered again." Sir Carr had become importunate, had told her that "he could not live always at this rate," and had begun to be "a little un-civil." Such behavior was not to be endured from an "ugly beau garçon," and she had been forced to turn him away. But she hated to lose any friend, even a false one.

Without transition, she turned to random items of news. Mall Knight's mother had just died, and Mall had put up a mourning escutcheon no larger than that hung out by Lady Greene's bereaved family earlier in the year. Lord Rochester, in town for part of April, had returned to the country. Savile was suffering from an attack of pox, but he was "upon recovery" and had a chance to marry an heiress, who would find him a good husband—"if he holds up his thumb," said Nell wickedly. Lord Middlesex (now Earl of Dorset) was wasting his days drinking ale with Thomas Shadwell, the dramatist, and Henry Harris, an actor at the Duke's Theatre. Young James, Lord Beau-clerc, was getting ready to go to France, where there were excellent schools. Casually, as if she had no notion of what was going on, Nell mentioned that she was to sup that night at Whitehall with the King and Lady Harvey. But the mention of Lady Harvey reminded her that she too was supposed to be a politician. "Now let's talk of state affairs," she said, "for we [the Country Party] never car-ried things so cunningly as now, for we don't know whether we shall have peace or war, but I am for war, and for no other reason but that you may come home. I have a thousand merry conceits, but I can't make her [the blushing amanuensis] write 'em, and therefore you must take the will for the deed."

If Nell was fooled by such plotters as Lady Harvey, her friends were not. They knew that, in obedience to Montagu's instructions, Lady Harvey had formed an alliance with Mrs. Jane Myddleton, and that the two ladies were trying to "bring into play" Mrs. Myddleton's sixteen-year-old daughter, Jenny, a slender, lovely girl, whose father (said the gossips) was Ralph Montagu. Scenting the plot, Portsmouth succeeded in barring the Myddletons and their manager from the King's apartments, and Lady Harvey was working through the unsuspicious Nell.

Early in June, Henry Savile sent an account of the affair to Lord Rochester. Lady Harvey (he wrote), "having little opportunity of seeing Charlemagne upon her own account, wheedles poor Mrs. Nelly into supping twice or thrice a week at W. Chiffinch's and carrying her with her; so that in good earnest this poor creature is betrayed by her ladyship to pimp against herself, for there her ladyship whispers and contrives all matters to her own ends, as the other might easily perceive if she were not too giddy to mistrust a false friend." Of course Nell would pay no attention to a mere letter from Rochester, Savile concluded, but perhaps some directions might be sent to a third party —that skilful old warrior Lady Southesk, for example.

With the wisdom of an experienced courtier Rochester refused to meddle. In his reply he merely restated the advice he had given Nell years ago; in effect he counseled patience and watchful waiting. Somewhat doubtfully Savile accepted his friend's advice and did nothing. Meanwhile Nell went her cheerful way, sublimely unconcerned about her danger.

But Providence, disguised as the Duchess of Cleveland, was already at work on Nell's side. Returning to England in May, the duchess found that Montagu had betrayed her intrigue with Châtillon. Coldly received by the King, she could do nothing either for herself or for her ex-lover, Savile. Frustrated and bitter, she returned to France in a murderous mood. To her mingled joy and horror she found that during her absence Montagu had debauched her daughter—and the King's—Anne, Countess of Sussex, and had been living with her "in most open scandal to the wonder of the French Court." Cleveland poured out her malice and wrath in tumultuous letters to King Charles, who promptly sent reproofs and commands to his daughter. When Lady Sussex paid no heed to her father's letters he sent the Earl of Sunderland to replace Montagu as ambassador, and Henry Savile as his personal agent to discipline the wayward countess.

Suddenly the game of musical chairs came to an end, with Montagu flat on the floor. Hastily returning to England in July, Montagu found that he had over-reached himself; not only were his plots spoiled and his chances of preferment lost, but he was dismissed from all his offices and forbidden the Court. Unable to obtain an audience with the King and deserted by Danby, he reversed his vestments, fled to the arms of the Country Party, and became Danby's deadliest enemy. In the confusion of changing scenery and sides, the post of Secretary of State, the prize for which Montagu had plotted, remained in Coventry's possession (two years later he sold it to Sir Leoline

Jenkins). But several of the other players in the deadly little game moved to other chairs. In August Lawrence Hyde became ambassador to Holland and sold his place as Master of the Robes to a friend, Sidney Godolphin, who in turn sold his place as Groom of the Bedchamber to Lady Shrewsbury for her new husband, George Bridges. Early in the next year Harry Savile replaced Ambassador Sunderland in Paris, but with the lesser rank of Envoy to France. He was a very successful diplomat.

During the summer of 1678, Buckingham continued to dodge around, intriguing with everybody in sight and vainly seeking an empty chair. Lady Harvey shared the disgrace of her brother, Montagu, and found even the backstairs closed to her. Her protégé, Jenny Myddleton, damned by association, threw herself headlong into matrimony. Peacefully unconcerned about the whole complicated business, Nell Gwyn trotted off with the King in August to spend the rest of the summer at Windsor. Heaven protects the poor working girl.

Meanwhile, in the spring and summer of 1678, international politics and the war in Europe had come to a new crisis. France, which had been slowly crushing the confederacy headed by William of Orange, had declared a two months' armistice, and offered Holland a treaty of peace on very hard terms. In England the Country Party had been clamoring for intervention on the side of the Dutch, while prudently refusing the King's requests for money to equip an army and navy. Charles had been taking money from King Louis to stay out of Europe—and so had quite a few members of the Country Party—but he was using the money to build up a standing army. By marrying his niece, the Princess Mary, to his nephew, William of Orange, he had in effect declared for the Dutch, and he had even sent a brigade of 3,000 men to aid the confederates. He was trying to strengthen his own position at home and abroad, bring the war in Europe to an end by threats of intervention, and stay out of war himself.

The Country Party, fearful of standing armies and "popery and wooden shoes"—the symbols of slavery—did everything it could to spoil the King's game. When it blocked his request for funds early in the summer, King Louis thought he had nothing to fear, withdrew his offer to Holland, and set his armies in motion. In July, King Charles countered with a desperate bluff: he sent emissaries to Holland offering an alliance unless France agreed to peace. Exhausted by six years of war, Louis agreed to quit for a while. On July 31 the Treaty of Nimuegen was signed. Holland was saved, but France was left with vastly increased territories and power. England remained torn by internal dissension, a prey to all kinds of doubts and fears.

But at Windsor, August and September were wonderful months. The weather was hot and dry; the days were calm. Parliament was prorogued until October; Portsmouth stayed at Whitehall, tearing down and rebuilding her lodgings; Buckingham lived in Nell's Pall Mall house except for the times when he flitted mysteriously across the channel to France on some new, wild project; the wicked Montagu had ceased from troubling for the nonce; and, on the surface at least, all the world was at peace. What with hawking and fishing, the company of the King, her small sons, and her many friends, Nell had a happy summer.

But for those who chose to look, there were evil omens: eclipses of the sun and moon—perennial portents of disaster—rumors of fires, uprisings in Scotland, and midnight massacres in the making. When King Charles brought his Court back to London in late September he found his council listening to a strange tale told by one Titus Oates, an unfrocked clergyman with a broad red face, long chin, vast mouth, and brazen voice. He described an international conspiracy by the Pope and his prelates, the King of France, and hundreds of English Catholic lords to assassinate the King, place the Duke of York on the throne, and impose the Catholic faith on England by fire and sword. Charles scoffed at the whole business, laughed at the talk of murderers with foot-long knives and silver bullets, and took his family off to Newmarket. Over London the storm grew blacker, but on the northern downs the weather was still fair.

At Newmarket Nell enjoyed herself as usual with the exciting races, the parties, dances, shows by strolling players, and all the fun the little town could provide. One day she even took a side trip to see near-by Cambridge, accompanied by Lord Dorset's friend and agent, Fleetwood Shepherd. The gentle pedagogues at Cambridge University had one eye for beauty and one for Court favor; they entertained her royally and scratched up some hasty verses in her honor. She was accustomed to literary adulation. Earlier that year a notable scholar, one Robert Whitcomb, had dedicated to her his *Janua Divorum*, a collection of lives of gods and goddesses. He informed the literate world that Nell had the "primitive wisdom" of Apollo, the "pristine wit" of Mercury, the "greatness of mind" of Juno, the "delicate beauty" of Venus, and the "God-like courage and brave spirit" of Hercules. For some reason Whitcomb did not think to compare her with Diana.

On October 16 the Court returned to London. The next day the body of Sir Edmund Bury Godfrey, the magistrate who had taken Oates' first deposition about the Catholic plot, was found on Primrose Hill, Hampstead. His collar was twisted about his neck as if he had been strangled; there were dark bruises on his breast; and his own sword was thrust through his heart. On October 21, as a wave of hysteria flooded England and washed to the farthest corners of the island, Oates was called before the House of Commons to declare what he knew about Godfrey's murder and the existence of a popish plot. The storm had broken.

XII
The
Great
Panic
1 6 7 8 – 1 6 8 0

X I I

FOR TWO YEARS England engaged in a vast witch-hunt, motivated by blind terror, spurred on by the lies of Titus Oates and his fellow informers, Tonge, Bedloe, and Prance, and whipped to fury by the leaders of the Country Party, who, if they did not invent the so-called Popish Plot, used it to the fullest for their own ends, careless how many innocents might die. On the flimsiest possible evidence three men were hanged for Godfrey's murder; yet to this day the real criminal has not been certainly identified. Fourteen Roman Catholics—lords and commoners—were executed for complicity in the plot. Thirty-eight priests were condemned to death; of these twenty-one died in prison, three were executed, and fourteen were reprieved. Of all the victims of the panic, only one, Coleman, the Duchess of York's secretary, was guilty of a crime—in his case no more than a foolish correspondence with a French Jesuit.

Everybody—except, of course, the King and the cynical Country lords—believed in the plot and lived in deadly fear of phantom cut-throats and French invaders. All men went armed; ladies carried pistols in their muffs; sentries patrolled the Houses of Parliament; and cannon loomed in a wide circle about Whitehall. Daily from the headquarters of the Country Party, the Green Ribbon Club at the King's Head Tavern in Temple Bar, came fresh "discoveries," and new rumors of fires and bloody outrages.

The funeral of Sir Edmund Bury Godfrey on October 31, 1678, was brilliantly stage-managed. Seventy-two clergymen marched before the bier on its way to St. Martin's Church, and a long procession of citizens followed. The mob was so heated "that anything called Papist, were it cat or dog, had probably gone to pieces in a moment." The preacher who delivered the funeral oration was guarded by two "thumping divines," who stood beside him in the pulpit and peered suspiciously about the church. The congregation trembled and wept as the orator raged against Rome.

November 5, the anniversary of the Gunpowder Plot, gave the Country Party another opportunity. There was a great procession that night, with effigies of Godfrey and the Pope, men dressed as friars and priests, boys with squibs, flaring torches, and pots of incense, and a grand finale in Fleet Street when his holiness (with live cats squalling in his belly) was committed to the flames of a great fire. That night all good Protestants lighted bonfires, and the zealous had images and fireworks. Nell Gwyn entertained the residents of Pall Mall with a pope-burning under the leafless elm trees at her front door. The effigy of the prelate "sat in a great chair, with a red nose half a yard long, with some hundreds of boys throwing squibs at it." Since little James was in France, Nell had only one small boy of her own to throw fire-crackers. It was fun to watch the excitement, even though the November air was sharp.

It was during this period of crisis that the two opposed political parties acquired the names they were to bear for the next two centuries. The members of the Court Party, loyal monarchists, were called Tories by their enemies because of their supposed link with the Catholic "Tories" of Ireland—"bog-trotters," or "wild Irish." In retaliation those of the Country Party, republicans, were called Whigs because of their strength in Presbyterian Scotland, where "whig" was sour whey. The Whigs were also called "fanatics" and "mutineers," and they called themselves "True Blue Protestants" in the sublime conceit that a Tory Protestant was tinged with the scarlet of Rome.

While they entertained the multitude with blood and circuses the Whigs pushed on their grand designs: to oust Danby, to exclude the Catholic Duke of York from the succession, and to replace him as heir-presumptive with the empty-headed but Protestant Duke of Monmouth. The first aim was easily achieved. In December, 1678, Ralph Montagu produced his hoarded letters from Danby with their evidence that the King and his Treasurer had offered to betray Holland to France for a mere £900,000. The furious Commons impeached Danby at once, and only a prorogation saved him.

Bowing before the storm, the King dissolved Parliament early in 1679 and ordered a new election. To appease the Whigs he sent the Duke of York into temporary exile, dismissed Danby, and named Lord Sunderland, a crafty neutral, Principal Secretary of State. But the overwhelmingly Whig Parliament which met on March 6 howled for Danby's blood and the exclusion of the Duke of York. Although the King gave Danby a full pardon, he was impeached again and sent to the Tower. To further appease the frantic Commons, the King appointed a new Privy

Council, dominated by Whigs and with Shaftesbury as President. He was willing to do almost anything to save the succession, but the arrogant "mutineers," flushed with success, refused to compromise. On May 22 the Commons passed an Exclusion Bill. Fearful that it might pass also in the House of Lords, the King prorogued Parliament and later dissolved it again. He had no great love for his brother, but he knew that a change in the succession would lead to the downfall of monarchy.

During that fearful winter and spring Nell Gwyn was the only one of the King's ladies (except, of course, the long-forgotten Moll Davis) who had nothing to fear. The others were Catholics and for a while they lived in mortal terror. Even Queen Catherine, accused of plotting to murder the King, hardly dared show her face outside Somerset House. Cleveland was indicted as a popish recusant; Mazarin was accused of complicity in the plot. The Duchess of Portsmouth, both Catholic and French, was the most hated person in the land. It was charged that she was "privy to the murder of Godfrey" and "out of zeal for her religion spat in Sir Edmund's face as he lay dead," that she and the King were preparing to flee to France, and that she was guilty of monstrous lechery not only with courtiers but even with her own blackamoor boy. The Whig libelers threw their foulest invectives at her, and the House of Commons seriously proposed chopping off her pretty head. But to Shaftesbury she was small game; he was hunting "tigers and bears and birds of prey," not "cony-catching."

On the seesaw of public opinion Nell rose as Portsmouth fell. Preserved in the amber of tradition is a pretty story. At this time a goldsmith was making an expensive service of plate for the King to give Portsmouth. The news spread abroad and people crowded his shop daily to see the plate and "to throw out curses against the duchess." Some, more violent, wished the silver melted and poured down the duchess's throat. All agreed in saying "it was a thousand pities His Majesty had not bestowed this bounty on Madam Ellen."

It was only by virtue of religion and friendship that Nell was on the popular side; as usual she took no interest in the great issues of the day. The friends who had guided her career from her earliest days on the stage were nearly all professed Whigs or, like Lords Dorset and Rochester, they leaned toward republicanism. Henry Savile, younger brother of the Whig Lord Halifax, curried favor with both sides, and Lawrence Hyde, the one staunch Tory among Nell's friends, hated Portsmouth with Whiggish fervor. Nell was not betraying the King when she entertained Whigs at her house. He encouraged her to do so; for there he could meet his enemies, learn their minds, and deal with them man to man. The Whigs used her as a pipeline to the King (not realizing that a conduit works both ways), and she, in her simplicity, saw them only as honest, patriotic gentlemen (very kind to poor Nelly) who were trying to save the King from the claws of Portsmouth and the grim wolf of Rome.

As the symbol of pure, Protestant Womanhood, Nell was courted, fawned on, and flattered in prose and verse. In April, 1679, Aphra Behn, dramatist, feminist, and Whig, dedicated a new play, *The Feigned Courtesans*, to Nell. "When you speak," gushed Aphra, "men crowd to listen with that awful reverence as to holy oracles or divine prophecies, and bear away the precious words to tell at home to all the attentive family the graceful things you uttered, and cry 'But, Oh! she speaks with such an air, so gay, that half the beauty's lost in the repetition.'" At about the same time an anonymous poetess who called herself "Ephelia" concluded a panegyric "To Madam G." with these lines:

> So bright your beauty, so sublime your wit,
> None but a prince to wear your chains is fit.
> I could wish something, but all Heaven's store
> Cannot afford one single blessing more;
> Honor nor wealth you want, nor any thing,
> Unless I wish you a perpetual spring
> Of youth and blossoming beauties, such as may
> Make all your envious rivals pine away.

The fair Ephelia had no notion of Nell's troubles. Wealth, indeed! When the Commissioners who replaced Lord Danby took over the Treasury they found exactly £1. 2s. 10d. in the vaults. There was no more money from France, and Parliament, of course, refused to vote funds. Henry Guy (now Treasurer of the Exchequer) doled out cash to favored pensioners as fast as it came into his hands, but Nell's allowance of £5,000 a year was paid in driblets of £250 to £500 and was often six months in arrears. She was having trouble getting money from Ireland, too. Partly because of "stops" on Irish pensions, partly because Nell's agent was a knave, she kept her friend Sir Robert Howard busy all year with letters and warrants to get things moving again. Even sister Rose (now remarried) suffered, and Nell had to appeal to the King to get her £200 stipend restored.

Late in June, while Scotland flamed with rebellion and London rejoiced over the savage execution of five Jesuit priests, the King took his family to Windsor for the summer. Nell settled down in her old lodgings and economized on her housekeeping. Although the King rode often to Hampton Court near London for meetings with his Council, he spent most of his time at his usual amusements. He had made every possible concession to the Whigs; now he could only wait for the storm to blow itself out. A courtier, describing a typical summer's day at Windsor, wrote, "Little was done all day but going a-fishing. At night the Duchess of Portsmouth came [from London]. In the morning I was with the King at Mrs. Nell's."

On July 20 an accident relieved Nell of one of her financial burdens. According to local tradition old Madam Gwyn lived at Sandford Manor House, Chelsea. A rivulet, Sandy End, which divided Chelsea from Fulham, ran beside her house. It was a hot July day; the old lady was sitting in her garden beside the brook, consuming more than her normal quota of brandy. She nodded, lost her balance, and tumbled into the water. Her garments pulled the poor wretch from her alcoholic daze to muddy death.

Nell hurried to London at once and arranged for a splendid funeral. There would be no small escutcheon hung out for *her* mother. The author of "A Panegyric" assures us that the obsequies were magnificent:

> No cost, no velvet did the daughter spare;
> Fine gilded 'scutcheons did the hearse enrich
> To celebrate this martyr of the ditch;

> Burnt brandy did in flaming brimmers flow,
> Drunk at her funeral, while her well-pleased shade
> Rejoiced, even in the sober Fields below,
> At all the drunkenness her death had made.

Old Madam Gwyn was solemnly interred in the south aisle of St. Martin's Church, and her dutiful daughter ordered a monument erected to her memory before she went back to Windsor.

In a dozen lampoons and mock-elegies, written with the delicacy of a small boy chalking a fence, the Tory libelers taunted Nell with her mother's sordid death. The author of "Satire Unmuzzled" (1680), a catalogue of Court ladies suspected of lechery and Whiggery, dipped his pen in gall when he came to Nell:

> Now for a she-buffoon, who, as 'tis said,
> Crawled into the world without a maidenhead.
> It is most sure 'twas never had by man,
> Nor can she say where it was lost, or when;
> We must conclude she never had one then.
> Her mother grieved in muddy ale and sack
> To think her child would ever prove a crack;
> When she was drunk she always fell asleep,
> And when full maudlin then the whore would weep.
> Her tears were brandy, mundungus her breath,
> Bawd was her life, and common-shore her death.
> To see her daughter mourn for such a beast,
> 'Tis like her life which maketh up one feast;
> Of all her jokes this mourning is the best.

Nell had more important matter than libels to worry about. In August the King was stricken by a fever so nearly fatal that the Duke of York was summoned home from

Brussels. He arrived at Windsor on September 2 to find his brother recovered; cured, ironically, by doses of "Jesuits' powder"—quinine. A battle now flared between the two rivals for the succession, York refusing to leave England unless Monmouth too was exiled. Charles was a just man with a sense of humor. He sent Monmouth, the glorious victor of Maestrich, to Holland, and Catholic York to Presbyterian Scotland.

When the matter was settled, King and Court went to Newmarket. Blessed with fair September weather the courtiers ignored the storms raging elsewhere and gave themselves up to revelry. The King was in good health and better humor. Every day there was "the divertissement of the comedy, and at night nothing but dancing and merriment." Nell was one of the gayest of the jovial crew, wagering "very highly at races and cockpits," and entertaining everybody with her tricks. She was still slender and very delectable in boy's clothes. One morning she dressed up in periwig and breeches "with a horseman's coat" and swaggered out to the paddocks where the King stood chatting with his cronies. For a moment they failed to recognize her; then she saluted them with the exaggerated graces of the stage. Ods fish! 'Twas Nell! "His Majesty and Court were very pleased." Nell was a better actress than horsewoman; a few days later she "received much damage from the fall of a horse."

In October the Court returned to London. Suddenly taking the offensive, Charles prorogued the new Parliament to January, dismissed Shaftesbury as President of the Council, and dared him to do his worst. The Whigs retaliated with the "discovery" of the Meal-tub Plot, a supposed

Catholic conspiracy to discredit Oates and his fellow liars, which added new fuel to the fires of fanaticism. Outwardly undisturbed, the King took time on November 8 to attend the remarriage of the Duchess of Cleveland's son, the Duke of Grafton, to Lord Arlington's daughter—now twelve years old and ripe for consummation. A few days later Charles took Nell's older boy to Portsmouth to witness the launching of a new warship, named the *Burford* in the child's honor. However worried he might be, the King went about his affairs with his usual calm.

The Whigs used every device they could think of to frighten or cajole him into accepting Monmouth as his legitimate son and heir. On November 17, the anniversary of Queen Elizabeth's coronation, they paraded a hundred thousand howling people through the streets of London behind effigies of Godfrey, the Pope, and the Devil. With a set face Charles watched the spectacle from a goldsmith's window. Two weeks later, counting on his well-known love for his oldest son, the Whigs brought Monmouth back to London, to the accompaniment of bells, bonfires, and a snowstorm of pamphlets.

The King was furious at this open flouting of his commands. When he refused to see his son, deprived him of all his offices, and ordered him to leave England again, Monmouth turned to Nell Gwyn for help. She responded nobly; Monmouth was her friend and in trouble. He found a refuge in her house, hid in her closet when the King came to see her, and continued to hope for an audience with His Majesty. Nell pleaded with the King again and again, begging him only to see Monmouth, who, she said, had grown "pale, wan, lean, and long-visaged merely because he was in disfavor." The angry monarch "bid her be quiet, for he would not see him." Such goings-on amazed the French Ambassador, who could never understand the quaint ways of the English; he wrote to King Louis of his astonishment that Monmouth "every night sups with Nelly, the courtesan who has borne the King two children, and whom he daily visits."

It was all a waste of time. The King would not be moved, and Portsmouth, to whom Monmouth appealed in desperation, replied coldly that she would do nothing for him "so long as he was an enemy to the King and to her." After two weeks of skulking about the Court and hiding in closets, Monmouth retired to the country. One effect of the futile episode was to make Nell even more popular with the London mobs. Her championing of Monmouth, "the Protestant Duke," gave her a blunt but distinctive title, "the Protestant Whore."

The Whigs, who fed the city on miracles, swelling tidbits of news into banquets of rumor, were quick to make use of a small episode involving Nell early in December. In Hyde Park one day her lead coach-horse came too close to Henry Wharton, a hot-headed lieutenant of the Coldstream Guards. Wharton drew his sword and avenged his dignity by running the horse through with one heroic lunge. (Nell complained to the King, who banished Wharton from Court.) It was easy to build this episode into a mighty piece of tittle-tattle; it took but a little slurring of sounds to turn "Mrs. Nelly, her horse," into "Mrs. Nelly, the whore." Within a few days there were widespread rumors that Madam Gwyn was missing, murdered by sword or poison, another victim of the wicked Papists.

On December 17 the editor of *Mercurius Domesticus* issued an official denial: "Several false and ridiculous reports being spread abroad concerning Madam Ellen Gwyn, as to her death or absence from her house, we are assured that there is no ground for such a report, the said Madam Gwyn being now at her own house in health, and has not been absent from it."

All through the winter and spring of 1680, while Parliament was prorogued again to October, and Whig and Tory jockeyed for position, Nell continued to champion Monmouth's cause. The Tory poets retaliated by calling her such interesting names as "she-buffoon," "puddle Nell," a "withered whore," a "hair-brained whore," and "the darling strumpet of the crowd." (The Duchess of Portsmouth fared no better at the hands of the Whigs, whose mildest term for her was "the damned, dirty duchess.") One day late in February Nell was sitting in a side-box at the Duke's Theatre when a drunken partisan "came into the pit and called her whore" to her face. Nell was not unused to the epithet, but her escort, Thomas Herbert, the Earl of Pembroke's younger brother, objected in the usual fashion. "There were many swords drawn and a great hubbub in the house."

In March the Duke of York ventured down from Scotland for a visit, and Monmouth, who had been drumming up Whiggery in the west, hurried Londonward also. This time the King strictly forbade Nell to receive Monmouth at her house; he barred also some of the more obnoxious Whigs, notably Lord William Cavendish and Mr. Thomas Thynne. Nell obeyed the letter of the King's commands, but the Countess of Orrery offered her house as a meeting

place, and often Nell supped there with Monmouth, Cavendish, Shaftesbury, and Buckingham. The conferences accomplished nothing. Helpless with Parliament prorogued,
many of the Whig leaders resigned from the Council in
disgust and sulked in their taverns. For six months there
was an ominous calm, the dead spot in the center of the
storm.

Perhaps, if the Whigs could not build, they could destroy. There was the Duchess of Portsmouth, their constant
enemy, arrogant, rich, living in splendor, and secure so
long as she held the King's love. Hopefully Buckingham
tried once again to supplant her with a new mistress. His
plot was doomed from the start, not because Portsmouth
was powerful but because Charles was weak. He was fifty
years old, debilitated by attacks of fever, and sterile as the
result of gonorrhea; after Moll Davis's daughter, now
nearly seven years old, he had fathered no more children.

Nevertheless Buckingham would try his luck. He formed
a new cabal: his sister Mary, Dowager Duchess of Richmond (who had long hated Portsmouth); her sister-in-law,
Lady Mary Howard; Nell, who still hoped to be a countess
and was willing to be at either end of a new intrigue; and
finally Lawrence ("Lory") Hyde, now First Commissioner
of the Treasury (a Tory, but another of Portsmouth's enemies). Their destined victim was Jane Lawson, niece of
the Duchess of Richmond's third husband, "Northern
Tom" Howard. The Duchess of Richmond (who con-
descended to "converse with Nell" in a noble cause) managed pretty Jane.

A Court satire, entitled "The Angler" in allusion to the
King's fondness for fishing, warned Jane of her danger:

O yet consider e're it be too late
How near you stand upon the brink of fate.
Think who they are who would for you procure
This great preferment to be made a whore:
Two reverend aunts, renowned in British story
For lust and drunkenness with Nell and Lory.
These, these are they your fame will sacrifice,
Your honor sell, and you shall hear the price:
My Lady Mary nothing can design,
But to feed her lust with what she gets for thine;
Old Richmond making thee a glorious punk,
Shall twice a day with brandy now be drunk;
Her brother Buckingham shall be restored;
Nelly a countess, Lory be a lord.

Mistress Lawson paid no heed to warnings. She was not alone in her desire to become "a glorious punk." Among other contenders for the title were Carey Frazier, daughter of Sir Alexander Frazier, the King's physician, and Elizabeth Jones, daughter of the Earl of Ranelagh and backed by the Irish interest. That spring and summer the traffic of bawds, managers, and maidens congested the backstairs. But King Charles, living in domestic bliss with his trio of trollops (Portsmouth, Mazarin, and Nell), was not to be tempted. One by one the candidates resigned; Mesdames Frazier and Jones took husbands, and Jane Lawson, finding her secular efforts of no avail, turned to a nunnery.

Early in June, while Nell was at her busiest with plots and cabals, trotting from Windsor to London to attend meetings of the Monmouth coterie, besieging the Irish authorities about her pension, and hiring a new agent and majordomo, James Frazier, shocking news came from

France. Little Lord James was dead. Just two years ago Nell had written of his preparations for his journey to France, for him the land of no return. He died "of a sore leg" and part of Nell died with him. No more details about his death and funeral are recorded. In the growing anxiety of the times, with Whitehall flooded by Whig-inspired petitions for a meeting of Parliament, and with new rumors of uprisings, rebellions, and foreign wars to report, the gossips paid little heed to the death of an eight-year-old child or the grief of his mother. For a while Nell tried to continue as a politician, but her heart was no longer in her work. She retired to Windsor for the rest of the summer and sought diversion and peace. To add to her melancholy, on July 26 her old friend and counsellor, Lord Rochester, surrounded by weeping women and praying parsons, died. He was thirty-three, just three years older than Nell.

Sobered, but by no means crushed, Nell was partially consoled by the King's gift of a fine mansion at Windsor. Not far from Windsor Castle, Burford House was a large, well-appointed dwelling, with pleasant gardens sloping to the south. Deeds of September 14 conveyed it to Nell's trustees, Lord Dorset, Sir George Hewitt, Sir Edward Villiers, and William Chiffinch, "in trust for Ellen Gwyn for and during her life, and after her decease in trust for Charles, Earl of Burford, and the heirs male of his body." Even after Nell took possession, the Treasury continued to pay for major repairs and for such improvements as "a brick wall for Madam Gwyn's garden on the south side of her house at Windsor." It was a noble gift indeed; now Nell had two fine houses—but only one son.

In the autumn, after a long lull, the winds of politics

began to rise again. Shaftesbury had secured London for Whiggery by contriving the election of a fanatic Lord Mayor and two republican sheriffs. The election of one sheriff, Slingsby Bethel (Dryden's "Shimei" who "did wisely from expensive sins refrain") was helped by a rumor that he was married to Nell Gwyn! Since the sheriffs chose all juries, the Whig victories assured the conviction of anyone accused of complicity in the Popish Plot. Now, as the time for Parliament to meet drew near, the Whigs gave a royal welcome to Monmouth on his return from another progress in the west, circulated stories of a black box which contained proof that his mother, Lucy Walter, had been the King's wife, whipped the London mobs to fury against York and popery, and set out once more to "popularly prosecute the plot." For a while even the Duchess of Portsmouth flirted with the Whigs, lured by the foolish hope that her son, the Duke of Richmond, might be named heir to the throne if York was legally disabled.

Parliament met on October 21. The House of Commons passed a new Exclusion Bill on November 11, and shouting mobs carried it to the House of Lords. There it was debated for six hours at white heat. Deserting his party, the Earl of Halifax upheld the cause of constitutionalism in a series of brilliant speeches and defeated the bill almost single-handed. The ranting Whigs demanded Halifax's dismissal from the Council, declared York incapable of holding public office, pushed the Popish Plot trials, and talked ominously of a republic.

It was the most critical period of King Charles's reign. A comet shaped like a sword-blade struck terror to the hearts of the ignorant and reminded the wise of a similar omen before the bloody revolution of '41. They had reason to be concerned. In the depths of the city Lord Shaftesbury was planning civil war. The London mobs were constantly tossed about by rumors. They shrieked with joy whenever a new victim of the plot was executed at Tyburn or on Tower Hill—hanged, disemboweled, and quartered. But the King refused every demand from the rampant Whigs. To give way to the clamor for exclusion would be to loose a flood of new demands which would sweep monarchy into limbo. To resist was to take the chance of revolution. With a lean and hungry Court, an empty Treasury, and war threatening on the continent, he chose to resist. On January 10, 1681, he first prorogued and then dissolved Parliament.

XIII

Counter-winds

1 6 8 1 – 1 6 8 3

XIII

THE WHIGS were so strongly intrenched in London that King Charles summoned his next Parliament to meet on March 21, 1681, at Tory Oxford. In February, after bitter protests at this unusual proceeding, the Whigs mounted a new campaign of lies, libels, and obscene songs. As usual Nell and the Duchess of Portsmouth figured in the lampoons as good versus evil, and some of the attacks against the Catholic mistress were so vicious that she was literally frightened into illness and talked of fleeing to France. One ingenious Whig contributed an imaginary canine conversation between Nell's "Tutty" and Portsmouth's "Snap-short." The burden of their lap-dog snarling was that Nell was "a good commonwealth's woman," a Protestant who had never "to make her own private gains endeavored the ruin of a nation," while Portsmouth, a spy for France and Rome, was one of "Pharaoh's lean kine" who had "almost devoured a kingdom." Snap-short held doggedly to one point: his mistress (Portsmouth) was "a whore of the greater magnitude."

On March 14, outwardly carefree and debonair, King and Court drove to Oxford through ways lined by Life-Guards. Revolution was in the air, but the King behaved as if on holiday. A day or two after his arrival he went, with Nell on one arm and Portsmouth on the other, to see a play, *Tamburlaine the Great*. Cheerfully he greeted the

Whigs who thronged into Oxford armed to their gnashing teeth. Although he scoffed at rumors that the fanatics planned to seize him and hold him a prisoner until he agreed to their demands, there were always guardsmen at his heels.

Mobs of both parties roamed the streets, and battles were common between blue-ribbon Whigs and red-ribbon Tories. One day a Whig mob mistook Nell's coach for Portsmouth's and surrounded it, howling threats and curses. Nell stuck her head out the window and called sweetly, "Pray, good people, be civil, I am the *Protestant* whore." Immediately the mob showered blessings on her sanctified ringlets and allowed her to pass.

King Charles made it clear to Shaftesbury that, although he was willing to accept a Protestant regency for his brother (if and when York inherited) he would not yield an inch on the actual line of succession. Inflamed by passion, prejudice, and power, the Whigs were not interested in law and justice; they bawled for Monmouth and decked themselves with ribbons stamped "No Popery, No Slavery." When they introduced a new Exclusion Bill in the House of Commons, the King (who had just concluded a secret treaty for a French subsidy) decided on dissolution again.

Since the first hint of his plan might be the signal for an uprising it was kept secret from everyone but his Council. On the morning of March 28 he strolled to the House of Lords followed by a sedan-chair conveying his ceremonial garb. Suddenly appearing in the Lords, wearing robes and crown, he summoned the Commons, who came pouring in, exultantly convinced that he was about to yield. They were struck dumb by the Lord Chancellor's terse, "It is His Majesty's royal pleasure and will that this Parliament be dissolved; and this Parliament is dissolved." Before the stunned Whigs could gather their wits, King and Court were well on the road to Windsor.

This was the last Parliament elected during the reign. In the next few months England, already sickened by bloody excesses, recovered from panic and plots, and the winds blew counter—toward monarchy and passive obedience. Aided by £400,000 from Louis XIV, spread over three years, King Charles paid his debts and fattened his Court. In return for this modest subsidy, Charles promised not to interfere with any of King Louis' imperialist schemes, so long as the French refrained from further attacks on Holland. He also agreed that if a new Parliament insisted on exclusion, he would dissolve it again. King Louis feared that, if the situation became too dangerous, Charles might agree to exclusion but substitute William of Orange for Monmouth as his heir, thus uniting England and Holland in a permanent league against France.

Now, in a storm of petitions expressing abhorrence of Whiggery, King Charles took a bitter revenge against his enemies. Whig informers lost their pensions, were fined for *scandalum magnatum*, and trembled for their lives. When the Grand Juries of London consistently refused (with an "Ignoramus") bills charging such scoundrels as College, Rous, and Fitzharris with high treason, the King's lawyers secured a change of venue and Tory juries convicted the poor wretches on the evidence of Tory informers. It was a lie for a lie and a head for a head. Quoth the King grimly, "At Doomsday we shall see whose arse is blackest."

With the Whig defeat Nell had no further interest in

politics, and there were no more cabals and conferences at her house in Pall Mall. Her friends, Monmouth, Buckingham, and the lesser Whig lords went into hiding for a while, fearing the King's vengeance. Shaftesbury was accused of high treason, freed on bail by an "Ignoramus" jury on November 24, and thereafter so hampered by the King that the following year he fled to Holland, where he died on January 21, 1683.

There were still Whig plots and tumults in the City, but outside London walls the days were calm. Once again Whitehall and Windsor came back to something like normal; there were cards, plays, dances, music, and races in season—but pale ghosts of the mad, lusty days of the past. As before, courtiers and mistresses strove for royal favor and preferment. In April, 1681, much to Nell's disgust, Portsmouth's son, the Duke of Richmond, was installed as a Knight of the Garter. But Nell was not without profit in her own country; sometime during the year King Charles gave her valuable leases of land in Bestwood Park, a crown property near the village of Arnold in Nottinghamshire.

The members of the King's little family continued in their ways, each according to character. Moll Davis remained in retirement. The Duchess of Cleveland, still living in France where she spent her fortune on a series of lovers but gave no new cause for scandal, made rare trips to England to bully the King for money. The Duchess of Mazarin, only an annex to the harem, amused herself with gamesters, sots, and sages. As always Portsmouth was the political power. The King's ministers—even Hyde and Halifax, who hated her—found it advisable to be at least civil, and Sunderland courted her shamelessly.

Nell carried on as court jester and entertainer. Particularly at Windsor, where the King loved to spend the long months of summer, it was her function to furnish amusement for His Majesty by bringing together at Burford House the liveliest members of the Court. Some of these were old friends—the Earl of Dorset, Fleetwood Shepherd, Henry Savile (now Vice-Chamberlain of the Household), foppish Sir George Hewitt, mad Harry Killigrew, George Etherege the poet (now knighted, married, and in the Duke of York's service), Peg Hughes, Mall Knight, and wanton Lady Arundel (née Lady Mary Mordaunt). Sir Carr Scroope, alas, died in November, 1680. Among new friends were Charles Grenville, Lord Lansdowne, a gay young spark much in love with Mall Knight; the aptly named William Dutton Colt, Prince Rupert's Master of the Horse; Lieutenant Stint Duncombe of the King's Foot-Guards, very attentive to Nelly; Henry Lumley, famous for nonsense; Charles Talbot, the young Earl of Shrewsbury (son of Nell's old friend, the countess); and dozens more.

There were professional entertainers, too, people like her former colleague, the actor Jo Haines, who claimed in a verse epistle addressed to the King that Charles was his debtor,

> Imprimis, in Scotland, for converting of Whigs,
> In England for Pindaric poems and jigs,
> At Dame Ellen Gwyn's for moving your laughter,
> A presage that some good was to follow after.

At London, Windsor, or Newmarket, Nell kept open house for her friends, and the King could always drop in, assured of jests and jollity. By day he went to Portsmouth's lodgings for business (and often to take a nap), but he devoted many of his nights to Nell, mirth, and sometimes love.

Usually his visits were only for innocent merriment, but the pious and prudish would never think so. In September, 1681, while the Court was at Newmarket, a delegation of Oxford aldermen were walking with the King in the fields when Nell passed them with a cheery, "Charles, I hope I shall have your company at night, shall I not?" The chaste aldermen misconstrued the harmless invitation and were shocked; one of them told the story with horror for months afterward, saying that he had "often heard bad things of the King," but now his own eyes had seen them.

The law students of London were no such prudes. The Christmas festivities at the Inner Temple were celebrated with wassail and revelry by thirty-two "gentlemen under the bar" from December 17, 1681, to January 19, 1682! On January 12 they invited Nell to one of their rowdiest entertainments, and in token of their admiration presented her with a gift of candy. In the record of their revels stands the solemn notation: "for sweetmeats for Madam Gwyn, £1."

But many respectable men—even good Tories—were as shocked as the Oxford aldermen by the King's frivolous Court and his multiplicity of queans. On January 24, 1682, sour John Evelyn witnessed the Duchess of Portsmouth's entertainment of the Moroccan Ambassador and his retinue. The guests sat at a long table, "a lady between two Moors," and among the ladies (Evelyn was pained to note) were "the Duchess of Portsmouth, Nelly, &c., concubines and cattle of that sort, as splendid as jewels and excess of bravery could make them." The "concubines and cattle" were put to shame by the Moors—grave, courtly men, who drank no wine.

Significantly it was Portsmouth and not Queen Catherine who entertained ambassadors. In all respects but one Portsmouth was queen and her reign was absolute. In the spring of 1682 she was so well established that she could risk a brief vacation abroad. On March 2 she set forth for her native land, "with seventy in family and £30,000 advance money." The Court of Louis XIV greeted her with the honors reserved for royalty.

The moment her back was turned, the Whig poets began their yapping. In March, 1681, a visitor to the English Court, Philippe de Vendôme, Grand Prior of France (a handsome sinner in shepherd's clothing), had fallen in love with the duchess. The gossips suspected an intrigue, and Portsmouth's trip abroad was gleefully explained as caused by the King's jealousy. In "A Dialogue between the Duchess of Portsmouth and Madam Gwyn at Parting," Nell, the constant nymph, was made to reprove her rival:

> . . . You, to your eternal praise and fame,
> To foreign scents betrayed the Royal Game.
> Witness the Prior [who] on your bosom lay,
> And in that posture did your lust betray,
> For which now with a pox you're sent away.

Portsmouth's excursion inspired also a pair of prose satires on a now-hackneyed theme: the conflict between the two mistresses. In "A Letter from the Duchess of Portsmouth to Madam Gwyn on her Landing in France" the fictional duchess boasted that in the Channel Neptune himself had made love to her, and for a moment she was tempted, thinking to see her son Richmond "Master of the Sea-horse as well as at land." But it occurred to her that Nell would be a more appropriate mistress for Neptune because of her "extraction"—mud. To this insult she added some horrid remarks about Nell's family and old Madam Gwyn's well-remembered death.

In "Madam Gwyn's Answer" Nell, as usual, got the better of the argument. She wondered that Portsmouth escaped drowning, but "he that's born to be hanged will never be drowned." As for the pretensions of young Richmond, "I have a little lord . . . that may for ought I know prick your bladder and let out that ambitious wind. Both sprung from one branch, and why should not he hope for something, as well as yours gape for all. There's little difference by the mothers' side if we search the Keroualle family in France and mine in England." True, Nell's mother had died in a ditch, "but what then? She was a soul, she loved brandy, and as for your papa, his lodging in Wiltshire [at the brutish Earl of Pembroke's house] was but in a pig-sty. If I came from a drunken family, you sprung from a swinish race, and pray what's the difference when our pedigree is summed up?"

While libelers dripped acid and Portsmouth went a-progress through France, King Charles and his Court were at Newmarket, kept from their wonted sports by cold and rainy weather. Samuel Pepys, who had nearly lost his head during the Popish Terror, went to Newmarket early in March to greet the Duke of York, now at last permitted to return to England. Pepys was very welcome at Burford House where he often met the King. For lack of Portsmouth and her lodgings, Charles "took his repose" at Nell's house "once or twice daily." Pepys was very fond of Nell. Purely for sentimental reasons he preserved a three-quarter length engraving of her person as Cupid. She was dressed very simply—in an arrow and a pair of wings.

Portsmouth came back to England in July, plump and lusty ("Fubbs" the King called her fondly), and a naughty poet jeered,

> Now Nelly you must be content,
> Her grace begins to reign;
> For all your brat you may be sent
> To Dorset back again.

With her prestige heightened by her overseas reception the duchess was more insufferable than ever. When Phyllis Temple, one of the Queen's Maids of Honor, "spoke reflectingly" of her to a confidant who tattled, Portsmouth "went crying to the King, who complained of it to the Queen and said he would stop Temple's salary for it." Queen Catherine fretted under Portsmouth's arrogance, but if she dared protest she was considered "saucy."

While Nell, the jester, followed the King about in his restless round—Newmarket in spring and fall, Windsor in the summer—Portsmouth, the politician, tended more and more to stay at home, cabaling with the Duke of York and governing the kingdom. Nell lived in a happy world where horses, gamecocks, and hawks were more important than treaties and taxes, cards and flirtations were serious amusements, and the only news was gossip. Even the poets began to lose interest in her, and one of them confessed coarsely that,

> All matters of state from her soul she does hate
> And leaves to the politic bitches.
> The whore's in the right, for 'tis her delight
> To be scratching just where it itches.

In the summer of 1682 Windsor was delightful. In hot, brawling London, where the Earl of Danby (still a prisoner in the Tower) was suing for his freedom, and Lord Shaftesbury was vainly regrouping his forces for a fresh assault, Portsmouth plotted mighty schemes of state. There were elections for Lord Mayor and sheriff, suits and countersuits at law, trials of Whig informers, and executions for high treason. At Windsor all was gaiety: hawking and fishing, long rides in the cool forest-land, suppers and cards —ombre or basset—in the soft glow of candles. Mall Knight grew tired of flirting with Lord Lansdowne, "the gay, the sprightly, and the wise," turned her batteries on William Dutton Colt (an attractive, but remarkably crosseyed, gentleman), and compelled his submission. Bored by "lovely" Duncombe's attentions, Nell Gwyn broke up Mall's new romance and trotted off with Master Colt. There was a mighty quarrel between the two ladies; the King was called in as peacemaker; he awarded Colt "and all his eyes" to Nell and sent Mall off on a little mission to France. To the pleasure of the whole Court, Sir George Etherege immortalized the social saga in a wicked heroic poem, "Mrs. Nelly's Complaint," in which he pictured Nell as haunted by the ghost of absent Mall Knight and crying out in her terror,

> To France my baffled, squeaking rival's gone,
> And Colt and all his eyes are now my own.
> Should she pretend to what's so much my due,
> She might as well take lovely Duncombe too,

Duncombe by my great sway and power preferred,
For mounting me well first, now mounts the Guard.
Help, Church and State, to do a princess right,
Guard me from wrongs and exorcise this spright.
Even now in terror on my bed I lie;
Send Doctor Burnet to me, or I die.

Windsor was delighted.

At the end of August the King and a number of his courtiers—among them Nell Gwyn—rode to the little cathedral town of Winchester "to see the horse-racing there." A Court official sent ahead to locate lodgings for the visitors had no trouble persuading Dean Richard Meggott to give up a bedroom in the deanery for the King, but when he chose Prebendary Thomas Ken's house "for the use of Mrs. Gwyn" he met a stern refusal. The courtier hinted that the King would pay; but "not for his kingdom" would the doughty priest permit "a woman of ill repute" to enter his chaste abode. Fortunately Dean Meggott was willing to compromise with sin and offered Nell a room in his own house, close to the King's bedchamber.

Easy-going Nell was not offended, and King Charles was delighted by Ken's stout integrity. Two years later when the bishopric of Bath and Wells was to be filled, Charles looked over the applications (among them those of Ken and the pliant Dean Meggott) and cried, "Ods fish! Who should have Bath and Wells but the little fellow who would not give poor Nelly a lodging?" And so it was decreed—although, with nice irony, tradition gave Nell the credit. Sixty years afterward, the poet Edward Young begged the Duchess of Portland to help him to a bishopric, saying, " 'Tis certain Nell Gwyn made Dr. Ken a bishop."

Poor Nelly! In matters of preferment her influence was nothing; ambitious and hopeful as ever, she could not even get honors for her son and herself. For young Charles, a handsome twelve-year-old, dark like his father—she wanted the highest honors in the King's gift: a dukedom and the Order of the Garter. For herself, as always, she wanted the coronet of a countess. Twice during 1682 the honor of the Garter was almost in her grasp, in August when the Duke of Lauderdale's death vacated a place in the Order, and Lord Burford was mentioned as his successor, and again in November when the dying Prince Rupert "sent his Garter to the King, desiring Lord Burford might have it." In each case another candidate was chosen. As for the dukedom—Cleveland's youngest son, Lord Northumberland, was still only an earl; it was not until April, 1683, that the King was able to provide him with the title (and, more important, the estates) of a duke. Nell's son always came last.

In the autumn of 1682 money was more important than honors. Infected by the Court craze for gambling, Nell played for high stakes, in a single night losing £1,400 to the Duchess of Mazarin. There were times when she won, of course; nevertheless her losses over a few months made quite a dent in her purse. But she was in no danger of bankruptcy; on December 7 she paid Prince Rupert's executors £4,520 for a "great pearl necklace." She even had something to spare for charity. In November thousands of people were made homeless by a great fire at Wapping. On December 11 the King gave £2,000, "a person of quality £500, and Madam Gwyn £100" for the relief of the sufferers. Nell was still getting her pension from the Treasury in small (but more frequent) payments, and regular revenues from Bestwood Park and the tax on logwood; but her Irish income (on which, earlier in the year, she had borrowed £400) had stopped again, and she was forced to appeal to the Commissioners of the Treasury for an order commanding payment. The years had brought no financial wisdom to Nell; as with all ladies of fashion, it was "her maxim that to run o' th' score" with tradesmen was "a Court privilege."

Nell's charity was as impulsive as everything else in her life; she lived by heart, not by intellect. A famous story about her generosity rests on no reliable authority, but could be true. "Once, as she was driving up Ludgate Hill, she saw a poor clergyman in the hands of the sheriff's officers, and struck with compassion, she lighted from her carriage, inquired into the circumstances of his arrest, and paid his debt on the spot; and finding, on application to the vouchers he named, that his character was as unexceptionable as his misfortunes were real, she generously befriended him and his family."

In November King Charles, a good father to his numerous brood, proposed sending the Earl of Burford (of whom he was "extremely fond") to France for more advanced education. Young Charles had been well supplied with tutors, but he had never been away at school. Viscount Preston, who had replaced Henry Savile as Envoy to France, was ordered to prepare for Burford's reception; he was to take a larger house so that the boy would have an apartment to himself, and he was to provide teachers of mathematics and fortification—"the best that can be got." There was a constant bustle and stir in Pall Mall through

December and January, but Nell (who remembered only too well the tragic fate of little James) could not bear to part with her remaining son. She temporized, asked that "he should be delayed a little time in hopes of a setttlement to be made upon him," and finally kept him at home. As a compromise, Mr. Peter de Launé, formerly tutor to the Duke of York's children, was engaged to teach him French.

The new year came in attended by the usual festivities and promises of better times. With Shaftesbury in Holland and the Tory reaction complete, the government seemed safe enough, but the King's ministers were aware of the dangers from Whig fanatics and were constantly on guard. Charles refused to take precautions, riding in his sedan-chair across the Park on his regular visits to Nell in spite of reported strangers lurking in the shrubbery. Once, when the Duke of York protested at his careless freedom, Charles replied, "Ods fish! James, no man in England will take away my life to make you king."

In March he went as usual to Newmarket where three weeks later his stay was cut short by a fire which destroyed half the town, upset his plans, and caused his return to London two days ahead of schedule. Some forty fanatic plotters were upset too. They had planned an ambuscade at the Rye House near Ware—a hay-cart drawn across the Newmarket Road to block the royal coach, and a dozen muskets blazing from ditches and fields. It was not until June that the Rye House plot was exposed and the King learned by what a narrow margin of timing he had missed going to Heaven without benefit of clergy.

The wheel had come full circle; now there was a Protestant Plot. Once again there was hysteria, panic, and the shabby round of informers, "discoveries," and confessions. Twenty-one men were indicted by a Tory Grand Jury for complicity in the plot, including the King's still favorite son, the Duke of Monmouth. Twelve fled and were never captured. One, Lord Essex, cut his throat in the Tower. Seven were condemned by Tory juries, savagely executed, and their reeking quarters stuck on spikes over London gates. Frantically denying that he had ever plotted his father's death, Monmouth went into hiding again.

The Tory revenge was complete, but no one was any the happier. The King's stern, deeply lined face reflected his bitter mood. In August he retreated from London to Windsor, but there was no peace for a father brooding over the treason of a beloved son. The Court, too, in a "great consternation on the late plot and conspiracy," was deeply shocked; Monmouth, gay, spirited, and handsome, had been a universal favorite. Of all the King's family, it was Nell who most nearly shared his sorrow. Monmouth—half-brother to her own son—had been her intimate friend for years, and although he was her senior by some nine months, she loved him with almost maternal affection. Only four years ago she had sheltered him in her home and pleaded his cause with the King. It was a gloomy summer for Nell, too. To add to her melancholy the last of August brought news of the death of Charles Hart, the actor, her "Charles the First."

But gloom could not long survive at the Court of not-so-merry King Charles. As the bitter autumn gave way to the coldest winter in man's memory, the winds of conflict died down, and the year went out in an anticlimax of small events. Monmouth came out of hiding, made his submission, confessed his part in the conspiracy, was pardoned, and then retracted his confession. In a passion, Charles consigned him to hell. He fled to Holland instead. The Duke of Buckingham, repenting his Whiggery, made overtures to the Court. Madam Mazarin, deeply affected by the loss of a lover (slain by her nephew in a duel), considered retiring to a nunnery and was dissuaded by friends who pointed out that nunneries were dull. Nell Gwyn received dishonorable mention as "a Church of England's Whore" in a new libel, "The Ladies March." Her good friend Lady Arundel (whose husband was now Constable of Windsor and was soon to become Duke of Norfolk) struck up a liaison with the young Earl of Shrewsbury. The Grand Prior of France, caught practically *in flagrante* with the Duchess of Portsmouth, was given twenty-four hours to leave the kingdom. By the blessed whim of Fate, the royal yacht assigned to waft him across the channel was named *The Fubbs*, after the duchess. Whitehall was normal again.

XIV

Rue with

a

Difference

1 6 8 4 – 1 6 8 5

XIV

THE WINTER of 1684 was so severe that the sea was frozen for two miles from shore, and the Thames was so solid that a "Blanket Fair" was held on the ice, with booths, sports, games, and ox-roasts. In the bitter frosts at the turn of the year, old Henry Jermyn, Earl of St. Albans, gave up the ghost, vacating an ancient and honored title. The King was quick to take advantage of the fact; on January 5 he granted his beloved son, Charles, Earl of Burford, the title of Duke of St. Albans, with all the rights and privileges pertaining to that exalted rank.

St. Albans' creation was accompanied by other signs of his nobleness. The King installed him in lodgings in Whitehall, and to support his new dignity gave him an allowance of £1,500 a year. (Nell continued to draw £5,000 a year for herself.) As guarantees of future prosperity he was granted the offices of Chief Ranger of Enfield Chace and Master of the Hawks in reversion (inheritance) after the lives of the current incumbents. At the same time the canny King arranged a marriage for the boy with Diana de Vere, the little heiress of the Earl of Oxford. (The wedding ceremony was not performed until April 13, 1694.) Finally, that St. Albans' honors might "not unaccompanied invest him only," the King acknowledged Moll Davis's daughter by naming her Lady Mary Tudor and granting her "the place and precedency of the daughter of a duke of England." A goodly king and a careful father.

At last Nell's boast that her son was as fit to be a duke as any of his half-brothers was justified, and her dearest ambition was fulfilled. She swelled with pride and happiness. For weeks "my lord duke"—a beautiful, mouth-filling phrase—was the burden of her conversation. In a sense she lost the boy when he moved across the Park to Whitehall, but she could see him daily throughout the winter, and at Windsor he lived with her in Burford House. Although he was not quite fourteen, he was treated as a man, with his own household of servants. Nell flourished in the aura of his splendor, especially when he appeared with his father on formal occasions. For instance, there was the time that spring when the Bishop of Rochester preached before the King at Whitehall, and after the sermon His Majesty and three of his tall sons, the Dukes of Northumberland, Richmond, and St. Albans, went up to the altar and took communion under the eyes of the whole Court and a bevy of stately bishops. It was a sight to bring tears to three fond mothers' eyes.

On April 14, at Burford House, Windsor, Nell dictated one of her rare letters—full of "my lord dukes"—addressed this time to Mrs. Frances Jennings, an old friend who was acting as her dressmaker and London agent. The bulk of the letter was a number of instructions to Mrs. Jennings, with some gentle chiding for past remissness. She was to finish some garments Nell had ordered, including a mantle which was to be lined with "musk colored satin." She was to ask Lady Susan Williams (another old friend, a widow now engaged in trade) to send some "gold stuff" and with it a note for Nell to sign so that Lady Susan could get her money from Mr. Trant (Commissioner of the Excise Of-

fice); and "Pray tell my Lady Williams that the King's
mistresses are accounted ill paymasters, but she shall have
her money the next day after I have the stuff." (A knight's
widow was not to be treated as an ordinary tradesman.)
Mrs. Jennings was to send Beavour, a jeweler, Coker, a
haberdasher, and Poietvin, an upholsterer, to Windsor for
instructions. Nell wanted to buy a ring as a farewell present
for Cleveland's son, the Duke of Grafton, before he left
to join the French army besieging Luxembourg. (Louis
XIV was at it again, this time attacking the Spanish Netherlands.) "My lord duke" of St. Albans was planning on
going to France with his half-brother, and the King was
"mighty well pleased" that Mrs. Jennings' son-in-law, Edward Griffith, was to accompany him. Poietvin was to bring
down a number of things Nell had ordered, especially "my
lord duke's bed." St. Albans, "the duke" (how she loved
that title!), had recently arrived at Windsor, bringing
Nell's new and much admired "crochet of diamonds," and
she loved the jeweled clasp all the more because her noble
son had brought it.

Scattered among instructions were comments and news-
items, set down just as they occurred to giddy Nell. "The
bill is very dear to boil the plate [in the usual cleansing
solution of red clay, salt, and alum] but necessity hath no
law." "Monsieur Lainey [de Launé, St. Albans' tutor] is
going away"—to France. "My service to dear Lord Kildare"—a friend and neighbor in St. James's Square. "I have
continued extreme ill since you left me, and I am so still.
I believe I shall die." "My service to the Duchess of Norfolk [reported pregnant after seven years of marriage] and
tell her I am as sick as her grace, but do not know what I

ail, although she does, which I am overjoyed that she goes on with her great belly." (The Duchess of Norfolk's great belly proved to be only the wind of rumor.)

Nell ended her letter on a thoughtful note, the whimsical complaint of a middle-aged woman (she was thirty-four) who loved youth and laughter. Here were all the young men leaving Windsor to join the French army, and to Nell it was "a sad slaughter," but, remembering the departure of another young man for France—Portsmouth's lover, the Grand Prior—she hastened to add, "they are none of my lovers." The simple truth was that she was "loath to part with the men." She concluded in her usual friendly fashion, "Mrs. Jennings, I love you with all my heart, and so goodbye."

St. Albans, still too young for the pomp and circumstance of glorious war, stayed at home after all, and did not finally go to France until January of the following year, when he set forth on the customary grand tour (France, Spain, and Italy) with a tutor, Mr. de Gachon. Dr. Lower, a Whig physician who attended Nell frequently and during his ministrations managed to "pick out of her all the intrigues of the Court," restored her to health. For the rest of the year she continued in her usual happy courses: following the King in his wanderings, wagering on races, gambling at Lady Mazarin's house or in the Groom Porter's lodge at Whitehall, attending parties, dances, and the theatre. Her income was paid regularly, and, as usual, spent well in advance. In December she made a long-term investment, buying the lease of a house in Priest Street, Windsor.

Meanwhile the insatiable Duchess of Cleveland came out

of retirement to whet the Court's appetite for scandal. Returning to England in March, 1684, she took a new lover, a scapegrace actor named Cardonnel Goodman, known to his underworld cronies as "Scum." After a few months Goodman distinguished himself by conspiring to poison two of her grace's sons, Grafton and Northumberland. He was tried, convicted, and fined £1,000. The fine was duly paid and besotted Cleveland continued to nourish the Borgia in her bosom. Something over a year later (in April, 1686, when she was forty-five years old) she gave birth to her seventh child, a son, christened "Goodman Cleveland" by the fascinated gossips. Of course, even while she was indulging her lechery with her rakehell lover, the duchess was dunning the King for money; wearily he paid his debts and closed his eyes to her revels.

England was at peace and prosperous. Content with his dogs, hawks, and horses, and shuttling regularly back and forth between Nell's house and Portsmouth's lodgings, the King left business to his ministers and pursued his usual rounds—Windsor in the summer, Winchester in September, Newmarket in October. Aging rapidly and tiring more easily, he was still cheerful and full of plans for the future. He gave no sign that he was growing restive under petticoat rule—indeed, when Portsmouth was seriously ill in November he hastened to her bedside, and government stood still until she recovered—but he was thinking of new directions for his policy and new faces at his council table. The Duke of Buckingham was again "coming much into favor at Court"; the Duke of York, Portsmouth, and Lord Sunderland—the extreme Tories—were gradually losing control to such moderates as Lord Halifax; and, at the

King's orders, secret overtures were made to Monmouth in Holland. There was even talk of calling a Parliament.

Among other projects revolving in the King's devious mind was a plan to make Nelly a countess. Although he had no precedent for raising a base-born commoner to the peerage, the thing could be done, and now, with his enemies dead or in hiding, was the time to do it. Portsmouth, loaded with wealth and honors, could hardly object, and Nell's old enemy, Lord Danby, finally released from the Tower, was powerless. Nell had strong friends in high places: Henry Guy, Henry Savile, Sidney Godolphin, Lord Halifax, and Lawrence Hyde, now Earl of Rochester and President of the Council.

Secretive as ever, the King hesitated to reveal his plans to Nell, but, as she told his brother some time in the following year, he hinted to her that "the world should see by what he did for me that he had both love and value for me." However in some fashion the secret leaked out, even to the title designed to crown Nell's long and faithful service —Countess of Greenwich. But between the King's good intentions and his performance came the consequence of years of hard living, hard drinking, and disease.

On Sunday night, February 1, 1685, John Evelyn was a witness to "the inexpressible luxury and profaneness" of the Court at Whitehall, with King Charles "sitting and toying with his concubines, Portsmouth, Cleveland, and Mazarin, &c." (The *et cetera* was base-born Nell, whose name the aristocratic Evelyn could hardly bring himself to write.) He remarked also on "a French boy singing love songs in that glorious gallery, whilst about twenty of the great courtiers and other dissolute persons were at basset round

a large table, a bank of at least £2,000 in gold before them."
When the party broke up later that night, Nell bade her
royal lover goodbye and jogged homeward across the Park
in her chair, serenely unaware that she would never again
see him alive.

On the morning of February 2 (Nell's thirty-fifth birthday) the King fell in a fit as he was dressing. Unaware of
the nature of his ailment—chronic kidney disease—his physicians rushed to his aid with phlebotomy, plasters, and
purges. For four days he was in almost constant agony, not
only from periodic uremic convulsions, but also from the
torture of blistering, scarifying, and cupping, and from
massive doses of every known drug, from cream of tartar
to quinine. Throughout he remained patient and uncom-
plaining. Outside the palace a vast crowd gathered, waiting
silently for news. There was no place for Nell at the King's
bedside; the nearest she could come to him was the royal
antechamber, crowded by a throng of anxious courtiers.

On Thursday, when it became clear that the end was
not far off, Portsmouth and the Duke of York helped
Charles achieve his secret longing: to die in the Catholic
faith. Father Huddleston (his old comrade on the flight
from Worcester many years ago), brought to his chamber
by a secret door, administered the last rites of the church
and left him at peace with God. Thereafter, until late the
next morning, his mind was clear. "He often spoke quite
aloud to the Duke of York in terms full of tenderness and
friendship; he twice recommended to him the Duchess of
Portsmouth and the Duke of Richmond. He made no mention of the Duke of Monmouth, good or bad." While his
mistresses wept in the antechamber, the tearful Queen, his

friends, and his children knelt at his bedside. He spoke tenderly to them all, and once, with a touch of his old wry humor, murmured that he was sorry to be so long in dying. Once again he recommended his children to his brother's care and added, "Let not poor Nelly starve." Thereafter he lay dozing, "and after some conflicts, his physicians despairing of him, he gave up the ghost at half an hour after eleven in the morning, being 6 February 1685, in the 36th year of his reign and 54th of his age." A few hours later his successor, King James II, was proclaimed at Whitehall Gate. The loyal citizens shouted with dutiful joy and trudged away, shaking their heads sadly. For all his faults, Charles had been a good king.

No one is less pitied than a dead man's mistress. However real her grief, she must wear her rue with a difference. As ladies in waiting, King Charles's mistresses could don the customary solemn black worn by all the Court, but they could make no further show of sorrow. Envoys sent to "condole the death of the late King" were received by the Dowager Queen "on a bed of mourning, the whole chamber, ceiling and floor, hung with black," but when Nell Gwyn and Portsmouth sought to deck their rooms in mourning they were forbidden. The duchess was not permitted even "to use that sort of nails [studs] about her coach and chair which, it seems, is kept as a distinction for the royal family on such an occasion, and had else been put on by her." The King's bastards were members of the royal family; their mothers were not.

In the privacy of their own homes the ladies who had shared the King's bed longest and with most profit to themselves and to the English peerage sorrowed for his passing.

Each had loved him in her own way. Even to Cleveland his death was at least as painful as that of a husband, or a lap-dog, while to Nell and Portsmouth it was tragedy, poignant and unalloyed. For seventeen years in Nell's case, for fifteen in Portsmouth's, Charles had been lover, husband, friend, and keeper. He had given them and their children wealth, jewels, houses, and honors. In return Nell had given him all her heart with unstinting devotion; even Portsmouth had loved him in her fashion. At his death the two women lost influence, prestige, and all hopes for the future. Portsmouth's reign was ended, and Nell's long-sought coronet remained an unsubstantial dream.

Of course all the King's ladies suffered in purse. Moll Davis, clouded by obscurity, had little to lose and not long to live. In 1687, some time after she married her daughter to Francis Radcliffe, later Earl of Derwentwater, her house in St. James's Square passed into other hands, and Moll was lost in the mist of time. The Duchess of Mazarin had much to lose and a strong reason to "shed floods of tears": the King's death ended her allowance of £4,000 a year. King James gave her a small pension, which was continued by his successor, but she dwindled rapidly into an old age of cards and brandy, moved eventually to a small house in Chelsea, and died in squalid poverty on June 2, 1699, in her fifty-third year.

Through three successive reigns the Duchess of Cleveland clung like a leech to her pension—£4,700 a year out of the Post Office—but with no one to badger for additional cash she spent the rest of her life deeply in debt. She moved in a violent sub-world of gamesters, sharpers, and rakes, and as her beauty waned she was reduced to taking

her lovers from among her domestics. At sixty-four, shortly after her first husband's death, she married, on November 25, 1705, General Robert Fielding, a rogue who
committed bigamy when he promised to "love, honor, and
cherish" her. When his crime was discovered there was a
scandalous lawsuit which ended with the marriage an-
nulled and Fielding in prison. Disappointed and bitter, the
duchess took her frustrated lusts to a small village in Middlesex, where she died "of a dropsy" on October 9, 1709.

Three days after King Charles's death, the Duchess of
Portsmouth, fearing Whig reprisals, fled to sanctuary at
the French Ambassador's house. In her panic she wanted
to sail for France at once, but King James promised her his
protection, offered her an allowance of £3,000 a year, and
insisted that she remain in England until she had paid her
debts and returned some crown jewels in her possession.
Reassured, she returned to Whitehall, and her greed over-
came her fears. Rejecting the King's proffered pittance with
scorn, she fought long and hard to retain the £19,000 a
year granted her by King Charles and the £25,000 a year
she claimed as her dues from the Irish revenue. She was
permitted to keep the first but not the second. When she
sailed for France in August her total wealth included the
ducal fief of Aubigny in France, granted her by Louis
XIV, large sums invested in France, £5,000 a year from
properties in England, £19,000 a year from the Post Office, a magnificent collection of jewels and plate, and literally shiploads of furniture, coaches, sedan-chairs, and household goods.

The echoes of her fall from power had hardly died
away in February, 1685, when the Whig poets were in the

streets with their mock-elegies. "The Duchess of Portsmouth's Farewell" presented moral Nell Gwyn lecturing her sinful rival, while the sad duchess lamented "the wretched state" of her affairs. In "A Pleasant Dialogue between Two Wanton Ladies of Pleasure" Nell scolded Portsmouth for her greed, lust, and pride, and the duchess declared her intention of returning to France and setting up as a bawd. "Portsmouth's Lamentation; or, a Dialogue between Two Amorous Ladies, E.G. and D.P." pictured Nell as rejoicing over her rival's fall and giving sage advice, while Portsmouth complained at having to pay her debts:

> From hence I thought for to convey
>   What in this land I gained,
> But I am here confined to stay,
>   And now my credit's stained.

Poor Nelly's credit was not stained—it was wiped out. Heedless of a day of reckoning, she had "run o' the' score" with tradesmen until she was thousands of pounds in debt. Now, aware that her pension ceased with King Charles's death, her creditors ravened at her door, and King James paid no attention to appeals for the renewal of her allowance. She owned valuable properties, but since they were entailed upon her son they could not be sold, and they could be mortgaged only with his consent. She hesitated to sell her personal possessions, knowing quite well that, although in time King James might pay her debts, he would never replace pearl necklaces and silver bedsteads.

The new King was a strict, formal man, surrounded by guards and priests, and very busy preparing for the spring session of Parliament; she could not appeal to him in person. However, James Graham, Keeper of the Privy Purse, carried messages back and forth. The King had her in mind, but for the moment he offered only vague promises: he would take care of her "business" in due time—as usual Nell came last. Reluctantly, under the pressure of clamorous threats, Nell mortgaged her Bestwood Park estates for some £3,500, borrowed from her bankers, Child and Rogers, about £6,000 on her jewels and plate, and persuaded Henry Guy to advance her £1,000 from the Exchequer.

Even these large amounts were not enough to satisfy all her creditors. When all her cash had been doled out, she was still in debt to the amount of £729. 2s. 3d., and the vindictive Shylocks of the city had her outlawed. She was in no danger of debtors' prison, but her credit was worthless and would remain so until her debts were paid to the last farthing. Meanwhile, with a large establishment to maintain and her income cut by £5,000 a year, she had very little to live on. Sometime in May she sent King James a passionate little note which began "Had I suffered for my God as I have done for your brother and you, I should not have needed either of your kindness or justice to me." She begged him for an interview, and urged him not to do anything about her affairs until she had a chance to speak to him. Fate had balked her of the coronet she had set her heart on; now she must strive mightily to save her hard-won wealth—for her own sake, of course, but more for the sake of her noble son, "my lord duke."

XV

Joy

in

Heaven

1 6 8 5 - 1 6 8 7

X V

SOMETIME in May, 1685, King James took a few moments from the cares of state to consider Nell's "business." By nature he was neither generous nor forgiving, and he had no reason to love the little Whig who had been so outspoken in support of his enemy, the Duke of Monmouth. But King Charles had urged him not to let poor Nelly starve, and James was at least a man of honor. Therefore he sent Mr. Graham to Nell with a considerable (but unspecified) sum of money and a number of "kind expressions" and assurances for the future.

Nell was surprised and pleased. Her answering letter began, "This world is not capable of giving me a greater joy and happiness than your Majesty's favor." She was grateful not only for the money, which, she said extravagantly, had brought her "out of the last extremity," but also for the "great comfort" of his pledges. In return she promised, "All you do for me shall be yours, it being my resolution never to have any interest but yours, and as long as I live to serve you, and when I die, to die praying for you." No more Whiggery! The old, friendly, tolerant days were gone, but she could not help reverting to them wistfully as she thought of the dead King. "He told me before he died," she said, "that the world should see by what he did for me that he had love and value for me. . . . He was my friend and allowed me to tell him all my griefs, and did like a friend advise me and told me who was my friend and who was not." James could be kind, but he could never be her "friend" in any sense of the word.

With enough money on hand to tide her over until the King's promises could be carried out, Nell took the cash to Windsor and let the credit go until autumn. She was at Windsor when the Duke of Monmouth, accompanied only by a hundred or so adventurers and desperadoes, landed in the west at Lyme Regis (June 11), declared himself king and his uncle a usurper, and called upon all loyal subjects to rally to his standard. With many others Nell watched fearfully from afar as thousands of Protestant yeomen, armed with ancient muskets, swords, pikes, and even scythes, flocked to join Monmouth, eager to depose a Catholic king; and the King's Guards and militia hurried to the scene of the revolt. For three weeks there were skirmishes and minor battles as the two armies maneuvered. Then, on the night of July 6, Monmouth threw his forces in a surprise night attack against the royal army at Sedgemoor, and had it not been for the alertness of General John Churchill (second in command) the crown of England might well have changed heads. As it was, the rebels were crushed and routed; two days later Monmouth was found asleep in a ditch and captured.

There was no need to try a traitor caught red-handed in the act of treason. Monmouth had one brief, painful interview with King James and then was sent to the Tower to be executed. This time there were no kind-hearted ladies to plead his cause. Nell could only mourn—but in secret—when, on July 15, the misguided pretender bared his neck to the headsman's axe. She had loved the man.

But her volatile spirits could not long remain depressed. Summer was a time for gaiety; all England quickly forgot the brief rebellion, except in the west, where mad Judge Jeffreys presided over the "Bloody Assizes." The King and Court, following the custom set in the previous reign, spent the summer at Windsor. Nell still had "a thousand merry conceits," and dozens of intimates to share them with.

One of her best friends, Mary Howard (née Mordaunt), the twenty-six-year-old Duchess of Norfolk, invited her often to Windsor Castle for Cards. That summer my lady duchess (tired of the Earl of Shrewsbury) was flirting with a handsome, Anglo-Dutch adventurer, Mr. John Germaine, aged thirty-five, and said to be an illegitimate son of William II of Orange (if so, he was half-brother to the then Prince William). Nell was the duchess's confidant in the affair and willing either to make sport herself or help it at need.

One day in August the Duke of Norfolk's duties took him on an extended trip to Portsmouth. The night of his departure, the duchess invited Nell, Germaine, and Colonel Henry Cornwall for a foursome at cards. In spite of the chill of the evening, two of the players were warm with ardent anticipation. So far the duchess had not yielded to Germaine's advances, but now her eyes glittered, her face was flushed, and her bare shoulders and bosom were moist under the powder. Nell watched her with half-envious amusement; the Dutch Lothario had made love to her, too. At one time in the course of the game, the two ladies went to "the Green Room" to repair their complexions, and Nell was overheard to say that "the dog [Germaine] would have lain with her, but she would not lay the dog where the deer [King Charles] laid." However—alas for fidelity!—her chief reason for refusing Germaine was that "she knew my lady duchess would have him." She had to make her boast: she could have had him herself, but she would not be her friend's rival.

The Duchess of Norfolk made no answer—none was needed—and the two went back to their cards. When the party finally ended and Nell and Colonel Cromwell left, Germaine secretly sent his footman for clean linen and spent the night in the arms of his charming duchess. The next morning her grace, who as wife of the Constable of Windsor held a daily levée, ordered a fire built in her husband's bedchamber, left Germaine asleep in her own bed, and prepared to receive callers. She was a picture of bland innocence as she lay in bed with a maid combing her hair.

Impatient for the bawdy details, Nell was the first caller. "Good morning to your grace," she said, "how did you rest last night?" "Very well," replied the duchess, with a frown and a side-long glance at the maid. Nell paid no heed to the warning and asked about Germaine's health. The Duchess of Norfolk said virtuously that she knew nothing of the gentleman's condition, and, to turn the conversation, complained of her hair being out of order. Merrily Nell commented that it had been a hot night with her grace, hot enough to put her hair out of powder and curl too! At this point in came Colonel Cornwall, who winked at Nell, bowed to her grace, and said, "How doth Mr. Germaine?" "Why do you ask me?" snapped the duchess. Said Cornwall, "He did not lie at home last night." Before the duchess could answer, Nell said, "I question not but he will come out by-and-by like a drowned rat." And sure enough, after a while in came Germaine, proudly showing off his alibi of clean linen.

To Nell, the comedian, the Duchess of Norfolk's adventure in adultery was only a cause for merriment and salty jesting. Unfortunately the Duke of Norfolk had no such sense of humor. Emboldened by success, the duchess continued her liaison, failed to take precautions against surprise, and a month later was "found in bed with one Germaine, to her great scandal." Norfolk sent her abroad for a year, tried a reconciliation, failed, and then arranged a legal separation. Thereafter the duchess lived secretly with Germaine until 1700, when, after several lawsuits and bills in the House of Lords, Norfolk was granted a divorce. Then she married her lover.

While Nell was teasing the lickerish Duchess of Norfolk at Windsor, another duchess, Portsmouth, was sailing for France in a ship laden with her loot. Although she returned to England from time to time to look after her affairs, she had no further dealings with Nell. Rich and respected, Portsmouth bought a house in Paris and for some years lived in grand style, forever reminding King Louis of her distinguished services in the cause of France. But in 1689, when William and Mary succeeded James II, all her English pensions were cut off, her creditors fell upon her, and she realized at last that the wages of sin are debt. King Louis saved her from want by a series of decrees forbidding foreclosure on her goods and chattels. She retired to her country estates and spent the rest of her long life in penitence and poverty, dying on November 14, 1734, at the age of eighty-five.

In September, 1685, King James, now firmly established on his throne and well supplied with funds by a sullen Parliament, again turned his attention to Nell's affairs. His first action was to pay the £729. 2s. 3d. to "several trades-men, creditors of Mrs. Ellen Gwyn, in satisfaction of their debts, for which the said Ellen stood outlawed." In addi-tion he gave Nell a Treasury note for £1,300 in Septem-ber, and in December two cash payments of £500 each as "bounty", out of the Secret Service funds. Most important of all, he settled on her a pension of £1,500 a year, be-ginning with January 1, 1686. Later in that year he began paying off her mortgage on the Bestwood Park estates. By the time the final payment was made on October 18, 1687, the total (with accumulated interest) came to £3,774. 2s. 6d. He refused, however, to pay Nell's personal note to Child and Rogers. At the time of her death that indebted-ness amounted to £6,900, which was paid off in part by the proceeds from the sale of her plate and in part by a gift of £2,300 from the King.

Following the precedent set by his brother, James re-fused to trust giddy Nell with too much cash in hand. His agents, Richard Graham, Sir Stephen Fox, and Francis Gwynne (Secretary of the Council and no relation to Nell), acted as her trustees, handled most of the money, and saw that it reached its proper destinations. One reveal-ing document shows something of the King's caution. The Treasury note for £1,300 acknowledged on its face the (purely fictitious) loan of that sum to the Treasury by Francis Gwynne. The note was to bear interest at seven per cent per annum, and to be paid from a tax on imports. On a folded sheet used as a cover for the note Gwynne wrote, "My name is herein used in trust only for Mrs. Eleanor Gwyn, whose money this is." In short, Nell could not cash the note without Gwynne's endorsement. On May 14, 1686, she talked him into assigning the note to her, and three days later she cashed it with Charles Duncombe, the banker.

Nell had to adapt herself to a less extravagant way of life, a process made easy by the fact that King James affected "neither profaneness nor buffoonery," and "the face of the whole Court was exceedingly changed into a more solemn and moral behavior." There was no more reckless gaming, and the open keeping of mistresses was frowned on, the King setting a good example by exiling his latest mistress, Katherine Sedley (Sir Charles Sedley's daughter), to Ireland, after first creating her Countess of Dorchester. Nell's old friends of "the merry gang," the wild, dissolute Wits of her youth, were rapidly disappearing. Rochester and Scroope were dead, and Sir Charles Sedley had reformed; Sir George Etherege went off as Ambassador to Ratisbon; Lord Dorset departed for his country estates, taking Fleetwood Shepherd along; Buckingham retired to Yorkshire, amused himself a-hunting, and died of a fever on April 16, 1687; Harry Savile disagreed with James's pro-Catholic policies, resigned, went to France for a surgical operation, and died on October 6, 1687; Henry Guy, still a bachelor, was busy heaping up wealth; only mad Harry Killigrew remained untouched by time. Some of Nell's feminine friends were still with her, but Mrs. Mary Young was dead; Lady Harvey was in retirement; Peg Hughes had returned to the stage; Lady Shrewsbury and Arabella Churchill (now Mrs. Charles Godfrey) were devoted to domesticity; and in 1686 the Duchess of Norfolk was in a French nunnery.

It was a very different world. There were no rivals for Nell to fight with, humiliate, and outshine, no royal lover to entertain (at considerable expense), and nothing to work for. Without interest or influence, Nell could do nothing to get further honors for her son. King James was kind to his nephews, but he had a bastard of his own, James Fitzjames, Duke of Berwick, to promote. It was not until 1718, in the reign of George I, that St. Albans gained the long coveted Order of the Garter—for his own merits, not his mother's services.

Changed as it was, the world still held pleasures for Nell —music, plays, fashions, friends, her son (who returned from the grand tour in 1686), and the daily bustle and excitement of life. From the autumn of 1685 to the spring of 1687 the gossips almost forgot her. We learn that at some time in this period the public workhouse painted a coat of arms for her, "per pale, arg. and or, a lion rampant, azure." Evelyn recorded with a sneer the rumor that she had turned Catholic, and failed to record the fact that she remained a staunch Protestant. Occasionally a libeler mentioned her in passing, usually as "old Nelly," "one of the wrinkled rout," "ugly-faced Nelly," and the like—epithets which were cruel enough but based on some measure of truth. She was thirty-six, and the normal life span in Restoration England was not more than forty years. In a period ignorant of sanitation, dietetics, and dentistry, and almost without medicine, a woman of Nell's age had little hope of retaining her youthful beauty. Add also that she had long suffered from the most dreaded of occupational diseases, acquired from one of her earlier lovers and rapidly approaching its last stage, with hardening of the arteries and high blood pressure as its warning signs. Increasingly of late years there had been periods of sickness, with slower recovery after each attack as the weakened machine ran down.

Early in March, 1687, Nell was stricken by apoplexy, with resultant paralysis of one side of her body. For a few weeks her recovery was doubted and one gossip even reported her death, but in April there were encouraging signs of improvement. In late May apoplexy struck again, and this time the doctors saw no hope. The elm trees in Pall Mall came into full leaf and grew dry and brittle in the heat of summer, but Nell lay helpless in the great silver bed, with its cupids, eagles, and crowns. She had many visitors, of course—her son, her sister Rose Forster, Lady Lucy Sandys, Mall Knight, Dame Margery Fairborne, and many another friend and neighbor. Clergymen, scenting a lamb to be saved, came to point the way to Heaven; chief among the shepherds were Nell's chaplain, John Warner, and Dr. Thomas Tennison, rector of St. Martin's Church.

Could there be salvation without penitence? Could there be penitence without awareness of sin? As a good Protestant and Whig, Nell had gone to church with reasonable regularity, paid her assessments, and donated to the poor. True, she had given her heart and body to more than one man, but she had been faithful to each in his turn. Loving pleasure herself, she had spent her life giving pleasure to others, as actress, entertainer, and mistress. In her large and generous way she had made many people happy and had consciously injured no one, except, perhaps, that weeping willow, Portsmouth. True, she had been a whore, but what then? Whoring was in fashion; it was no more than a craft or trade. Dimly she knew that she had sinned, but use and custom had long ago suppressed all sense of guilt. Dr. Tennison, a man of "a most holy conversation, very learned and ingenious," labored to open Nell's eyes. To her bedside he summoned all the hosts of hell in a preview of purgatory, its sulphurous and tormenting fires. Only repentance, confession, and piety could save her. Shrinking from the flames, Nell repented in anguished tears, saw the light of Heaven break, and spent her last days "in hopes of a joyful resurrection."

On July 9 Nell made her will (signing with her customary "E.G."), commending her soul "into the hands of Almighty God," and bequeathing her worldly dross to her son. As executors she appointed four old friends: Henry Sidney; Lawrence Hyde, now Earl of Rochester; Sir Robert Sawyer, the Attorney-General; and Thomas Herbert, now Earl of Pembroke, once her chivalrous defender in the Duke's Theatre. In October she added two codicils to the document. By that time she was so completely paralysed that she could barely talk; therefore the codicils were not signed but only "attested and acknowledged."

The gossips who judged Nell to be worth about £100,-000 ("a great many say more, few less") were not exaggerating; certainly she possessed "a considerable estate," thanks largely to the foresight of King Charles who had tied up all her properties with trusts and entails. Her will merely referred to her "houses, lands, tenements, offices, places, pensions, annuities, and hereditaments" with no inventory or estimate of values, but her Pall Mall house alone was worth at least £10,000, and Burford House at Windsor, a much larger building with extensive grounds, was worth twice as much. Then there was Bestwood Park, her incomes from Ireland, the logwood tax, and other investments; and all her personal property, mortgaged and unmortgaged. St. Albans could hardly grudge the £1,500 or so which Nell gave to friends, kinfolk, and charity.

To her sister Rose, Nell gave a total of £400, plus £40 to Rose's husband for a mourning ring. Captain William Cholmly, Nell's "kinsman," was to have £100. She gave her executors £100 each, and John Warner and Dame Margery Fairborne £50 apiece for mourning rings. Her physicians, Drs. Harrell, Le Fèvre, Lower, and Lister, were each to receive £20 in addition to the amount of his bill, and Dr. Harrell's nephew (his assistant) was to have £10. She ordered that all her servants should be given a year's wages and mourning clothes, and singled out two of them for additional gifts: John Berry, porter, £10, and Bridget Long, "who had been her servant for divers years," £20 a year for life. She even remembered her two nurses, Anne Edling and Elizabeth Hawkes, with "ten pounds each and mourning, besides their wages due them." Finally she provided for a mysterious pensioner, "Lady Hollyman," who was to have her dole of "ten shillings a week continued to her during the said lady's life."

Nell's gifts to the poor of St. Martin's Parish were not large, but the subjects of her charity were purposefully chosen. In pious remembrance of her father's death at Oxford she entrusted Dr. Tennison with £100 "for taking any poor debtors . . . out of prison, and for clothes this winter, and other necessaries, as he shall find most fit." To this she added a request that the Duke of St. Albans would "lay out twenty pounds yearly for the releasing of poor debtors out of prison every Christmas day." Then—an unusual bequest in a bigoted age—she gave Warner and Tennison £50 for the use of the Catholic poor of the parish —to show her charity toward those who differed from her in religion.

Through the slow months of autumn Nell clung to life with surprising tenacity, wasting almost visibly day by day. At last, on November 14, 1687, at ten o'clock at night, her brief candle flickered out. Three days later she was buried in the chancel of St. Martin's Church with all the pomp and expensive panoply (cost: £375) befitting the mother of a royal duke. To a large congregation of her sorrowing friends Dr. Tennison preached a funeral sermon on the daring text, "joy shall be in Heaven over one sinner that repenteth, more than over ninety and nine just persons who need no repentance."

She was hardly in her grave when a pair of eager poetasters, with their eyes on St. Albans' purse, produced their elegiac tributes. "Laurinda, a Pastoral on the Lamented Death of the Incomparable Madam Gwyn" expressed "in dewy verse" the grief of a poet who mourned Nell's passing in such restrained lines as these:

> 'Twas always spring, for when the sun retired,
> Her warmer beams the vocal groves inspired,
> Her cheerful looks the winter's rage beguiled,
> Her smiles made summer, and she always smiled.

The author of "An Elegy in Commemoration of Madam Eleanor Gwyn," writing in even dewier verse, suggested that

. . . some may cast objections in and say
These scattered praises that we seek to lay
Upon her hearse are but the formal way.
Yet when we tell them she was free from strife,
Courteous even to the poor, no pride of life,
E'er entertaining, but did much abound
In charity, and for it was renowned;
Not seeking praises, but did vain praise despise,
And at her alms was heard no trumpet noise;
And how again we let them further see
That she refused and hated flattery,
And far from her dissemblers did command,
We may have hopes her fame for this will stand.

Could he have looked down through the centuries, our poet would have been astonished to see how long Nell's fame for kindness, humility, and charity has lasted. Convinced that she was "a good sort," one of their very own kind, and attracted by the romance of her rise from rags to riches, the English-speaking people have long cherished her as "pretty, witty Nell," the impudent little comedian who became a great lady and never lost the common touch. Today her name is used to glorify tea-shops, restaurants, apartment houses, taverns, and a brand of marmalade!

But the real Nell Gwyn was even more human and lovable than the legendary figure. Her worldly success was due far more to spirit than to flesh; she was no lustful Laïs or mercenary Messalina. She never maddened men with her beauty; she tickled them with her wit. Unfortunately her contemporaries recorded all too little of her conversation and too few of her *bon mots*. Moreover, her way of speaking and gesturing, the tone of her laughter and the joyous spontaneity of her whimsies—as ephemeral as the art of the actor—could not be recorded. She spoke her "graceful things . . . with such an air, so gay," that we can only lament that "half the beauty's lost in the repetition."

Friendly and kind, witty and giddy, honest and loyal, Nell was above all ambitious and hard-working. By nature humorous, pleasure-loving, and frankly carnal, she chose prostitution as an honorable and lucrative profession in an age when the successful courtesan was socially approved. Brought up in the rough schools of bawdyhouse and Restoration theatre, she quickly grew skilled in the art of pleasing, and with honest realism she employed her skill to get far more out of life than her birth and breeding warranted. Although she never attained her ambition to be a countess, she kept the affections of King Charles II for seventeen years against formidable competition, founded a line of noble descendants entitled to wear the bar-sinister on their shields, and left her son rich in dignities and property. She earned every bit of her success.

Appendix

NELL'S LETTERS

NO LETTERS in Nell's handwriting have ever been found. The six printed here were all dictated to amanuenses. They are taken verbatim either from the originals or from authenticated copies. The original of Letter I is in the Widener Collection, Harvard College Library. The originals of Letters II and III were found in Kilkenny Castle, Ireland, and first printed by Gordon Goodwin in his edition of Cunningham's *Nell Gwyn* (1908). Letter IV is from a copy of the original made by the Reverend William Cole on November 16, 1774. The original has since disappeared; the copy is in British Museum Additional MS. 5847. The originals of Letters V and VI are in B.M. Additional MS. 21, 483. Although without address or signature, the context clearly indicates they were from Nell to James II. The handwriting is suspiciously like that of the amanuensis (perhaps Nell's maid, Bridget Long) who wrote Letter I.

I

[Nell Gwyn to Lawrence Hyde, June, 1678.]

pray Dear Mr Hide forgive me for not writeing to you before now for the reasone is I have ben sick thre months & sinse I recoverd I have had nothing to intertaine you withall nor have nothing now worth writing but that I can holde no longer to let you know I never have ben in any companie wethout drinking your health for I love you with all my soule the pell mel is now to me a dismale plase sinse I have uterly lost Sr Car Scrope never to be recovrd agane for he tould me he could not live allwayes at this rate & so begune to be a littel uncivil which I could not sufer from an uglye baux garscon   Mrs Knights Lady mothers dead & she has put up a scutchin no beiger then my Lady grins scunchis   My lord Rochester is gon in the cuntrei   Mr Savil has got a misfortune but is upon recovery & is to mary an airres who I thinke wont wont have an ill time ont if he holds up his thumb   My lord of Dorscit apiers wonse in thre munths for he drinkes aile with Shadwell & Mr Haris at the Dukes house all day long   my lord Burford remimbers his sarvis to you   my Lord Bauclaire is is goeing into France   we are a goeing to supe with the king at whithale & my Lady Harvie   the king remembers his sarvis to you   now lets talk of state affairs for we never caried things so cunningly as now for we dont know whether we shall have pesce or war but I am for war and for no other reason but that you may come home   I have a thousand merry conseets but I cant make her write um & therfore you must take the will for the deed   god bye   your most loveing obedient faithful & humbel

sarvant

E G

II

[Nell Gwyn to James, Duke of Ormonde, Lord Lieutenant of Ireland, September 4, 1682.]

My Lord

This is to beg a favour of your Grace, wch I hope you will stand my friend in   I lately gott a freind of mine to advance me on my Irish peñcon halfe a year's Pay^mt for last Lady Day (wch all People have rec^ed but me) and I drew bills upon Mr Laurence Steele my Agent for ye Pay^mt of ye money, nott thinking but long before this ye bills had been paid: but contrary to my expectation I last night re^cd advice from him y^t ye bills are Protested, & he cannot receive any money without yor Grace's Positive order to ye Farmers for it.

Your Grace formerly upon the King's Letter (wch this inclosed is the coppy of) was so much mine and Mrs. Forster's freind as to give necessary orders for our Pay^mts, notwithstanding the stop. I hope you will obleige me now, upon this request to give yor direcõns to ye Farmers; y^t we may be paid our Arrears; and what is growing due & you will obleige

My Lord

Your Grace's most humble

serv^t to command

Ellen Gwin.

III

[Nell Gwyn to Richard, Earl of Arran, eldest son of the Duke of Ormonde and Deputy Lord Lieutenant of Ireland, November 26, 1682.]

My Lord

I hope yor Lords^hp will now obleige me so much as to stand my Freind. I have wth much Importunity gott ye Lords of the Treãry to give an order to my Lord Ormond to cause the Arrears of my Peñcon stopt in Ireland to be paid what is due to me to last Michãs with my sisters Mrs. Forster & others whome their Letter mencõns: my Agent is Mr Laurence Steele to whom I have sent this letter to diliver to your Lordshp hoping for my sake you will be pleased to give him a speedy dispatch in this businesse & obleige your Lor^shps most humble servant to command

Ellen: Gwin

IV

[Nell Gwyn to Mrs. Frances Jennings, April 14, 1684.]
  These
    For Madam Jennings
      over against the Tub Tavern
        in Jermin Street   Windsor
          London   Burford House
                             Aprill 14
                              1684

Madam.
    I have receiv'd y^r. Letter, & I desire y^u would speake to
my Ladie Williams to send me the gold Stuffe, & a Note with
it, because I must sign it, then she shall have her Money y^e
next Day of Mr. Trant; pray tell her Ladieship, that I will
send her a note of what Quantity of Things I'le have bought,
if her Ladieship will put herselfe to y^e. Trouble to buy them;
when they are bought I will sign a Note for her to be payd.
Pray Madam, let ye Man goe on with my Sedan, & send Potvin & Mr. Coker down to me, for I want them both. The Bill
is very dear to boyle the Plate; but Necessity hath noe Law.
I am afraid M^m. you have forgott my Mantle, which you
were to line with Musk Colour Sattin, & all my other Things,
for you send me noe Patterns nor Answer. Monsieur Lainey
is going away. Pray send me Word about your Son Griffin,
for his Majestie is mighty well pleasd that he will goe along
with my Lord Duke. I am afraid you are soe much taken up
with your owne House, that you forgett my Businesse. My
Service to dear Lord Kildare, & tell him I love him with all
my Heart. Pray M^m. see that Potvin brings now all my
Things with him: my Lord Duke's Bed &c.   if he hath not
made them all up, he may doe that here for if I doe not get
my Things out of his Hands now, I shall not have them until

this Time Twelve-month. The Duke brought me down with him my Crochet of Diamonds, & I love it the better because he brought it. Mr. Lumley, & everie Body else will tell you that it is the finest Thing that ever was seen. Good M^m. speake to Mr. Beaver to come down too, that I may bespeake a Ring for the Duke of Grafton before he goes into France.

I have continued extream ill ever since you Leaft me, & I am soe still. I have sent to London for a D^r. I believe I shall die. My Service to the Dutchesse of Norfolk, & tell her I am as sick as her Grace, but doe not know what I ayle, although shee does, which I am overjoyed that shee goes on with her great Belly.

Pray tell my Ladie Williams, that the King's Mistresses are accounted ill-pay-Masters, but shee shall have her Money the next Day after I have the Stuffe.

Here is sad Slaughter at Windsor, the young Men's taking y^r. Leaves & going to France, & although they are none of my Lovers, yet I am loath to part with the Men. Mrs. Jennings I love you with all my Heart, & soe good by.

E. G.

Let me have an Answer to this Letter.

V

[Nell Gwyn to James II, April or May, 1685.]

had I suferd for my God as I have don for y^r brother and y^u I shuld not have needed ether of y^r Kindnes or iustis to me

I beseecch you not to doe any thing to the setling of my buisines till I speake wth you and a poynt me by Mr Grahams wher I may speake wth you privetly   God make you as happy as my soule prays you may be, y^rs

VI

[Nell Gwyn to James II, April or May, 1685.]

S^r

    This world is not capable of giving me a greater ioy and happyness then y^r Maties favour not as you are King and soe have it in y^r power to doe me good having never loved y^r brother and y^r selfe upon that account but as to y^r persons had hee lived hee tould me before hee dyed that the world shuld see by what hee did for me that hee had both love and value for me and that hee did not doe for me, as my mad lady woster,* hee was my frind and alowed me to tell him all my grifes and did like a frind advise me and tould me who was my frind and who was not   S^r the honour y^r Ma:^{tie} has don me by Mr Grahams has given me great comfort not by the present you sent me to releeve me out of the last extremety, but by the Kind expressions hee mad me from you, of y^r Kindnes to me wch to me is above all things in this world having God Knows never loved y^r brother or y^r selfe interestedly, all you doe for me shall be yours it being my resolution never to have any interest but y^{rs}, and as long as I live to serve you and when I dye to dye praying for y^u.

*Margaret Somerset, Dowager Marchioness of Worcester, spent her life in genteel poverty, petitioning vainly for the return of £91,500 which she claimed her husband had spent in the King's service before the Restoration. She lost her wits about 1679, and was known thereafter as "the mad Marchioness of Worcester." She died in 1681.

BIBLIOGRAPHICAL NOTES

I

THE MOST useful biographies of Nell are Peter Cunningham, *The Story of Nell Gwyn*, ed. Gordon Goodwin (1908) and A. I. Dasent, *Nell Gwynne* (1924). For materials on her family and background see the *Calendars of State Papers Domestic*; E. B. Chancellor, *The Annals of Covent Garden* (n.d.); Sir Francis Fane's unpublished "Commonplace Book," Shakespeare Library, Stratford-on-Avon; and Samuel Pepys, *Diary* (1893). The best versions of the satires quoted are found in British Museum Harleian MSS. 6913, 7319.

II

For the background of the years 1650-1660 see Arthur Bryant, *King Charles II* (1933); Gilbert Burnet, *Bishop Burnet's History of His Own Time* (1723); Julia Cartwright, *Madame* (1900); A. I. Dasent, *The Private Life of Charles II* (1927); Allan Fea, *Some Beauties of the Seventeenth Century* (1907); Philip Sergeant, *My Lady Castlemaine* (1911); and H. D. Traill, *Social England* (1903). On brothels and bawdy-houses see Pepys, *Diary*, and Ned Ward, *The London Spy* (1703). For the theatre see W. R. Chetwood, *A General History of the Stage* (1749); Edmund Curll, *Betterton's History of the English Stage* (1741); Leslie Hotson, *The Commonwealth and Restoration Stage* (1928); and William Van Lennep in *Joseph Quincy Adams Memorial Studies* (1949). For satires see Harleian MS. 7319.

III

Bryant, *Charles II; Calendars of State Papers Domestic;* Dasent, *Nell Gwynne;* Anthony Hamilton, *Memoirs of Count Grammont,* ed. Gordon Goodwin (1903); Pepys, *Diary.* For stage and acting see Curll, *Betterton's History;* Montague Summers, *The Restoration Theatre* (1934), *The Playhouse of Pepys* (1935); and the prologues, epilogues, and stage directions of contemporary plays. The description of the audience is an imaginative reconstruction. For Dryden's friends see Winifred, Lady Burghclere, *Buckingham* (1903); V. De Sola Pinto, *Sir Charles Sedley* (1927); Brice Harris, *Dorset* (1940); and J. H. Wilson, *The Court Wits of the Restoration* (1948).

IV

Eleanor Boswell, *The Restoration Court Stage* (1932); Burghclere, *Buckingham;* Daniel Defoe, *A Journal of the Plague Year* (1722); John Evelyn, *Diary* (1906); Hamilton, *Grammont;* Harris, *Dorset;* Allardyce Nicoll, *Restoration Drama* (1923); David Ogg, *England in the Reign of Charles II* (1934); Pepys, *Diary;* V. De Sola Pinto, *Rochester* (1935); Traill, *Social England;* Anthony Wood, *Life and Times* (1900). For a comment on *The Chances* see Nathaniel Lee's preface to *The Princess of Cleve* (1689); on Nell's new suit see *Notes and Queries,* 2nd Series, VII, April 9, 1859; for Lady Honora O'Brien see Historical Manuscripts Commission, *Le Fleming MS.*

V

The Bulstrode Papers (1897); Burghclere, *Buckingham;* Burnet, *History;* Curll, *Betterton's History;* Fane, "Commonplace Book"; Richard Flecknoe, *Euterpe Revived* (1675); Nicoll, *Restoration Drama*; Pepys, *Diary*; Pinto, *Sedley*; *Savile Correspondence* (1859); and Eliot Warburton, *Prince Rupert* (1849). For Nell's dance with Lacy see Evelyn, *Diary*, the letters of Mrs. Evelyn. For her part in *The Virgin Martyr*, see *N & Q.* CXCIII, February 21, 1948. For her rôle as Pulcheria see Montague Summers, *Essays in Petto* (n.d.). Accounts of the Killigrew-Buckingham quarrels appear in HMC, *Seventh Report*, and *The Review of English Studies*, XII, 1936.

VI

Burghclere, *Buckingham*; Burnet, *History*; Bryant, *Charles II*; Dasent, *Charles II*; K. C. Hurd-Mead, *A History of Women in Medicine* (1938); H. M. Imbert-Terry, *A Misjudged Monarch* (1917); Ogg, *England*; *The Rochester-Savile Letters* (1940); and Sergeant, *Castlemaine*. For Nell's residences and the birth of her son see Fane, "Commonplace Book"; Wood, *Life and Times*. On the Roos case see Burghclere, *Buckingham*; Edward Hyde, Earl of Clarendon, *Life* (1761); *The Poems and Letters of Andrew Marvell*, ed. H. M. Margoliouth (1927). For Keroualle see Cartwright, *Madam*; H. Forneron, *Louise de Keroualle, Duchess of Portsmouth* (1887); and the anonymous *Francelia* (1734). This brief biography is a mixture of fact and fiction.

VII

Burghclere, *Buckingham*; Cunningham, *Nell Gwyn*; Dasent, *Nell Gwynne*; John Dennis, *Familiar Letters* (1721); Evelyn, *Diary*; Fane, "Commonplace Book"; Forneron, *Keroualle*; *Francelia*; J. J. Jusserand, *A French Ambassador at the Court of Charles II* (1892); Marvell, *Letters*; *Rochester-Savile Letters*; Sergeant, *Castlemaine*; and Wood, *Life and Times*. For Nell's house see the deeds in the Pierpont Morgan Library,

New York, or my description, *N & Q*, CXCIV, April 9, 1949; see also A. I. Dasent, *The History of St. James's Square* (1895); N. G. Brett-James, *The Growth of Stuart London* (1935); Pepys *Diary;* and *Savile Correspondence* (Pepys' friend, Sir William Coventry, paid £1,400 for the leasehold of the house in October, 1667). On Nell's portrait see C. H. Collins Baker, *Lely and the Stuart Portrait Painters* (1912). The story of Nell and her footman is quoted from Henry Fielding, *Tom Jones* (1749). For the Coventry case see Marvell, *Letters;* Ogg, *England; Journals of the House of Commons;* and satires in *Poems on Affairs of State* (1716). For Lady Clanbrassil see *Calendars of State Papers Domestic; Conway Letters* (1930); and G. E. C., *Complete Peerage.* For young Hughes see HMC, *Rutland Papers;* for Keroualle see HMC, *Seventh Report,* and *The Secret History of the Reigns of K. Charles II and K. James II* (1690).

VIII

Burghclere, *Buckingham;* Burnet, *History;* Bryant, *Charles II;* Dasent, *Charles II;* Evelyn, *Diary;* Fane, "Commonplace Book"; *Francelia;* Forneron, *Keroualle;* Marvell, *Letters;* Pepys, *Diary;* Sergeant, *Castlemaine; Williamson Letters* (1874); Anthony Wood, *Athenae Oxonienses* (1813). The portrait of Nell as a shepherdess (or an excellent copy) is in the Columbus Art Gallery, Columbus, Ohio. It has been over-painted to cover Nell's bare breast. On Cleveland, Mulgrave, and Savile see *Calendars of State Papers Domestic; Essex Correspondence* (1913); *The Conduct of the Earl of Nottingham* (1941); and *Rochester-Savile Letters.* For Buckingham's affairs see *Conway Letters;* HMC, *Sixth Report* and *Ninth Report.* For Rochester see Gilbert Burnet, *Life of the Earl of Rochester* (1680). For Nell's warrants and pension see HMC, *Third Report* and *Calendars of Treasury Books.* On Pepys and Nell see *A Descriptive Catalogue of Naval Manuscripts* (1926).

IX

For Nell's income see *Calendars of Treasury Books; Secret Service Accounts of Charles II and James II* (1851). The collection of Nell's household accounts was originally seen by Cunningham, who printed the silversmith's, sedan-chair maker's, and chairmen's bills in his *Nell Gwyn*. For the bill from the Duke's Theatre see *The Harvard Library Bulletin*, Autumn, 1950. Thirty of the original collection of bills are now in the Ohio State University Library. For additional information on customs and manners see Arthur Bryant, *The England of Charles II* (1935); Pepys, *Diary*; G. S. Thompson, *Life in a Noble Household* (1937); Traill, *Social England*; F. P. and M. M. Verney, *Memoirs of the Verney Family* (1907). See for other items *Williamson Letters* and Colley Cibber, *Apology for the Life of Mr. Colley Cibber* (1740).

X

Bryant, *Charles II; Bulstrode Papers;* Burghclere, *Buckingham; Calendars of State Papers Domestic;* Cunningham, *Nell Gwyn;* Dasent, *Nell Gwynne;* Evelyn *Diary;* Forneron, *Keroualle; Hatton Correspondence* (1878); Lewis Melville, *The Windsor Beauties* (1928); and Sergeant, *Castlemaine*. For Nell's jokes see Fane, "Commonplace Book"; and HMC, *Second Report*. For her Privy Chamber appointment see Samuel Pegge, *Curialia* (1791); her quarrels with Portsmouth, *Lettres de Madame de Sévigné* (1862); her gifts, pensions, and deeds, HMC, *Ninth Report, House of Commons Journals, Calendars of Treasury Books*, and the deeds in the Pierpont Morgan Library. For the poems quoted see Waller, *Works* (1744); *Poems on Affairs of State;* and Harleian MS. 6914.

On Rochester see Fane, "Commonplace Book"; *Rochester-Savile Letters;* and *Francelia.*

XI

Andrew Browning, *The Earl of Danby* (1944); Bryant, *Charles II;* Burghclere, *Buckingham; Calendars of State Papers Domestic; Essex Correspondence;* Forneron, *Keroualle; Hatton Correspondence;* HMC, *Seventh Report* and *Ormonde Papers;* Marvell, *Letters;* Ogg, *England; Rochester's Jokes* (n.d.); *Savile Correspondence;* Wood, *Life and Times.* On Nell's friends see Allan Fea, *King Monmouth* (1902); *Rochester-Savile Letters;* Wilson, *Court Wits;* HMC, *Rutland Papers; N & Q,* 8th Series, XI, January 23, 1897. For Montague's plots see Browning, *Danby; Rochester-Savile Letters;* Sergeant, *Castlemaine;* G. Steinman Steinman, *A Memoir of Mrs. Myddleton* (1864).

XII

Bryant, *Charles II;* Burghclere, *Buckingham;* John Dickson Carr, *The Murder of Sir Edmund Godfrey* (1936); Julia Cartwright, *Sacharissa* (1901); Dasent, *Nell Gwynne;* Forneron, *Keroualle;* H. C. Foxcroft, *Life of Halifax* (1898); C. B. R. Kent, *Early History of the Tories* (1908); Narcissus Luttrell, *Brief Relation of State Affairs* (1857); *Lady Russell's Letters* (1854); *Verney Memoirs;* H. E. Woodbridge, *Sir William Temple* (1940). On Nell's finances see *Calendars of Treasury Books; Calendars of State Papers Domestic;* and HMC, *Ormonde Papers.* On her mother's death see HMC, *Buccleuch MS;* Thomas Faulkner, *Description of Chelsea* (1829); C. J. Fèret, *Fulham Old and New* (1930); and the satires quoted in Chapter I. For the goldsmith story see *The London Chronicle,* August 15-18, 1778. "Ephelia" published her works as *Female Poems on Several Occasions* (1679). For

Nell at Newmarket see Lady Newdigate-Newdigate, *Cavalier and Puritan* (1901); All-Souls MS. 171, Bodleian Library. On Nell and Monmouth see HMC, *Ormonde Papers* and *Seventh Report;* Cartwright, *Sacharissa;* and *Diary of Henry Sidney* (1843). For the death of Lord James see HMC, *Seventh Report;* Anthony Wood, *Fasti Oxonienses* (1815). For Bethel see *N & Q,* 7th Series, IX, March 15, 1890; for Nell's Windsor house see *N & Q,* 2nd Series, VIII, October 29, 1859. The satires alluded to all appear in Harleian MSS. 6913 and 7319.

XIII

J. L. Anderton, *Life of Thomas Ken* (1851); Bryant, *Charles II,* and *Samuel Pepys, the Years of Peril* (1935); *Calendars of State Papers Domestic; Calendar of Inner Temple Records* (1901); Cunningham, *Nell Gwyn;* Evelyn, *Diary;* Forneron, *Keroualle;* HMC, *Seventh Report; Lady Russell's Letters; Letters of Humphrey Prideaux* (1875); Luttrell, *Brief Relation;* Roger North, *Examen* (1740); *Roxburghe Ballads* (1883); Warburton, *Prince Rupert.* For the story of "the Protestant Whore" see James Granger, *A Biographical History of England* (1775); deeds to Bestwood Park are recorded in B. M. Additional Charters, 15,862-64; on Nell's pension see HMC, *Ormonde Papers;* for her gambling see Theophilus Lucas, *Memoirs of Gamesters* (1714); on Edward Young see HMC, *Bath MS;* for Nell's charity see Anna Jameson, *Memoirs of the Beauties of the Court of Charles II* (1851). The satires quoted are in Harleian MSS. 6913, 7317, and 7319.

XIV

Bryant, *Charles II;* Burnet, *History; Calendars of State Papers Domestic;* Raymond Crawfurd, *Last Days of Charles II* (1909); Sir John Dalrymple, *Memoirs of Great Britain* (1773); Dasent, *Nell Gwynne,* and *St. James's Square;* Evelyn,

Diary; Allan Fea, *James II and His Wives* (1908); Forneron, *Kerouaille;* Luttrell, *Brief Relation;* Sergeant, *Castlemaine.* For St. Albans' lodgings see *N & Q,* CLXII, September 10, 1932; for his trip abroad see *Calendars of State Papers Domestic* and HMC, *Downshire MS.* For mourning customs see Evelyn, *Diary,* and HMC, *Ormonde Papers.* On Nell's finances see *Calendars of Treasury Books;* Dasent, *Nell Gwynne;* HMC, *MS in Various Collections;* and *Secret Service Accounts.* For ballads see *Roxburghe Ballads,* and *Bagford Ballads* (1878).

XV

Burghclere, *Buckingham;* Cunningham, *Nell Gwyn;* Dasent, *Nell Gwynne;* Evelyn, *Diary;* Fea, *King Monmouth;* Forneron, *Kerouaille;* Harris, *Dorset;* Luttrell, *Brief Relation;* Wilson, *Court Wits.* For Germaine and the Duchess of Norfolk see *A Complete Collection of State Trials* (1809-28); and *The Norfolke Divorce* (1700). For Nell's finances see *Secret Service Accounts; Calendars of Treasury Books.* The Treasury note for £1,500 is in the Ohio State University Library. For libels mentioning Nell see Harleian MSS. 6914, 7319, and *Poems on Affairs of State.* For her coat of arms see *N & Q,* 2nd Series, V, January 2, 1858. On Nell's sickness and death see Charles MacLaurin, *Mere Mortals* (1925); *Hatton Correspondence;* HMC, *Downshire MS; N & Q,* CLXIII, September 10, 1932; *The Letter-Book of Sir George Etherege* (1928); for elegies see Harleian MS. 7319, and *A Little Ark* (1921).

Index

INDEX